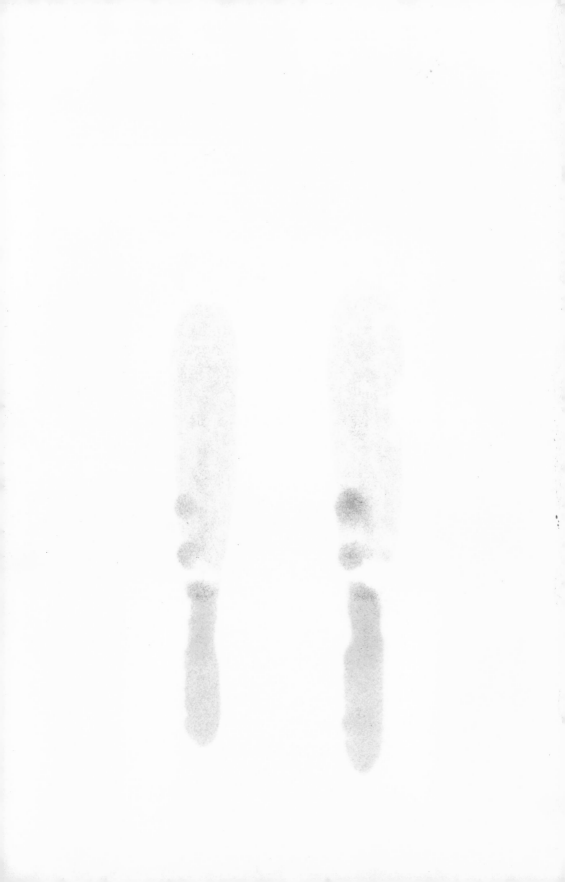

To Katy—who knows why.

Acknowledgments

I have researched at numerous archives over the last twenty years, and nowhere have I found more friendly and helpful people than those who work under the able direction of Dr. Benedict K. Zobrist at the Harry S. Truman Library. My greatest debt is to librarian Elizabeth Safly and archivist Erwin Mueller—Elizabeth for her unwavering charm and infectious good humor despite my many demands upon her (including her help in deciphering blurred passages from Harry Truman's now-faded World War I letters), Erwin for being the most outstanding research archivist of my acquaintance. Pauline Testerman, in charge of audiovisual, also gave willing assistance, as did Vicky Alexander, Dennis Bilger, Patty Bressman, Robin Burgess, Mildred Carol, Donna Clark, Harry Clark, John Curry, Nell Flanagan, James Fuchs, Philip Lagerquest, Warren Ohrvall, and Doris Pesek.

To my beloved friends, Dr. and Mrs. Robert E. Bruner of Kansas City, I am deeply appreciative. They not only gave me use of rare, recently found Truman family letters (Virginia Bruner is kin to the President), but as their houseguest during my frequent trips to the Truman Library I have been spoiled irreparably by, among other favors, their giving me the keys to their automobile.

Olive Truman, widow of General Ralph E. Truman, is another dear friend, and Olive generously detailed for me her husband's close relationship with his cousin Harry. Martha Ann Swoyer, the President's niece, graciously invited my wife and I to her family's Fourth of July picnic (which unhappily we couldn't attend), and sent me a copy of an essay her uncle Harry had written as a youth.

Others intimately involved with the Truman story have helped, including the President himself, with whom I talked two decades ago as a college history student. More recently, the President's daughter, Margaret Truman Daniel, shared her remembrances with me, as did Dr. Wallace C. Graham, W. Averell Harriman, Mrs. Herbert H. Haukenberry, Francis G. McGowan, John Martino, Charles Murphy, Mrs. Samuel I. Rosenman, Florence and Mary Spottswood, Dr. John Steelman, and Mr. and Mrs. Robert Weatherford, Jr.

My colleagues at Northern Arizona University, from President Eugene M. Hughes on down, were most supportive. Help with travel and clerical expenses came from Academic Vice-President Joseph W. Cox, Graduate Dean Henry Hooper, and Arts and Science Dean Charles E. Little. The Organized Research Committee granted me a research stipend, and my department chairman, Delno C. West, Jr., gave me released time from teaching. Paula Gussio, of NAU's public information office, assisted with photographs. Fellow historians William H. Lyon, Dwight E. Mayo, William J. Roosen, and Andrew Wallace drew upon their respective specialties to help define unfamiliar terms Harry Truman used in his correspondence as a land and mineral speculator and as a soldier in France.

My longtime friend Franklin D. Mitchell of the University of Southern California critiqued early chapters, as did my son, Gregory E. Poen. Both encouraged me during the book's formative stages. Later on, Robert H. Ferrell of Indiana University, who has edited other portions of the Truman collection, cooperated by sharing information about his concurrent research and publication activity.

The people at Putnam's also deserve thanks— my editor, Ellis Amburn, along with his assistant, Fred Chase, were most helpful and congenial. Then, too, copy editor Mary Kurtz did an excellent job alerting me to passages where confusion or inconsistency prevailed.

Finally, my wife, Kathryn, to whom this book is dedicated, proofread the manuscript, buoyed my spirits, and remained my best friend, even though

for months my green-eyed word processor trans-
fixed my gaze and made exorbitant demands upon
our time together.

M.M.P.
Flagstaff, Arizona
July 27, 1983

Contents

Letters Home by

Harry Truman

Introduction

My first two encounters with Harry Truman differed in setting and circumstance, but in each I watched an adventuresome man smiling his way through uncertainty. In one, on a balmy October evening in 1950, he stood in an open convertible dressed in a white panama suit, waving a presidential greeting to crowds lining San Francisco's Market Street. He had just returned from his Korean War strategy talks with General Douglas MacArthur on Wake Island. In the other, eleven years and one season later, he sat behind the wheel of his car as a private citizen bundled in a heavy overcoat, trying to navigate a snow-swept, icy street in his hometown, Independence, Missouri. Both times, true to his nature, he was a man on the move.

Venturing out, embracing the unknown, was a lifelong habit with Harry Truman. Whether an

8,000-mile flight to a remote Pacific island or a short drive across town, HST loved to experience new places. "I like to take trips—any kind of trip," he wrote from retirement about the time I first met him at the Truman Library. Next to reading, he considered travel his chief recreation. "And traveling," he judged, "has taught me almost as much as I have learned from books."

Fortunately, Truman also liked to jot down what he had seen along the way. Several years ago, while compiling *Strictly Personal and Confidential: The Letters Harry Truman Never Mailed,* I discovered at the Truman Library a host of letters he wrote home. Scattered through hundreds of archival boxes, they, along with other travel-related notes, had never been published. When I brought these materials together, they formed, like chips in a mosaic, a panoramic portrait of an amazing personality. Pungent, humorous, often petulant, they reveal an evolving, maturing Harry Truman experiencing a unique, personal odyssey.

At first, I planned to visit every place the President's lifetime meanderings had taken him. I'd already been to most of the states in the union and to Canada, Hawaii, and Wake Island, so I started by paying a visit to the Air Force Museum in Dayton, Ohio, to examine his presidential airplane, the *Independence,* named after his hometown. Then I went to Key West, Florida, to look over his favorite vacation spot.

But when I got back to the Truman Library, the vastness of my task overwhelmed me, especially when I came across a speech note written in his later years in which HST reflected, "I've been from Aroostook, the potato county in Maine to San Diego, California; from Seattle and Bellingham, Washington, to Key West, Florida; from Minnesota to Louisiana, and all the states in between east, west, north and south. . . . I've [also] been to many countries in Europe, South and Central America." That did it! I decided I'd best experience Harry Truman's travels through his notes and letters.

Except for an interesting and happy set of circumstances, most of the letters in this book would have been destroyed. While the President saved everything—including laundry slips—for history, his wife Bess and his sister Mary Jane wanted these letters reduced to ashes. In her book *Letters From Father,* Margaret Truman recalls the time her father found her mother throwing letters into the fireplace. When he admonished her to think of history, Bess replied, "I have."

"He couldn't do a thing with my mother," Margaret informed me. The Truman family physician, Dr. Wallace Graham, told me that "Mrs. Truman destroyed many of them. She said 'They're warm enough the way they are, and they're nobody else's business!' So she burned them."

But I'm convinced that Bess burned only a small fraction of her husband's letters. Because he wrote her so often, sometimes twice a day and over a fifty-year period (I estimate around 1,500 letters), because their old fourteen-room house in

Independence boasts a cavernous attic and numerous nooks and crannies that could handily accommodate cast-off furniture, clothing, and knick-knacks (and, as it turns out, over 1,200 "Dear Bess" letters), and because the President ordered copies made of still others when he prepared his memoirs, all but a few escaped the flames.

More serious was the destruction wrought by Miss Mary Jane Truman. "My Aunt Mary Jane burned her letters—which was a disgrace, I thought," Margaret Truman told me one night as we sat in her New York apartment. "I practically didn't speak to her after that. She had no business doing that." Apparently Harry's sister did it more out of anger than from a desire for privacy. Having never married, living out her last thirty years alone without husband or children, Miss Mary Jane went to her grave in 1978 an embittered woman. Harry had gone off to build a career in politics. Vivian, her other brother, had married, raised a big family, and had a farm of his own. And what had Mary Jane done? Because Harry and Vivian expected it, she stayed home and looked after Mamma. With vengeance in her heart, she destroyed hundreds of Harry's letters.

In a final spiteful thrust shortly before her death, Mary Jane schemed to torch what letters remained. She knew that a batch Harry as President had written her and Mamma still existed because he had "borrowed" them from her while working on his memoirs back in the 1950s. So, cane in hand, she appeared at the Truman Library one afternoon.

Her brother's body now lay in the Library court-yard. Could she have her letters back? Rose Conway, the President's longtime secretary, dutifully handed them over, about a hundred in all, neatly written on green White House stationery. Miss Mary Jane took them home and built herself a nice fire.

What she didn't realize, nor did I until recently, is that every one of those letters survives. I found typed copies in the President's memoirs files, held together in a loose-leaf binder sandwiched between other notes, and I've included some of them in this book. "Dear Mamma and Mary," most begin, and whoever typed those letters thirty years ago meticulously preserved comments HST scratched on the envelopes when, preparing his memoirs, he reread them.

I learned also that another collection of Truman writings thought to have been destroyed still exists. Martha Ann Swoyer, the President's niece, has in her possession the earliest known essays penned by Harry Truman. In the middle of an interview with her, she asked me to turn off my tape recorder. She left the room, and when she returned she carried two oversized books with padded covers. Saying not a word, Mrs. Swoyer placed them in my lap, then rejoined Jim, her equally silent husband, to await my reaction. At first glance I thought they were high school annuals. I opened one and realized that here were Harry Truman's long-lost high school theme books. The penmanship was beautiful; his world history notes looked like a college honor student's; his English compositions spoke of duty, honor, and courage. I later received from Mrs. Swoyer copies she had made of several of these essays, and one is printed here for the first time.

Nor until recently did I discover that letters written by the President's mother and paternal grandfather have survived. Virginia Colgan Bruner, a cousin of Truman's (and along with her husband, a good friend of mine), telephoned me one day and said, "Monte, I've got some old family letters here, I'd like you to look at." We placed those letters on the kitchen table, Virginia and I, and we found the oldest and rarest of all Truman family correspondence. Harry's Aunt Emma was Virginia's grandmother, and in her letters we found correspondence between her and Harry's grandfather Anderson Shipp Truman that dated back a hundred years. We also came across the only letter existing penned by the President's mother, Martha Ellen Truman. A unique find, these early family letters are also included here.

Other discoveries beckoned. Margaret Truman, confronted with her mother's failing health several years ago, asked that an inventory be made of her parents' house in Independence. So the Truman Library sent a team to sort through the attic of the big old house at 219 North Delaware. In addition to uncovering hundreds of "Dear Bess" letters, they found boxes stuffed with dozens of long forgotten "My dear Daughter" letters.

"[My father] always told me not to burn up letters and any papers that I might have. And I didn't," Margaret had assured me earlier. This unexpected discovery confirmed what she had said.

But the new letters required a decision. Margaret had just published *Letters From Father,* which contains letters her dad had written her over a span of three decades. Now there were lots more, and these new ones had been written over an even greater time period. Following her mother's death in October 1982, Margaret, in harmony with her father's liberality, signed these intimate and loving letters over to the public domain. I learned about them two days after they became available when I arrived at the Truman Library hunting pictures for this book. I found the pictures, but I prolonged my stay and spent most of the time making copies of these delightful letters. Needless to say, I expanded this book to include them.

Then too, three of the President's cousins also saved their letters, and they are on file at the Truman Library. Ethel and Nellie Noland, schoolmates of Harry and Bess, preserved a rich lode of letters and postcards. And because Cousin Harry loved to tease the girls, his correspondence with them, even from the battlefield in France during the First World War, is filled with humor and good fun. Ralph Truman, who rose to the rank of general in the National Guard, also turned his Cousin Harry's letters over to the Library, and they speak of politics and shared wartime experiences.

But for Harry Truman, voluminous letter writing was not enough. He also left behind a stack of "diary" notes, along with other sketches describing places he visited and people he met. Penned often on hotel stationery, he wrote these either during his hotel stays or when he returned home (he collected hotel stationery like others collect matchbooks). During his first political job as a county administrator, he searched his soul about political ethics and rampant corruption on stationery bearing the letterhead PICKWICK HOTEL, a now defunct Kansas City landmark. During his senatorial years, he penned a 34-page account of his experiences as a soldier. After he became President, he started making entries in a formal White House diary. He even added to these by jotting random notes on any paper he found handy, whether a banquet placemat or a railroad dining car's menu. And because Harry Truman believed that the only good history is history based on all the facts, he saved it all.

There are those, however (and members of the Truman family are among them), who believe he shouldn't have. The letters are too intimate, the language too salty, and they portray Harry as a racist. Now that they've been found, it would have been better, they think, had Margaret not opened them to public scrutiny.

In defense of Harry Truman's philosophy of history and his daughter's decision to abide by it are those like Charlie Murphy. No Truman associate was closer to HST than Murphy, and I talked with him one night in his Washington, D.C., law office. He spoke from behind a small desk tucked in the corner of a dimly lit back room. The secretaries had long before departed, and I knew the old gent had worked at that desk for many hours. A lamp illuminated his oval face. He looked tired and I felt apologetic for being there. But his recollections proved sharp, and I sensed his pleasure at recounting past political battles and warm personal friendship.

I mentioned a letter I had come across in which the President had instructed an aide to cooperate fully with his biographer. He didn't want anything held back, he said, and he told his assistant, "If I come out all right, I'm lucky." That showed, I surmised, that Harry Truman really wanted to be judged on the record, without any cover-up. "He really didn't need any cover-up," the old counselor told me with a knowing smile. "I have always felt that the more we can do to get the story out just like it really is, the better it will be. I think the story is that good myself."

It is.

I

Horatio

Dear Daughter:

Your fine letter came this morning and your dad was surely glad to get it.

I do wish you and your mother were here in spite of cannons. A little boy about your age came out to the firing point yesterday, and when the big guns went off he almost climbed the flagpole. I think he was more scared than you'd have been. Someday I hope you don't mind them and will come and watch your daddy shoot, and see how it is done.

I am glad you are practicing [the piano] because I would be disappointed if someone should say that the reason Margaret Truman can't play is because her daddy is trying to teach her and he doesn't know how. I want you to know how, but I can't do it for you.

You have to work for yourself if you expect to accomplish anything. And I surely want you to be as good as the best in everything you undertake except smoking cigarettes, and I hope you'll never do that. I've never yet seen a smoking woman that

10

I'd have around me for a minute.

I am glad you are walking everywhere and I hope you'll be entirely well when I get home next Sunday.

Kiss your mamma for me and tell her I still look for letters.

Your loving
Dad

Known years later as "Give 'Em Hell Harry," in family matters this one-time army reserve officer on summer encampment remained to the end of his days a sentimental man, a loving man. His letters home show an unbounded devotion to his wife, Bess, and their daughter, Margaret.

Harry also had love enough to share with the rest of his kin. Among them were cousins Ethel and Nellie Noland, who lived just down the street and around the corner from Harry's boyhood home in Independence, Missouri. Three quick turns on their doorbell's handle and the Noland girls would come rushing "because we knew it was Cousin Harry and we would have a lot of fun." He taught the girls' little sister "Chopsticks" on the parlor piano, lightheartedly joshed Nellie, who took things a bit too seriously, and joined in on plans for a Sunday picnic. "He was a good sport, we just had a lot of fun," Ardis Haukenberry, the Noland sisters' niece, remembers.

They went to high school together, Harry and Bess, Ethel and Nellie, and there his cousins gave him the nickname Horatio, from Shakespeare's

Hamlet, *the play about a Danish prince who had difficulty making up his mind. Hamlet's trusted friend Horatio was different; like Cousin Harry, he wasn't fuzzy-minded. Once you've studied a problem, Harry believed, you needed, with courage, to do something.*

And by his sophomore year, Independence High School's Horatio could explain what courage meant. Written at the age of fifteen, the following is the earliest known essay penned by this future President.

[English Note Book, 1899]
"Courage"
Behavior is the Mir[r]or in which
each man shows his
image.
Emerson

The virtue I call courage is not in always facing the foe but in taking care of those at home. Courage does not always come in battle but in home communities.

I once read a little story of a man who displayed great courage when the Plague was in London. When the Plague first arrived the people were so scared that they left the city, or when a person in a family took sick the house was shut up and a red cross put upon the door and no one allowed to go out but the doctor. The people were so scared when one of a family took it that they would do nothing but scream and would do nothing the doctor said.

This young man put on a doctor's wig and went and waited on the sick. He saw that the doctor's orders were carried out. He took the Plague but got well. I call this courage in the highest degree.

I call it courage in Robt. Morris when he gave up all his fortune for the help of the Americans of whose freedom he was in no way assured, and who when they did get it let him die in poverty.[1]

Thus ends my short composition on what I call courage.

A true heart, a strong mind, and a great deal of courage and I think a man will get through the world.

Putting family needs first came naturally to Harry; he'd learned by example from his parents. Soon after John Anderson Truman and his bride, Martha Ellen, took up housekeeping in Lamar, Missouri, in 1882 (where Harry was born two years later), John's papa, Anderson Shipp Truman, moved in with them. "I have a nice room. Just the right size for me. I have a nice stove in it," the family patriarch assured his daughter Emily.

Anderson Shipp had settled in western Missouri from Kentucky in the 1840s. A widower crippled by arthritis when he moved in with his son, he penned a letter that, stained and hardly readable, Virginia

[1]Morris helped finance the American Revolution, and later went broke through an ill-fated land purchase.

Colgan Bruner discovered a century later among her grandmother Emily's correspondence.

True to the old man's original prose, this rare document reads:

Oct. 18th '82
Lamar
Barton Co., Mo.

My dear Emma and Roch[2] . . . ,
We have got Sister fixt up and in good hands. . . .

Where I have seen our neighbors, they are very kind and sociable and friendly.

I have nothing new to write you as being a stranger I have not been out in the county yet. This city is a nice town. It is a good deal like Independence. Some very nice buildings, and a good deal of business down here.

We have six churches here. Almost all of the denominations that is common is represented here. The Baptist has the lead, that is the most numbers at this time. They have a young preacher. . . .

Emma, you must not let Murray[3] forget me . . . remember your dear old Pa.

A. S. Truman

Harry, whose middle initial "S" stands for Shipp as well as for Solomon, after his maternal grandfather, Solomon Young, was four years old when Pappa Truman died. He remembered him as a

---

[2]Emily and Rochester Colgan, his daughter and son-in-law.
[3]Murray Colgan, his grandson, father of Virginia Bruner.

God-fearing Baptist "who set the women of his family on a pedestal and kept them there." It was a trait his grandson inherited.

The family moved to Independence, and because the Presbyterian Church was close by, Harry's mother enrolled him in its Sunday School. There he met his lifelong love, Bess Wallace, granddaughter of a prominent Independence merchant. She was the "prettiest sweetest little girl" he'd ever seen, but he was so shy he didn't talk to her for five years.

A few months after Harry graduated from high school, his livestock-trading father lost their house around the corner from the Noland sisters. The family moved to Kansas City, and instead of going to college, Harry, true to his definition of courage, went to work to keep his younger brother and sister in school.

His first job found him pumping a railroad hand-cart down a stretch of newly laid Santa Fe track as a timekeeper for a railroad construction crew. When that job ran out after the new Santa Fe section was completed, Harry tried his hand at various things: wrapping newspapers in the basement of the Kansas City Star, *ushering at a theater, finally clerking at a bank for seventy-five dollars a month.*

But he always saved out enough change for a stage show, and he didn't forget his hometown cousins. Here, in his earliest known letter, Harry (alias Horatio) beseeches Ethel and Nellie to travel down the twelve-mile "Dummy Line" that connected Independence by rail to Kansas City. In addition to the theater, he also promises to perform some matchmaking for Nellie.

[Kansas City, Mo.]
Feb. 2, '04

My Dear Cousins:
I'll meet you at EBT & Co.'s Walnut St. entrance on Sat. Feb. 6, '04 at 2:15 P.M. and have *him* along if possible (that's for Nellie). If not he'll come to the theater *later.*

I shall expect you all to go home with me and stay till Sunday. Anyway, if you can do so write me at home, 2108 Park. I think if you will go home with me to supper [that] Mr. H.[4] will too.

I understand that Mr. Beresford[5] is exceedingly good, so don't fail to come. I've *already* got the seats, so if you fail I'll have to take some hobos and I don't want to do that.

Write immediately if you'll stay till Sunday to—

Horatio

After Harry quit his bank job to take up farming on his grandmother's farm southeast of Kansas City, hobos (who stalked the railroad tracks and countryside) were once again on his mind as he penned a letter to Bess. "I was scared to an inch almost, but it was all for nothing. I didn't even see a hobo," he reported after walking home in the dark beside the train tracks. He signed this, one of

---

[4]A fellow bank clerk, remembered only as Mr. Henderson.
[5]Harry Beresford, popular stage actor.

*his first courtship letters, "Most sincerely, Harry."
It would take him seven years and two hundred and
twenty-seven additional letters to Bess before he
changed to "Yours forever, Harry."*

*It wasn't shyness alone that controlled young
Truman's pen. He felt that unless he made good,
unless he became a successful businessman, he
was unworthy of Bess's hand. At every turn, Bess's
mother, Madge Gates Wallace, reminded him that
the Wallaces stood among Independence's social
elite.[6] So, whenever Harry visited Bess, he tried to
impress Madge Wallace. "I am glad your mother
like[d] my efforts on the piano," he wrote. "I am
ashamed of it myself. But you know a farmer can't
be a pianist, much as he'd like to be."*

*There were lots of things a farmer couldn't do.
Returning to the family farm near Grandview after
rendezvousing with Bess to see a show in Kansas
City, he wrote her about some of them.*

Grandview
Monday P.M.
[June 10, 1912]

Dear Bess:
I am at last answering your letter. It was my intention to answer it when it first came but I could think
of nothing of interest to say to you and kept putting
it off until suddenly it was no use to write because

[6]Bess's grandfather, George Porterfield Gates, had
amassed a sizable estate by supplying flour and grain to
wagon trains heading west along the Santa Fe trail.

I'd beat the letter.

Do you know I waited fully ten minutes on the corner for that dad bloomed car? Think of wasting ten good minutes on the corner on Sunday night. I did my level best to miss the train—walked all the way from 9th & Walnut to the depot and still had four minutes. It was my idea [that] if I could have legally missed the thing to see if you'd go to Fairmount with me today. Did you go?

It really was a good thing I got home, though. We plowed corn this afternoon and I was much in demand. I raked the yard this morning, that is a large part of it. Our yard is about the size of yours and when I go to clean the grass off it, I usually start before breakfast and quit after supper.

There was a little old meadowlark [sitting] on the telephone wire and every time I'd stop to observe the scenery he'd say "Pretty boy. Go right back to work." I finally made him change his base of operations and nag the hired man.

There are some birds who haven't any consideration for a person's feelings. There's one that says "Oh my, what a poor hay pitcher" when we make hay. It gets very exasperating when it's kept up all day long. Black birds say "Jack. Jack. Jack, the Champion." Crows swear terribly if you know what key they're talking in and happen to be in a cussing mood yourself. It takes a pretty fluent cusser to understand all they say. I couldn't, you know.(?)

. . . [The corn] has to be plowed, you know, whether school keeps or not. We are also anticipating (spelled right?) a hay crop this week too. Would have had it up by this [time] if it hadn't been for the rain. We ought to have dry weather this week, though. You know, the moon changed in the evening. When it changes before dinner it's a sign of rain. Didn't work last year, though. As Mark [Twain] says, all signs fail when it's dry so it's best to carry your own bottle. . . .

I wish we had an [auto] machine, if it was only a Ford. I am almost tempted sometimes to get papa to agree to sell the black horses and buy a dinky Ford. They'd do it.

If by any chance under creation I can go [to the auto races], would you? Don't you hesitate to go with someone else if they ask you because I'm sure I'll have to work. . . .

This is an awful excuse for a letter but won't you answer it soon? You know I only write to get your letters. Please think this is worth one.

Sincerely,
Harry

II

"This, Without the Paint, Looks Like My Joint"

Determined to get rich, the farmer thought he'd try his hand at land speculation on the northern Great Plains. The government still had some acreage for homesteading left, but not much, and so it conducted a drawing to determine the successful applicants, and a friend urged Harry to register.

"I'm getting ready for So. Dakota today," he wrote his sweetheart. Like Bess's mother, however, Harry held decided opinions on who were God's chosen. "I bet there'll be more bohunks and Rooshans up there than white men," he judged. "I think it is a disgrace to the country for those fellows to be in it. If they had only stopped immigration about twenty or thirty years ago, the good Americans could all have had plenty of land and we'd have been an agricultural country forever." Like Thomas Jefferson, he feared the city's impact upon society. "When it is made up of factories and large cities it soon becomes depraved and makes classes among people."

Sending the Noland sisters a postcard from Gregory, South Dakota, Horatio, with visions of becoming a land baron, jotted, "Here is where we did it. When we win we'll invite you up to see us." The girls never made the trip to South Dakota, because Harry didn't win the lottery. But news soon arrived of similar doings in Montana.

Having to see the family lawyer in Kansas City, Harry also used his journey there to gather information on how best to get to Montana.

[Grandview, Mo.]
[early September, 1913]

Dear Bess:

I saw [your brother] George today in K. C. I might as well have stayed in town for all the time I spent at home. It was necessary for me to see Boxley, principally to get touched for some money. It seems to be a very charming habit of his. In fact, as Bill Bostain[1] said in his famous high school speech, touching seems to be the proper description of interviews with lawyers. If dollars were tears, those gentlemen would certainly have their clients praying for a larger reservoir.

Besides the visit to Mr. B., I made one to the office of the Burlington [Railway] Co. [and] got about six volumes of literature and some information. Also, I visited the offices of the Rock Island, the C. M. & St. P.,[2] [and] the Chicago Grt. Westn.

[1]A high school classmate who apparently had oratorical talent.
[2]Chicago, Minneapolis, and St. Paul.

At each one I hid all the books I already had and received a new supply. I brought the literature home in a market basket. (There were apples in the bottom of it.) At each office I learned that the RR had the best and quickest way to go, although there was a difference of six hours in some of the schedules.

I have had half the fun of going now anyway, whether I get off or not. I've a notion that my name will be 9002 if there are 9001 claims, but I reckon I'd as well blow $60 for carfare as for booze. Since I don't drink, I can charge the 60 off to unrequited thirst and know that at least I'm obtaining more nearly value received.

I haven't any excuse to offer for not having called you up except that I went to Federman's twice to do it and couldn't get a phone. That is another time my intentions were good. Please credit. Of course, I couldn't possibly spend 5 cents. I hate to talk over a pay-as-you-enter phone because every time just as conversation is going good, down comes the key with a "time's up, another nickle please." To tell the truth, I hate to talk over the phone anyway. I'm always rattled and can never say what I want to. I like to use one only when I'm driven to it. I don't even answer one here at home when [sister] Mary's handy to it.

I hope George can get off to make the Montana trip. I'm sure we can have a good time even if we get nothing. Also, we'll probably get cooled off. I think [your other brother] Frank really wants to go too. My small brother says he's not going to spend money for a Pullman under any circumstances. I've a notion he thinks I'll buy one and offer him half. He's got another think coming. I'll sell him half. As dry as it's been and as hard up as I am, I'm going to be stingy even if he has got twins.[3] Papa's dying to go. I'll bet he does. Won't that be a conglomeration of Trumans?

Bess . . . I'm mad because I had to come home. The threshers were expected this afternoon and they *didn't* arrive. I might just as well have been at Independence, provided always, of course, you'd been home. It was most awful nice [of you] to say the breaks in the middle of the week were a pleasure to you. You bet I'm glad. They're seventh heaven to me.

Can I come Sunday? If we don't thresh, I shall have urgent business in town, I hope about Friday. Please consider this worth an answer.

Most sincerely,
Harry

Here's King René. You see, I wasn't bluffing.[4]

The Chicago Great Western had the best rail connections to Glasgow, Montana. With the train jolting and swaying, Harry's penmanship proved a bit shaky.

---

[3]Harry's brother Vivian had recently become a father.
[4]An enclosed clipping showed a statue of the fifteenth-century ruler of Provence and Anjou.

Dear Bess:

We have a full two sections anyway. Another boy came up just as we were ready to leave. We've been playing cards ever since we left K. C.—not Roman Cross either. I am tired riding already. There are three other young men in this section and we've been having a very good time. The other four are married. You can see how birds of a feather etc.

I wish very much that George could have come. Our berths came to $1.80 apiece for the trip up. If we can do as well coming back, our expense won't be very great. That will make about $36 for railroad fare. I guess we can eat on $10, so you see the expense will fall far short of $60. The crowd on this car is as good and as good-looking as any I ever saw on a standard [fare.] This is tourist [class], you know.

We have decided to take claims No. 1, 2, 3, 4, 5, 6, 7, 8. Of course, the one who's telling it gets one, and the rest have to take them as they come. We'll have $40 worth of fun.

I wish I'd told you to start a letter today to Glasgow, G. Del [General Delivery]. It sure will be a long wait till I get one. I am hoping you can read this one. This *Limited* (?) is making such a pace I can hardly write. I'll send you another from St. Paul. We wait 3 hrs there and I can do better.

Most sincerely,
Harry

From Minneapolis, Horatio wrote Nellie: "It is cold as an iceberg up here. They say it's been hot at one time, but I don't believe it."

From Glasgow, Montana, came word: "Here's where we registered. I am in line for No. 75,000."

Back on the Grandview farm a few weeks later, he informed Bess: "I got a paper from Montana yesterday just full of interesting things. It says that 34 bushels of wheat can be raised on the Ft. Peck land and that land is worth from $12 to $50 per acre. I am hoping for 320 of the $50 kind. Watch me get 160 of the $12 variety. Probabilities are that none will spell what I take."

He was right. Again, the numbers eluded him.

Undaunted, Harry cast about for another land deal. Wanting to marry Bess, yet having to apologize for urging her to marry him "and then not following up things with the proper sort of jewelry," he explained: "Financially, I'm $12,500 worse than nothing." "But," he promised, "I'm not going to be for long, and if you'll believe it, I know I can make things come [out] right yet."

His renewed search for success took him to the Pecos Valley in west Texas. "I am in Texas again. We are having some time," read the card he dispatched to Cousin Ethel from Fort Stockton in November 1915. He spent a lot of time that fall and winter jumping on and off trains across the southwest. At Sweetwater, a Texas town west of Forth Worth, he sent Nellie a picture postcard.

[early September, 1915]
I had to get up early and run three blocks to obtain this one. We are only supposed to stay here 5 min., but I thought it was worth the risk. *Ain't it grand!*

The "grand" building was Sweetwater's high school. Harry and Nellie had a running joke about her becoming a schoolmarm, and everywhere he traveled, he searched for pictures of schoolhouses. Failing that, he sent her jailhouses as a fitting substitute.

Once, unable to find a postcard showing either, he sketched for Nellie a "photo from 'Life,'" and captioned his artistic rendering "Co. Jail. Potiwatimie Co., Kansas." But the drawing more resembled the Tower of London. He added:

[Denison, Texas]
[Feb. 1, 1916]
We passed this place in the early morning, but I managed to get a photo of it. Thought perhaps you'd like one for your collection. Denison is approaching. Something of interest may appear.

At Fort Worth, the local high school caught his eye.

Feb. 3, 1916
Here is another building in which you should exhibit some interest. The inmates who run it get from $100 to $200 per.

Back in Fort Stockton, he found a postcard boasting a picture of the Pecos County jail.

Feb. 5, 1916

I'm stopping here. I haven't forgotten you. I can't find the high school so I'm sending a good substitute. Harry

His Uncle Harry, Harrison Young, lived with his sister's family on the Grandview farm. Harrison also owned some land and had saved some money, so his nephew hoped the old man might stake him to a slice of that prized Texas acreage. He finally convinced his uncle to go with him to see for himself the wonders of the Pecos Valley.

As their train chugged westward, Horatio wrote three cards to Nellie, the first sporting another of his artistic sketches (this time titled "Polytech Eufaula"), the second showing the Women's Penitentiary at McAlester, Oklahoma ("Here we are, identification and all. Very very interesting place"), and the last showing the train depot of Denton, Texas ("There's no jail in the burg. Here is the next best thing.")

"Uncle Harry seems to be enjoying himself," he informed Bess. "He is able to beat every big lie that is told in his presence by a bigger one. When he can do that, he's happy." But alas, the old gent didn't stay happy. The Pecos Valley chilled him to the bones, and he told Harry "if he ever thawed out," he'd not chance another visit there. "I have

about given up hope for this proposition now," the young land speculator admitted.

After delivering Uncle Harrison home, Harry turned to speculating in minerals. He borrowed $2,000 and bought a third interest in a lead and zinc mine in Commerce, Oklahoma, called the T.C.H. Mine (for Truman, Culbertson, and Hughes). He handled the company's books, and divided his time between the farm and the mine.

To save money, he even took over the job of night watchman at the mine. To hire one, he figured, would cost $2.50 a night. "So I bought me a cot and mattress for $4.50, and now I consider that I'm making $3.00 a night by sleeping in a better place than I was paying 50 cents for."

In an undated letter fragment to Bess, he wrote:

[Commerce, Okla.]
I must be noise-proof when it comes to sleeping. There's a 135-horsepower gas engine in one of these mills that's running all night. It makes a racket like the German army. The other one has a shaft hoister going all the time. It makes a noise like a rattle trap Met street car. Occasionally some water or something runs down out of one of the boilers here in the room, making a sound like a rat sliding off a tin roof. None of 'em affect my sleeping powers after 9 P.M.

Despite his prudence and hard work, the elements again turned against him. The mine's ground boss got drunk, their superintendent turned out *crooked, neighbors diverted their water supply, and hoisting equipment broke down constantly. Facing bankruptcy, Harry confided to Bess that "I shall join the class who can't sign checks of their own, I suppose. It is a hard nut to crack, but it has to be done. There was never one of our name who had sense enough to make money. I am no exception."*

"We are still hanging on by our eyebrows," he wrote from the mine three months later. "Just think' what a win would mean," he added, clinging to his vision of success. "All my debts paid (something that no one of the name ever accomplished), a city home, a country home, some automobiles and flying machines. . ."

But as he waited for a train in the Miami, Oklahoma, depot, located a few miles from his zinc operation, the end was near.

August 22, 1916

Dear Bess:
Your good brief letter came last night. I was sure glad to hear from you. I was afraid you wouldn't get mine. . . .

I am certainly sorry to miss the Fair. I was expecting to be there at least one day but I just can't leave here now. We made 3 tons of lead and 1½ tons of zinc yesterday. That amounts to about $285. If we can do that well three days a week, we can pay out. The ground boss expects to do better than that tomorrow.

I started to Neosho this morning to see one of the former owners of the mine and get a further time extension. I have missed two trains already but hope to catch the next one.

It turned cold down here last night and I overslept. Didn't get up until 6:30 and by the time I'd made a trip down underground and changed my clothes, I only had twenty minutes to come four miles. Just missed the taxi that would have caught the first train. Got over here to Miami five minutes after it left. Took a fool notion to go to the barber shop and missed the next one by half a block.

I am sitting in the station now and if this one gets by without me I'll give up the trip and go back to the mine. I might be better off and some RR fare ahead if I did that anyway. The old gink may turn me down. If he does, I'll still get a chance to come home broke.

I sure hope to see you Sunday if not sooner. I am going to look for another letter day after tomorrow. Be sure and send it because it's awful lonesome down here.

Most sincerely,
Harry

"The old gink" didn't turn him down, but despite the former owner's tolerance Harry's mine venture came to naught. "Closed it down yesterday after paying out the last cent I've got. There's nothing like going entirely busted while you're at it." Anyway, he conjectured, it was time to make "a new start."

Sending Cousin Ethel a color print showing a similar mining operation, Horatio had jested,

"This, without the paint, looks like my joint. Thought perhaps you'd like to see where I sunk my change."

III

"I Have Oil on the Brain"

[Muskogee, Okla.]
[Dec. 19, 1916]
[Nellie:]
I have forgotten whether I favored you from here
or not when I was going south. If I did, you can
simply destroy the old one. I have oil on the brain.

H—

*"You know," Harry mused shortly before his zinc
mine went bust, "a man's judgment is good or bad
accordingly as he wins or loses on a proposition."
Success resulted from "one big guess." And, he
vowed, "I'm going to keep guessing. Mamma says
that Grampa Young was cleaned out three times
that she can remember, but he came up every time
with something else."*

*That something else for Harry was an oil ven-
ture. One of his zinc partners had a friend named
David Morgan, a Tulsa oil man, and with a $5,000
loan cosigned by Mamma, Truman bought into
Morgan & Company. "Nearly every person I have
talked with lately is interested in some kind of oil
deal," he bragged to Bess. "I nearly bust to tell*

[them] what kind of one I'm in and then don't."

During his trip south with "oil on the brain," taken to check out oil leases in southern Oklahoma, he found another schoolhouse for Nellie.

[Vinita, Okla.]
[Dec. 18, 1916]

Here is a brand new one. I've passed here several times but have never had the opportunity to remember you. A Very Merry Holiday Season to you.

As ever, H—

The new year started on a promising note. Everyone seemed to need Harry's help, including the Masonic Lodge he had helped organize out in Grandview. Writing Bess on company stationery, with its letterhead printed in flowing old English, the farmer-turned-oil speculator exuded self-confidence.

Morgan & Company
Oil Investments
Corporation
Suite 703 New Ridge Arcade
Kansas City, Mo.

Jan. 12, 1917

Dear Bess:

How does this look to you? I have cancelled their order for this [stationery.] There'll be no more like it. It looks like patent medicine ads.

I am sending you the [theater] passes. I wish I

could see you tonight, but I have to be home to start the Masons off right this year. This is their first meeting this year.

I do wish you would come in and see what a busy man I am.

There are several collectors, the honorable president, and two stenogs waiting my royal pleasure right at this minute.

Here's waiting impatiently for Sunday.

Most sincerely,
Harry

For a commission, Morgan & Company handled purchase and lease of suspected oil-rich property in Kansas, Oklahoma, and Texas, and as a land syndicate it also sold shares. Bess even invested a few dollars in the enterprise. "The money is coming in by the basketful," the company's treasurer, one Harry S. Truman, could report.

With success in his grasp and marriage on his mind, he assured Bess:

I do wish I could have taken that walk with you. I have high hopes of taking a very long one with you very soon. Things look very encouraging at this place now. If I can only pay Mamma out, I'll sure be in a position for all the things I have told you of.

But then Harry lost confidence. Having just turned thirty-three, and bruised by his inability to salvage something from his defunct zinc invest-

ment, he sat depressed one midnight in a Kansas City hotel. Carrying on an imaginary conversation with his sweetheart, he let his mind wander over many subjects, including his country's recent entry into a world war.

WESTGATE HOTEL

Kansas City, Missouri
Sunday Night
[May 27, 1917]

Dear Bess:

The train was late. It didn't arrive until 10:15. Should have been in at 9:00. I didn't call up because I know you don't appreciate midnight calls.

This letter should have reached you at ten o'clock this morning but the one I had written sounded so bad that I didn't send it. In fact, it was both blue and mushy. They don't go well together or singly. This one may be as bad before I am through. If it is, I won't send it either. I have written you dozens of epistles you have never seen.[1] Whenever I'm particularly happy or particularly the opposite, an insane desire to tell you about it possesses me and I write you about it. Generally I'm never half so badly or so well off as . . . I first thought, and you are therefore not worried with

[1]Writing letters and then not mailing them was a lifelong habit with Truman. For those he wrote but didn't dispatch as President, see the editor's *Strictly Personal and Confidential: The Letters Harry Truman Never Mailed.*

35

knowing what a very erratic and unstable person I am.

You know, I have been badly disappointed today. That dad blasted [zinc] mine has been sold twice and has come back to me both times because the brother of the man who owns the land the thing is on happens to own the adjoining mill and wants my mine to run through it. (Can you comprehend that Dutch statement?) There is a Bertha M. Clay[2] plot connected with the thing. . . .

I seem to have a grand and admirable ability for calling tails when heads come up. My luck should surely change. Some time I should win. I have tried to stick. Worked, really did, like thunder for ten years to get that old farm in line for some big production. Have it in shape and have had a crop failure every year. Thought I'd change my luck, got a mine and see what I did get. Tried again in the other long chance, oil. Still have high hopes on that, but then I'm naturally a hopeful happy person; one of the "Books in brooks, Tongues in trees and Good in everything" sort of guys.

Most men are liars (I'm one myself on occasion . . .) and they all are when there's money in it. I was very very impressionable when I was a kid and I believed all the Sunday school books and idealist dope we were taught. And it's taken my twenty-

[2]Pseudonym for Charlotte Mary Brame, who wrote a number of adventure novels, including *The Earl's Atonement* (1885).

36

odd years to find that Mark [Twain] is right when he says that the boy who stole the jam and lied about it and killed the cat and sassed his ma grew up and became a highly honored citizen and was sent to Congress. [Twain] is absolutely right. The poor gink who stands around and waits for someone to find out his real worth just naturally continues to stand, but the gink who toots his horn, and tells 'em how good he is, makes 'em believe it when they know he's a bluff and would steal from his grandma.

I don't believe that. I'm just feeling that way now. If I can't win straight I'll continue to lose. I'm the luckiest guy in the world to have you to love, and to know that when I've arrived at a sensible solution of these direful financial difficulties I've gotten into, that I'll have the finest, best looking— and all the other adjectives in the superlative—girl in the world to make the happiest home in the world with. Now isn't that a real heaven on earth to contemplate? I think it is and I know I'll have just that in the not far off future, unless it is necessary for me to get myself shot in this war and then I'll still find you somewhere.

I dreamt that you and I were living in Rome when togas were the fashion. I am always dreaming of you. I'm never anywhere in a dream or out of it that I don't imagine you there too. . . .

You'll sure enough be bored when you get this if you do. But I just had to have a conversation with you. I can never say what I feel when I see you and anyway when a hard-headed American citizen gets to spouting his heart actions in Laura Jean Libby[3] periods, he just simply feels like an idiot, and I do but I mean all I've said about you and I'll keep hoping that J. S. Mullen[4] stays by us till we get a gusher and I can really show you how much I care.

Hope to see you right soon. Will have to go home tomorrow night to get a new set of collars etc., as my grip has all secondhand ones. Can I come over Tuesday night? Just remember how crazy I am about you and forget all the rest.

Most sincerely,
Harry

Many decades later, looking back on his experience as an oil man, Truman reflected in an unused draft of his memoirs that "the manpower shortage resulting from the imminence of the war" caused Morgan & Company to fold. Those companies that took over its abandoned oil leases went on to discover Kansas's famous Teter Oil Pool.

[Memoirs draft]

Thus Culbertson, Morgan and I, together with our shareholders, missed by a few months being beneficiaries of this great oil pool and the millions of dollars which it has already pro-

---

[3]Popular American novelist whose books espoused an idealistic formula for love and marriage.
[4]A Morgan & Company financial backer from Ardmore, Oklahoma.

duced from the leases formerly owned by our little company. If we had carried that well [in Greenwood County, Kansas] on down and opened up the Teter field ourselves, it is a cinch that I would never have become President of the United States. . . .

Actually, though, I believe that destiny had a hand in my participation in this [ill-timed] speculative venture. Otherwise, I might have exchanged a stormy career in politics, which carried me from the precinct to the Presidency, for the easy life of a wealthy oil man. And I don't think that would suit me at all.

IV

"I'm a Soldier Now"

He resigned as treasurer of Morgan & Company, packed his grips, left his sister Mary in charge of the farm with a hired man, and went off to war.

It was actually Harry's second hitch in the military. As a youth, he had wanted to attend West Point, but "flat eyeballs" kept him out of the regular army. So, at twenty-one he applied to a Kansas City national guard artillery unit. It had less stringent physical requirements, and after the medical sergeant gave him an approving nod on June 14, 1905, Henry could boast to Cousin Ethel, "I'm a soldier now."

His first stint as a soldier lasted seven years, and the summer encampments he attended gave the farmer from Grandview a variety of experiences, some of which he recalled on paper. His second year in the guard, his unit went to St. Joseph, Missouri:

[Diary, 1937]

It rained nearly all week at St. Joseph. The lightning struck the headquarters tent of the brigade and killed a sergeant and a private, so that the members of Battery B felt that some real war had been experienced. The principal diversion during that wet week was to dig holes in front of tents where the water was a foot deep over all, and let unsuspecting sergeants and second lieutenants fall into them.

He left the guard in 1912, and when he reenlisted after the war broke out, he was commissioned a first lieutenant and shipped to Camp Doniphan at Fort Sill, Oklahoma.
The colonel put Truman in charge of the regiment's canteen, and he launched his business with money collected at two dollars per man from each of the artillery batteries. Lieutenant Graballsky, they called him. That changed to "Curly Trumanheimer" when he teamed up with Sergeant Eddie Jacobson, a Jewish merchant from Kansas City.

[Camp Doniphan, Okla.]
[Oct. 17, 1917]

Dear Bess:
I am writing you in the canteen, the picture of which is enclosed. It is not a very good picture either, because it was taken the first day we moved into the building and things weren't very clean around the outside (or inside either).

The work still piles up. They find something new to do every day. Drill from seven-thirty to nine-thirty on the guns and all afternoon on horseback.

41

I have written you a letter every night and gave it to a nut to mail and he failed to do it. He gave them to me this morning. You should have heard the cussin' he got, or rather you should not have heard it. It would have to be edited to go into the Police Gazette. Some of those letters were works of art at the time of their composition but are stale dope now. . . .

I almost bought a carload of apples yesterday but they wouldn't take off enough on the price. I am some purchaser. Everyone says ours is the best canteen on the job. Jacobson is some manager. That's a grand combination, Jacobson & Trumanheimer. . . . I wrote checks until my bank account is as weak as Morgan & Co.'s used to be when I had paid for drilling rig, etc. I have taken in about $5,400 and bought some $9,000 worth of goods. I always manage to get back to the canteen no matter where I start to talk.

I sure wish I could see you. I'd almost desert to do it. I'm of the opinion that I'd better cripple Chas. Mize.[1] . . .

Send some of that cake. It never did get hard; it only had 15 minutes to work in after it arrived and it was sure good.

I am going to see that Uncle Frank doesn't beat you to the postman from now on if I have to sit up

[1]Mize's mother had invited Bess to accompany her on a visit to Camp Doniphan, but then delayed coming.

until 3 P.X.[A.M.] to do it. I'll send you some more pictures when they are done.

Your Harry

[Camp Doniphan, Okla.]
[Oct. 25, 1917]

Dear Bess:

This has been another fine day. Your letter came on time today. I'll admit that our mail service is bum all right but it is improving and I hope that very soon it will be in perfect running order. Father Tiernan is in charge and has built himself a fine tent to work in.[2]

Mr. Lee[3] and I have our tent boxed up now and it is like living in a house. The floor is bright and new and shows the dust awful plain, but I think we'll soon have it black enough so that will be remedied.

Our dust storms continue with charming regularity. Some of the natives are of the opinion that they will quit but I doubt it. . . .

Your enclosure is very fine.[4] I have had my hat

[2]Regimental chaplain, Father L. Curtis Tiernan, known affectionately as Padre, who also oversaw the mailroom.
[3]Jay M. Lee, who after the war wrote *The Artilleryman,* a chronicle of the 35th Division's artillery units' wartime experience.
[4]Bess's enclosure, probably a letter from a friend whose loved one served with Harry, has not survived.

stretched on the nice things she said about me. I only wish I could be half as fine as some people think I am. Then I'd know I wouldn't stay in Okla. all eternity.

I slipped up on your letter last night because I had no place to write. All our goods and chattels were scattered from here to yonder on account of getting into our new house. I am going to send this special on the bet that it may not appear until Sunday and I'll do your tomorrow's the same way. You may get them both on Sunday.

I am hoping to see you soon. You never can tell how the Commanding Officer is going to act but I am doing all I can to get away on Nov. 7. It looks good. Write every time you get a chance.

Yours Always,
Harry

"PERMISSION TO LEAVE REFUSED AT LAST MINUTE," *Harry had to wire home. Leaves were also cancelled at Christmastime. Stuck in camp, Curly Trumanheimer contented himself by writing letters.*

For Ethel and Nellie, he wrote:

December 24, 1917

My Dear Cousins:

Your good letter came several days ago and I certainly appreciated it. I had written you a couple of times before and could not understand why you hadn't answered. Several of my letters home and across the street were lost and I decided to send a school house. It had the desired result.

I have been going like a sewing machine ever since our arrival down here. They made me canteen officer, which means that I run a general store for the regiment. We sell everything from buttons to booze, or an imitation of it. Booze has been barred from the army, thank heaven, or I would have in all probability been court-martialed for refusing to sell it. We sell about $500 or $600 a day in candy, cakes, etc. Christmas knocks the socks off our business because everyone gets cakes from home.

The stockings and handkerchiefs were just what I needed. You couldn't have made a better selection if I'd been there to show you (which I'd surely have liked to be). I can't tell you how I'll appreciate the socks until I've worn them in the trenches one of these icy mornings. I get out and drill around and raise sand generally on horseback, on foot, and sometimes in an automobile. I have been wanting to go up in an aeroplane, but haven't yet.

I wish you could come down and see me while I'm here. Mamma and Mary were down last Saturday and Sunday. I was sure glad to see them. I nearly ran off and went home with them. They had a fine time but the weather was not very nice while they were here.

Please write to me whenever you feel inclined because I am always glad to hear from you and letters from home look mighty good. Remember me to everyone, especially all the family.

Thank you very much for the socks and

handkerchiefs. They are just what I need. And finally, write.

> Most sincerely, your cousin,
> Harry

Finally, in January, Harry got a one-week leave. "I have been pinching myself every day, saying, well what a grand kidding you gave yourself," he wrote Bess afterward. Instead of buoyed spirits after being home, he was more homesick than ever. "I didn't know how crazy I was about you until I went to leave," he told his love. "I'd give all I have or ever expect to have to see you tonight."

A blizzard hit Oklahoma, and Bess, not hearing from Harry for several days, sent him a wire. He replied:

NOTHING WRONG   LETTER EVIDENTLY MISCARRIED   WROTE YOU DAY BEFORE YESTERDAY TRAINS ALL LAID OUT AND DELAYED BY STORM WIRING YOU TODAY   VERY SORRY TO HAVE CAUSED SO MUCH WORRY   WILL WRITE YOU FROM NEW YORK SOON

Rumors abounded about their overseas departure date, and after sending Bess a second wire that day, he wrote her a letter.

> [Camp Doniphan, Okla.]
> [Jan. 15, 1918]

Dear Bess: I have your telegram today and I hope you have my two. I wouldn't cause you any worry for the world. It sure makes a fellow feel like he is someone to have the nicest girl in the world telegraphing to see if he is on his pins or not.

I have been the busiest mortal on the reservation since returning. They closed the canteen on the 10th and forced us to take an invoice right away and then opened up again. I had an awful time proving up because my Jew was in Kansas City. In addition to that I have had the Battery office to straighten out and the Battery mess to run. I have also had to attend drills morning and afternoon and go to school at night.

General Berry told us yesterday that we would have to learn the drill regulations by heart and do several other impossible stunts. It is my opinion that an elimination process is taking place preparatory to our going abroad. I mentioned in my wire that I would probably write you from an eastern port soon. You can put your own construction on it because we can't write about some arrangements that are taking place here.

I am very lucky, I think. You probably won't think so. Besides, I may get a physical and get sent home. I'd very nearly croak if I do, as badly as I would like to be home. . . .

I am going to get better about writing from this [time on], and when I can't write I'll wire you a night letter. I am looking for a letter today. I haven't written Mamma and Mary since I came down. Please forgive me this time.

Yours Always,
Harry

[Camp Doniphan, Okla.]
[Jan. 18, 1918]

Dear Bess:

Your letter came yesterday and I was very glad to hear that mine had arrived at last. . . .

I have been so busy, I don't have time to get homesick but I wish I could see you. You can't imagine how badly I wish it. But it can't be done now. When the war's over we'll make up for time lost. Remember, it has to be won and someone has to do it. I am sure you wouldn't have me be a slacker much as you'd like me to be at home. I know that's how Mamma feels, although she sure hates to see me go. If I get a kickout for incompetence then I'll know I've tried anyway, and I can stay at home with a clear conscience (I'd rather be shot though).

Yesterday was a grand day—your letter came and it also was one to make me feel all stuck up. Send one as often as you can. The days are grand when one arrives.

Yours Always,
Harry

Then it was Harry's turn to worry over missing letters.

[Camp Doniphan, Okla.]
[Feb. 16, 1918]

Dear Bess:

I haven't heard from you for five days and I am getting terribly uneasy. I am going to wire you to-

48

day if I don't hear. I got a letter last Tuesday saying that you didn't feel well, and I have been expecting every day to hear you were worse. I hope that you are not and that everything is all as it should be. I haven't heard from home for a week either.

They played me a bad trick at the bank up there the other day. My good friend Booth[5] called a $4,000 loan on me. Maybe you think I didn't unburden my mind on him. I am going to show him a thing or two some of these days.

I went out to fire [artillery] the other day along with the rest of the regiment's officers and by some hook or crook I was unlucky enough to observe more shots correctly than anyone else, and now I have to fire next time. I'm scared green because Gen. Berry always eats 'em alive after they fire. He's very expert at making a person shake in his boots. Capt. Pete was second and Lt. Patterson was third. There was evidently some mistake in grading the papers because you know very well that a person with a half-baked eyesight like mine couldn't see more shots correctly than one with real eyes. Anyway, I'm the goat. I guess it's very good experience though.

If I don't hear from you very soon I'm going to disgrace the service by going A.W.O.L. and finding out what's the matter. There was some joy in life when I got letters from home and from you but when they come from bankers and I am ordered to show my ignorance before the whole regiment,

---

[5]A hometown banker.

there's not much left. If I could only see you, I'd
be all in heaven.

Yours Always,
Harry

*Bess's letters started coming again, and he didn't
have to go A.W.O.L. But then Lt. Trumanheimer
got another scare. His commanding officer included him in a group put up for promotion, and
the qualifying exam, conducted by General Lucien
G. Berry, was an ordeal:*

[Diary, May 14, 1934]

His object was not to find [out] what we knew,
but how much we did not know. When we
could answer, it displeased him. But when we
couldn't, he'd rattle his false teeth, pull his han-
dlebar mustache, and stalk up and down the
room yelling at us, "Ah, you don't know, do
you? I thought you were just ignorant rookies!
Now, you aspire to be officers and generals,
sure enough, by becoming captains in the
United States Army. It will be a disaster to the
country to let you command men, etc. etc."

*Convinced he had failed, he urged Bess, "Please
don't say anything about it."*
*New rumors of imminent departure for overseas
filled the air, and his regiment was "again having
spasms of preparations to leave." Having once
packed and unpacked over a false alarm, Harry*

now kept his grips pretty much filled.

[Camp Doniphan, Okla.]
[Feb. 26, 1918]

Dear Bess:

Your two letters came yesterday and made me feel real good because yesterday was the meanest day we've had since last October. The dust was so thick you could hardly breathe. We had a Brigade Review. The men had to pitch shelter tents and made their blankets down in all the dust while the Division Commander and Inspector General looked on to see if they could. It was some review. I never saw so much artillery together in my life. Things went off nicely in spite of the weather. . . .

The overseas detachment is having special drills every day now, and I have an idea that they will be pulling out of here very soon. You never can tell though because we thought the same way last month.

I wrote Mr. Booth the meanest letter I ever wrote a banker and he agreed to renew my note. I was in a wrathy mood that day and I wrote one to Morgan & Co. that rather got next to them, and they came across in a handsome manner. I guess it pays to be mean sometimes. I am going to have a nipping disposition, I'm afraid, when the war is over.

The general told Lt. Marks last night that he passed [his promotion exam]. That gives me hope, for he didn't answer any more questions than I did.

I wish I could step in and see you now. I'll bet

51

you are sure lonesome with everyone gone to Platte.

I guess Webster really lost out.[6] They tell me it was because of his size.

Please write as often as you can and I'll do my level best to write real often. I'm glad you saw the vision of the two [captain's] bars. It makes me feel like winning.

Yours Always,
Harry

February yielded to March, and still he waited for word to leave. In the meantime, he bought a horse and sold his automobile, a 1911 Stafford. The horse, "a fine Kentucky-bred saddle animal, pretty as a picture and gentle as a dog," was offered by the colonel, who, preparing to transfer out, took only $100 for the prize which Harry shipped home to the farm. "You lucky Jew. You get all the plums that fall, don't you?" he quoted his jealous friends.

For his 1911 Stafford, called affectionately "Lizzie," which Trumanheimer had used to haul soda pop and things for the canteen, he received $200 from a "poor sucker." "I'd already charged her off to profit and loss, less the profit end," he gloated. "My former Jew clerk in the canteen watched me make the sale and then told me he still had something to learn in salesmanship."

---

[6]A fellow soldier, mustered out of the Army.

Then he got sick and feared he might be left behind.

[Camp Doniphan, Okla.]
[March 13, 1918]

Dear Bess:

Your letter came just now and made this a fine day. . . .

I have been confined to quarters with a cold. I guess there is no harm in telling now that it's over. The major doctor almost sent me to the base hospital one day when my fever went up to 102. I was out with the battery today and have been feeling fine. I was afraid if I went to the hospital the overseas detail would leave without me. They say that some people going through here twenty years hence will see some soldiers sitting on a pile of baggage expecting to leave suddenly, and that will be the overseas detail of the 35th Division still awaiting order to entrain. . . .

You don't need any new clothes to look good to me. You'd always look that way no matter what you had on. . . .

Yours Always,
Harry

The long-awaited orders finally came.
With the day's first light glimmering in the eastern sky on Thursday morning, March 19th, the phone rang downstairs at 219 North Delaware Street in Independence. "I asked a switchman at a shanty in the yard where the train stopped [in

53

Kansas City] if I could call up my mother and my girl," Truman described the moment. "The switchman was a patriot too. He said, 'Son, call hell and heaven if you want to and charge it to the company.'"

But Bess's mother wasn't as generous. "I am sorry to have disturbed your mother, but I hope she'll forgive me this time," Harry apologized afterwards.

When the troop train paused in Cleveland, Horatio found a schoolhouse for Cousin Nellie.

March 22, 1918

Here's one for your collection. I was so busy at [Fort] Sill I couldn't write home. Will do better abroad. We are here for this evening. H.S.T.

But he did better in New York City:

[March 26, 1918]

My Dear Cousins:

I am in the most touted town on earth, and it is a vast disappointment. I have stopped at the Mc-Alpin Hotel, been to the Winter Garden, walked down Broadway and 42nd Street at night, up 5th Ave. in the daytime, been on top of the Woolworth Bldg., crossed Brooklyn Bridge, been to a Chinese chop suey joint, rode the subway from the Battery to 130th St. [and also] the elevated. In fact, I've done everything I can think of trying to see something to turn my admiration hump into enthusiastic

clamor. But I feel like Mark [Twain] did when he went to Italy. I want to ask the New Yorkers if they ever saw the United States, and when they showed me Grant's Tomb, I involuntarily asked "Is he dead?" They (the N. Yorkers) stand and expect you to fall dead every time they pull one of their best press agent stunts on you, and if you don't, they are dead sure you are lacking somewhere.

The Waldorf and the McAlpin are no better than the Muehlebach or Baltimore [back home]. Broadway is not half as bright as [Kansas City's] 12th St. on any night, and besides it's all torn up, and half its length it looks as shoddy as an abandoned fairground in winter. I'll admit that 5th Ave. looks almost as well as Armour Blvd. on some of its length, but not half so well on the rest. 26 Broadway is an old-time office building like the Shiedley Bldg. in K. C., only taller, and Wall Street is an alley.

The view from the Woolworth Bldg is grand and magnifique though. You can see Old Lady Liberty holdin' up her torch to the incoming on one side, [and to] Jersey City, Hoboken, Weehawken, Long Island City, Brooklyn, Canada [and] Connecticut, if you can look that far, on the other. It is 792 ft. and 1 inch above the sidewalk. I don't know how the carpenters came to run in that inch, but that's what the book says the height is. I don't think it's any lower than that, if as low.

Some of Jersey City burned up today while we were on top of the bldg. It was a fine sight, even if some Hun ought to be shot for doing it.

This town, they say, has 8,000,000 people. 7,500,000 of 'em are of Israelitish extraction. 40,000 of 'em niggers and the rest are white people.[7]

Kansas City can produce more good-looking girls than two New Yorks. The show Sunday night at the Winter Garden couldn't appear at the Globe [back home] and get by. I am going to try Fred Stone[8] tonight, and if he falls down, I'm going to stay in camp till we leave.

You can write me: Det. 35th Division, Camp Merritt, N.J., and I'll get it. Remember me to all the family. I am sorry I haven't written sooner but I worked so hard when I went back [from leave] that Bess had to wire me to see why I didn't write. And the home people thought I was dead. Please forgive me.

Sincerely,
Harry

---

[7]This sentence, while still legible, was later scratched over, probably by someone other than HST.
[8]A featured actor at New York's Globe Theatre.

V

"Am Gone to France"

[Diary, 1937]

We sailed from New York on the *Geo. Washington* on Good Friday night at midnight. Another lieutenant who had been examined for promotion just ahead of me and I stood on the deck that night and watched the skyline of the great city disappear and we both had some very solemn thoughts. There were submarines to be avoided by the great liner, and then there were shells and rifle balls and gas and minenwerfers[1] and pneumonia and a lot of things ahead. We thought of all of them and discussed the situation very thoroughly. Then we went below deck and played poker all the rest of the night.

After about twelve or thirteen days sailing around the Atlantic we landed in Brest. The major and all the lts., except the three in charge of the enlisted detail, were taken to the Continental Hotel and six very pleasant days were spent learning how to drink French wine and

[1]German trench mortars.

what to eat. I wouldn't look at the French mademoiselles because I had gotten myself engaged before I left home and I tried and succeeded in being as clean in France as I knew my intended bride would be at home.

From Brest, Truman traveled inland to receive instruction on the French 75-mm cannon at Montigny-sur-Aube, a château owned by a rich silk merchant.

"Am gone to France," he had jotted Ethel before leaving the States. Once settled, he wrote the Nolands about his first weeks there:

Somewhere in France
May 7, 1918

My Dear Cousins:
You've no idea how very much pleased I was to get Ethel's letter from Camp Merritt. It was among the first I have received in Europe and was all the more highly appreciated for that.

You most certainly would have been raised to the nth power in my estimation (if you aren't already there) had you have gone to work at Mark Twain School. You'll never know how to appreciate Mark really and truly until you read his "Innocents Abroad" and "Tramp Ahead," and then get to come over on a government boat with all expenses paid, and an almost really truly salary in the bargain. . . .

Rode all around in a real French train. You know, they have little bitsy engines like we used to wind

58

up when we were kids, and their cars are all divided up crossways with the world . . . as some of our old open electric cars are, with seats clear across with a step along the side. Only two seats are turned together and boxed up with a door at each end.

The first-class [train] coaches have about four compartments and look like the buses they have in most small towns to meet the trains and haul people to the hotels at home. They are upholstered about like a Pierce Arrow limousine and ride very comfortably. The second-class ones are about like a Ford sedan, and the third-class ones are about like the front seat of a spring wagon. I was with a major and rode first-class.

I stayed at a hotel in the town were I landed. Had a room about the size of your dining room with the sitting rooms thrown in. The floor was as slick as glass; there was a marble wash stand a couple of meters long by about one wide with a couple of bowls and pitchers big enough to take a bath in, and a *cut-glass* water bottle. The bed was about six feet above the floor and they use pillows for cover. I had to orient myself every time I came in. There was a mahogany wardrobe with a full-length mirror in which I could admire myself in my Sam Brown belt (may the devil fly away with him).

I visited a castle said to have been started by old man Julius Caesar himself and occupied by various kings and queens of ancient times. I have since discovered that most French towns are saddled with some such musty old building with dungeons that had stakes stuck up to catch unlucky prisoners on, and that Caesar or Augustus or some other old Roman had something [to] do about [it]. (In all probability [they] never even saw or heard tell of it.)

Things age mighty quick over here. There is always a keeper who goes around with you for a small consideration, say ½ franc, nearly nine cents in real money. If you buy something, and give a five- or ten-dollar bill for it, you get back enough colored paper and big copper cents to load down a pack mule. The coppers are about the size of a half dollar and are worth ten centimes, two cents in money. A Frenchman can buy a paper, a square meal, a bottle of wine, and get some change for one, but it takes dollars and francs for an American to get along.

They are sure good to us though, and are the most polite people I ever saw. They don't seem to be able to do enough for us, especially here at school where they have been spoiled by having tourists and army officers around.

I am living at a real chateau with a park, a moat, and a cute little picture-book village out front. There are marble stairs, handcarved woodwork, and everything like you read about—and I'd give a lot for a base burner or some steam heat. There's a shower bath that has water right out of the Arctic Ocean in it.

Of course, the place was built back in 1550 by Catherine de' Medici or the Duc de Guise or Henry III, IV or Cardinal Richelieu or somebody or other who was ruling this glorious old country at that time. Some low-down cuss burned up most of it in 1789, and a rich silk merchant rebuilt it in 1903. There's a rock over the door with MVCL on it and I can't tell how much that is. Evidently 1650. I suspect that Henry of Navarre maybe or some of his three musketeers were all around here.

There's the cutest little [water] branch that runs down through rows of trees. It is about a foot deep and ten wide and the French call it a river.It is sure a pretty little stream. I took a walk through an adjoining chateau park the other day, and there was a swan and some green and white ducks floating on the river, and it sure looked like a picture.

There are old mills all over the country, both water and wind kind like Holland pictures show. You'd never think that war is raging in this same land. It is so peaceable and quiet and pretty. You never see any French men. It is only women and children and old men. The rest are whipping Dutchmen.

They are sure making soldiers out of us too. I never worked or studied so hard in my life. I'll be strong enough to be either county surveyor or a horse doctor when I get back.

About the only things that bother us any are the town clocks. There's one on the church, and one on the Hôtel de Ville. They are never together, and they each strike the quarter hours, and when the city hall clock strikes the hour it always hits off the four quarters on chimes and then strikes the hour. It'll wait about four minutes, and then bang away the hour again to be good and sure that everyone knows it's on the job.

The cussed old church clock is not far from our windows. (We have double French ones that Bertha M. Clay writes about.) The chimes are cracked and insist on going off five minutes late. The hours are struck on the church bell, a beautiful toned bell that can be heard I'm sure about 50 miles. It usually strikes two for twelve o'clock, and about eighteen or twenty for five AM. Sometimes it'll strike the whole twenty-four and then some about that time in the morning. Then, at 5:30, they insist on ringing it and another one for about five minutes. It sure creates a grand cussing bee in our room instead of prayers as it's intended to.

I am fat, healthy, and working hard, and I hope you are the same except for the first. Be sure and write because we're all crazy for letters. I'll write you as much and as often as the censor'll let me. Tell all the family hello.

Sincerely,
Harry S. Truman
1st Lt. 129 F. A.
American E. F.

Although at first he felt he didn't have anything new to tell Bess, he ended up giving her a pretty fair description of life in artillery school:

France, May 12, 1918

Dear Bess:
I am hoping for another letter today. Got one last Sunday and it put [so] much pep into me that I

passed this week's exams with flying colors. Even worked out my probabilities right, and that's some job. I'm getting a college education in geometry, trig, and astronomy. I can be county surveyor when I get back.

Everyone in the room is writing either to his girl or his mother. I am going to write Mamma too because Gen. Pershing has ordered everyone to, although I don't need any order.

There is absolutely nothing to tell you. I am in the same fix that Jack Hatfield's nigger was I told you about on the boat. If you didn't get that letter, maybe I'd better tell you again. This coon told Jack he wanted to write to Liza. Jack told him all right, and started the letter for him as "Dear Liza." The coon then said "I loves you." All right, Jack told him, he had that. "I loves you." Jack put that down for him. The coon scratched his head awhile and then said, "Your lovin' man, Henry." . . .

I could tell you lots and lots of events, but the devilish censor would only tear it up and you wouldn't get any letter. . . .

I heard that Bill Bostain was not far from here at an infantry school but that he had gone up to General Hdqts. so he may be on the front now for experience. They say it's great experience and that you learn more in a week than you knew all your life before. I expect it's so. Hope to find out some day but I'm far from it now.

Be sure and keep writing because it's sure lonesome over here when there's an hour to spare from work. I'll write as often as they'll let me. Even if I can only say I love you, I love you.

Yours Always,
Harry

After six weeks of schooling, he rejoined his regiment and discovered himself listed in the New York Times as having been promoted to captain. He also got a new job.

Angers, France
June 19, 1918

Dear Bess:

This is the grandest afternoon I've spent since I've been in France. I received seven, count 'em, *seven* letters from *you,* five from Mary, one from Boxley,[2] and one from Blair,[3] and a card from Miss Maggie.[4] I got them at noon today at regimental headquarters and then I had to come back to battalion hdqts. and have school for two hours and then read letters from home. I saved yours until last because I wanted the most possible enjoyment and worked things on a climax basis.

You've no idea what a grand and glorious feeling it is to have seven letters from the only girl in the world poked at you by a mail orderly. The latest possible date too, May 20 was one of them. I wrote you yesterday, but I couldn't possibly fail to write again today, even if something pops in the battal-

[2]Fred Boxley, Truman's lawyer in Kansas City.
[3]An unidentified correspondent.
[4]Harry's nickname for Bess.

ion. For fear you won't get the other letter, I'll have to tell you that I'm a Capitan in Uncle Sam's Armee. Didn't know it until I got back to the regiment. I am Adjutant of the Second Battalion. Some job; I have to teach school and do a lot of things I never thought I could.

I haven't heard of any of the 129th Field Artillery running away with French girls. Most of us have too much work to do to think of French girls and besides, speaking personally, when I'm not working, my mind is occupied with a girl in [the] U.S.A. of a kind they don't make in France or anywhere else.

Gee I wish I could see you, but our work is cut out for us and the sooner we accomplish our task the better for all the world and the sooner we'll get home. Americans are sure well thought of in France now and always will be, I hope.

It's sure good to hear of your going to the Shubert, driving down the country roads east of the world's capital (Independence) and doing other things like that. How I wish I could have been along.

I sure want that shirt but under present orders I guess I can't have it. No packages whatever will be shipped according to present instructions. Maybe they'll loosen up later and send us some. If they do, be sure and send it. I still have the sweater you knitted for me, and it is as good as new, although I've worn it a lot and certainly did appreciate it on the voyage over, and will use it a lot about two months from now. . . .

I just barely sneaked through at the school and now they've got me teaching Trig., Logarithms and Surveying and Engineering and a lot of other high-brow stuff that nearly cracks my head open to learn just before class and then if some inquisitive nut asks me a question, I'm up a creek and usually answer him by telling him he's ahead of the schedule and I'll tell him tomorrow. Then I'm safe to look it up and still have my prestige. Some system, I claim.

You wanted to know if I get plenty to eat. I should say I do. Though I would give six months' pay (and I get about 2 bushels of francs every month) for one Sunday dinner at your house. . . .

There was always a sufficiency, but I got so tired of that same old French flavor to everything that when I got back to the regiment and went down to the supply co. mess and they gave me stewed tomatoes plus rice and some real honest-to-goodness American coffee, I thought it was the best meal I'd ever eaten.

If I could come in to your house for dinner you'd probably have to send for a doctor when I got done doing justice to pie and cake and ice cream. I am getting fat over here though and walking about fifteen miles a day, so I guess the food certainly agrees with me. I never felt better in my life.

I'm going to have my likeness struck off on one of these French cameras if we stay here long enough, captain's bars, go-to cap, Samuel Brown belt, and everything. It's just like harnessing a horse now when I go to dress. I look like Siam's

King on a drunk when I get that little cockeyed cap stuck over one ear, a riding crop in my left hand, a whipcord suit, and a strut that knocks 'em dead. (Except that there's no one to fall for it.) Therefore like every good American soldier I have an insane desire to let the folks at home know how I look. . . .

I am writing you at every opportunity and telling you all the censor'll let me and I'm thinking of you always.

Yours,
Harry

I'm not learning any French. I have to study artillery too hard. I can tell 'em I don't understand and ask for des oeufs sur la plat and that's about all. I pronounce fromage, frummage, and says Angers like she's spelled, but the French insist on saying fro-maaj and Onjay. I'll never comprehend it.

From Angers, the regiment moved to Camp Co-ëtquidan near Guer, Brittany. There one day, the major called Captain Truman into his office and told him he'd been assigned to command Battery D. There wasn't a rougher, tougher group of men in the artillery, and Harry knew it. These wild Irish Catholics from Kansas City had gone through four previous commanders, and Harry had visions of disaster. "July 11, 1918 at 6:30 AM I took [over] the battery, and I was the most thoroughly scared individual in that camp. Never on the front or anywhere else have I been so nervous," he confessed to his diary.

The nervousness subsided, even though most of his men got drunk the night before they were to prove their firing ability on the French 75-mm. What's more, they "serenaded" the colonel, and ended up with sentries posted outside their billets.

Next day, despite the hangovers, Battery D passed its firing muster with high marks, and word filtered down that the C. O. had told Captain Truman that his boys ought to get drunk more often. "We'd play around on a lot of other things," Francis "Jerry" McGowan, a young corporal at the time, remembers, "but riding the horses or firing the gun, well we had pretty sharp boys who would get busy on those things."

Satisfied that he and his wild Irish battery could work together, Truman wrote:

[Camp Coëtquidan, France]
Sunday, August 4, 1918

Dear Bess:
Your letter of July 7 and one dated way back in April came yesterday and, of course, I was very happy and granted lots of favors to the battery. I told the mail orderly if he did not get me an Independence-postmarked letter, he needn't come around me for the day. You should have seen him smile when he found one. [He] immediately asked for a pass and got it.

The communiqué of today is sure a grand one,[5]

[5]Reference is to announced Allied victories in the nearly

and I am only scared to death the Dutch will get everlastingly licked before D Battery gets to unload a volley at them.

I shall be happy if I can only get to order my battery to fire one volley at the Hun if I get court-martialed the next day. You know that would be something really worthwhile. An infantryman can only shoot one bullet at a time with his little pop gun, but I can give one command to my Irish battery and put 848 bullets on the way at once.

You must think I'm clean gone *dizzy* sure enough talking about what me and *my* battery can do continually, but if my running of the thing turns out to be a success, I shall be the proudest person on earth. . . .

Your dream came near being fulfilled today. If I hadn't been a battery commander they would in all probability have sent me home as an instructor. I hope they don't do it until I have earned a gold service stripe and have seen the front, much as I would like to be home. I'd be forever apologizing for not having gotten to the front.

I am surely very glad to hear that your mother is better and I sincerely hope you have no more sickness or worry. Please don't worry about me because I have every reason to think that I'll safely return. My 194 men think right well of me and they are not going to let any Dutchman run away with me and there isn't a shell made that can crack my

completed Aisne-Marne counteroffensive against the Germans.

tin hat. Besides, we may not even arrive on the front until it's a sure thing.

I hope you got to make the trip home to see Mamma and Mary. The horse is out there and Mary says he is a dandy. I am glad he is, for the colonel simply made a present of him. . . .

Be sure and write as often as you can because I am always happy when your letters come. I wish I could see you. Oh how I wish it.

Yours Always,
Harry

Next day, itching even more to move to the front lines, Harry wrote the Nolands:

[Camp Coëtquidan, France]
August 5, 1918

My Dear Cousins and Aunt and Uncle and second cousins:

I received Ethel's letter a few days ago, and it made me real happy to think that anything I could write from over here would be so interesting. It seems to us who work so hard every day that everything is commonplace and that whatever we do we get stepped on by a major or a colonel or even sometimes by a general. But I reckon it is all for the one purpose—to make us fit to shoot at the Huns.

I wrote you a nice long letter from Angers and told you all about my having been made a captain and a lot of other irrelevant and unimportant details of things I'd been doing and [am] expected to. They had a box-headed censor over there and I am morally certain he destroyed that concient (can't spell it) effort of mine to be interesting and let you know what I was and had been doing. . . .

I'm the hard-boiled captain of a shanty Irish battery. It's an ambition I've always had to be a battery commander. Now [that] I'm it, I find it's mainly trouble and hard work. It's some satisfaction though when you've worked like Sam Hill half the night (and felt as if you'd have the whole organization and yourself too in the jug before sunset the next day) to see all the kinks unwind themselves and have the battery pull out of the park on time, get into position, and shoot the best problem on the row. That's what happened to me the other day. It was mainly good luck and excellent support from my competent lieutenants. I shot away some 611 rounds of ammunition. Enough to make some dozens of stenographer girls buy liberty bonds for the next year. And the best part of it was [that] the projectiles hit the target. . . .

Maybe I'll get shot by a Hun, but I think not. And maybe I'll get sent home for shooting up some infantry major's dugout, but I hope not. All we're scared of now is that old Gen. Foch[6] will chase the Hun over the Rhine before we get there.

Be sure and keep writing when you feel inclined because letters from home are very good to get, and don't worry about our hardships because "they ain't." We live in houses, eat all we can hold, and

[6]French General Ferdinand Foch, supreme commander for the Western Front.

work so hard we can't get into any devilment. So don't be uneasy. Remember me to everyone in the family and hope for me to shoot straight and hit only the enemy.

Sincerely,
Harry

VI

"If I Was a Sobsister . . ."

D Battery moved out for the front on August 18, 1918. Truman's first exposure to combat took place in the Vosges mountains.

Lest he forget, as soon as censorship lifted following Armistice Day, Harry set his battlefield experiences to paper. In a twenty-four page letter he wrote Bess (it is more like a diary), he spoke of his baptism to war.

Verdun, France
Nov. 23, 1918

We stopped in Saulxures a couple of days. One night I got an order to be ready to go up to the front and make a reconnaissance for the purpose of going into position at 4 AM the next morning. Every battery commander got the same order and there was great hubbub and excitement about going into position before the enemy for the first time. It did give me a real creepy feeling, one I shall never forget. Although I've gone into some real positions since then, I have never felt about them exactly as I did that first one.

We rode about 15 kilometers in a truck through some of the prettiest and hilliest country I ever saw to a town called Kruth which was full of German sympathizers and French soldiers. We got horses that had been sent up the night before and the real climb up the Vosges to our positions began.

It took us until noon to reach the headquarters of the French group commander and it was a steady climb all the way. The Huns were shelling a crossroad not far from those headquarters and I got to see my first enemy shell light, and it was not a very pleasant sensation. The SOS[1] or Camp Doniphan seemed very pleasant and very far away. . . .

I chose a place on the edge of the woods for the battery and a place further down in the woods for the kitchen. There is a rock road running down the side of the hill and it was about 200 meters straight up from this road to my kitchen. All the supplies, water, etc., had to be carried up by hand as well as all the material for construction. The battery was brought in over the ridge at night but that road could not be used any more because the position would have been given away to the Boche air photos. . . .

One of the men dropped a can of lard when they were bringing up the kitchen supplies from the lower road and it rolled all the way to the valley below, scattering lard on every tree it hit and finally

[1]"Source of Supply," military jargon meaning any place behind the lines, including back home in the United States.

74

landing a battered piece of tin at the bottom. One of the kitchen police went down the next day and gathered in the lard, getting a chunk from a tree and a chunk from a bush and maybe some on the ground. Anyway the cooks rendered out the sticks and saved a half a can of lard.

It was surely some steep hill and the trees were all full of wire entanglements. If a man had started to roll down he'd have been in shreds when he got to the bottom.

Well, I worked on that position and followed all the rules in all the books to the letter and never did fire a shot from it. I got ordered one day to go pick out a position some two kilometers closer to the Dutch lines and get ready to fire a gas barrage at him. I was supposed to have twenty-four hours to get ready but only had about six. My horses were seven kilos away and no phone to them. You should have seen the hurrying and scurrying I did to get into position and get adjusted and ready to fire.

I got ready and went up to the O. P. [observation post] and began my adjustment. That was my first shot at Heine and it was an event. The boys heard someway that I was going to shoot at the brewery and it was with great regret that they pulled the trigger. It was a mistake because I didn't shoot at the brewery, although I could have. They are saving the case of that first cartridge and I hope to see it engraved with the date, place, and event and installed with the other important things in D Bty's archives in Kansas City some day.

About that time, the German barrage started, and the first sergeant yelled "Run, fellers, run! They got a bracket on us!" Well, they ran but me and six or seven privates. Four horses were killed and the rest got away.

I rounded up my men and marched them out. When I passed regimental headquarters I asked the colonel if I should go back after my two guns and was told to get them the next day. I thought I was disgraced, but I wasn't. I found that most men and outfits either run or want to badly when under fire the first time.

My men decided I wasn't afraid and that I was lucky because none of them were hurt. They believed that all through the war. The major wanted me to court-martial the first sergeant, but I didn't do it. I broke him to a private and transferred him to B Battery.

[Dear Bess:]
[Nov. 23, 1918]

The boys called that engagement The Battle of Who Run, because some of them ran when the First Sgt. did and some of them didn't. I made some corporals and first-class privates out of those who stayed with me, and busted the Sgt.

[The battery withdrew to Kruth for a few days' rest, then moved north toward the Argonne front. First by rail, but covering most of the distance by foot, they arrived west of Verdun in the early morning.]

I finally got into position by daylight and then went up on the side of a hill in some woods and went to sleep. Got up about 3 in the afternoon and picked out another place to put my cot which was very lucky for me because that night my first choice was unmercifully shelled, and I'd be in small pieces now as would half my battery and my Lts. if I'd stayed there.

We spent the next day, which was [September] 24th, in digging trenches and preparing shelter for the men and figuring out ranges to different places to fire on. When we did finally fire they gave us targets, of course, that we'd never figured for.

Every night Heine shelled all the surrounding territory but missed me. He shot up Pete Allen's bed just after Pete had gotten out of it and blew out an ammunition dump and killed a man for Salisbury. They were both within two hundred meters of me but a shell never came any closer than that all the time we were there, but they lit on all sides of us and did shoot a hole through my kitchen stove pipe. I promptly moved the kitchen on the urgent request of the cook.

Well . . . the eventful day was Sept. 26 and at 3:20 AM I began firing a barrage that lasted until 7:20. My guns were so hot that they would boil wet gunnysacks we put on them to keep them cool, and I was as deaf as a post from the noise. It looked as though every gun in France was turned loose and I guess that is what happened.

At 8:30 I hooked up and moved out at the head of the second battalion 129 F. A. because I got ready first. Got out in no-man's-land and the colonel told me to go into action behind a hedge and walk out front and find if I could shoot up some machine guns that were playing hob with our infantry. I went along with Major Gates but found nothing to shoot at. Got shot at myself and after looking around about an hour we decided to go back.

When I got back to the battery I found that the Hun had a bracket on me, that is over and a short [of my position], and that I should get away from there as quickly as the Lord would let me. The colonel had ordered my Lt. to limber up and had taken the rest of the regiment around another way. I got hooked up before Heine started his fire for effect and started across no-man's-land crossways trying to get to a wood over behind Vauquois. As usual under such circumstances I got stuck and had to hitch in the men. We finally caught the rest of the column and the Hun began to shell again. They got a direct hit on one of Salisbury's wagons and completely wrecked it. One of my men was sitting in a shell hole and a dud lit right between his legs. If he hasn't a charmed life no one has.

The shelling finally got so bad we had to unlimber and wait for it to quit. There was a little hollow we had to cross, and, when it finally got dark, I hitched 12 horses on a piece and got across some way or other. It was 3 AM when I had finally gotten all my carriages but two into that wood. Those two [carriages] are out in no-man's-land yet I guess, because I never did get them.

That was the worst night I ever spent. Men went to sleep standing up and I had to make them keep on working because I had to be in position to fire by 5 AM the 27th. I got into position but the infantry advanced so fast I couldn't dig my trail holes deep enough to fire over them, so I didn't get to fire that morning.

Our battalion got orders to move forward that day and we went up through Cheppy and took up a position in front of Varennes. I was the farthest front battery that afternoon and I got instructions to fire on Charpentry and go up and observe the fire.

I went up and by some unaccountable mistake got ahead of our front line infantry, and I didn't even have a pistol. I got in a shell hole to observe fire and the infantry fell back and left me there. I fell back also and established myself an O. P. at a tank headquarters and . . . shot up a German battery in position, one moving out, and a German O. P., and I'm the only B. C. in the 129th who ever saw what he fired at, and I think that is some distinction.

We stayed in until Oct. 2 when we went back to a little dirty French town to rest, and I'll say we all needed it. Every one of us was almost a nervous wreck, and we'd all lost weight until we looked like scarecrows.

His cousin, Ralph Truman, served as operations officer of one of the 35th's infantry units, and when the fighting subsided the two got together to compare notes.

The Nolands also got a vivid picture of life on the Western Front.

Somewhere in France
November 1, 1918

My dear Cousins:

Your very highly appreciated letter came a day or two ago. I have been pretty busy or I'd have answered it the day it came. My battery hove 1,800 shells at Heine this morning before breakfast and I as bty. commander had to get ready for the job. . . .

Our cousin Capt. Truman distinguished himself in that drive. I saw him the other day and he told me all about it. I'll tell you when I see you. It is very interesting. I guess he'll be a major soon. I hope so anyway. He deserves it.

After we rested a few days they sent us back to a "quiet sector" to do a little position warfare—the kind I was educated for in all those fancy schools I went to. I have been living in a dugout with all the comforts of home, except that I'll get so used to going downstairs to bed that I'll in all probability have to sleep in the cellar when I get home.

I have quite a list of experiences here of late along a lot of different lines. For instance, I saw an American plane shoot up a Hun and he just went a-rolling to the ground in flames from about a mile up. They sent me out to the O. P. (observation post) to shoot up with my battery any venturesome

Huns who might come out to pick up the poor bird's remains. None came as long as it was daylight, and so, of course, I didn't do any shooting. I met Ralph while I was out watching for Huns. He was doing the same thing, only on a different place.

Just as I was getting all fixed up fine and dandy I had to move—which is usually the case—to another place further up the line. I am now in front of the most famous and hardest fought-for city in France.[2] They say that some 800,000 French [and] 1,000,000 Huns lost their lives here. It sure looks like it too. There are Frenchmen buried in my front yard and Dutchmen buried in my back yard, and gobs of both scattered over the whole landscape, which by the way is the most dreary outlook I've ever seen. There's one field over west of me here a short distance where every time a shell lights it plows up a piece of someone. I guess it must be Le Mort Hommes.[3] If it's not, it ought to be.

They say that the Hun put over 1,000,000 shells a day where the Crown Prince[4] was trying to go through. It sure looks it. The trees, evidently once beautiful forest trees, are mere trunks and stumps, some with a bare limb or two sticking out making them look like mute ghosts when the moon shines on them; as it was the other night.

If I was a sobsister or superstitious I could write you some things about the vista now before me that

[2]Verdun.
[3]Using fractured French, he means "dead men."
[4]Eldest son of Kaiser Wilhelm II.

81

would make your hair stand on end, or make you weep anyway.

I was in the city of Verdun day before yesterday and it is heartrending to look at it. Every house I saw had a shell hole in it, and if any didn't have [one] yet they were likely to have [one] any time because Heine sends them over with charming regularity.

There was a little old bobtailed switch engine, about the size of the one in Electric Park [back home], switching cars along a track about 500 yards [long]. And the Hun was sending a 210 [shell aimed at] about the center and just over the track with clock-like regularity. There was an American engineer on the thing and when this big old 210 would light, the little old engine would go toot! toot!, chase to the other end of the switch lickety-split, wait until the next 210 [hit] and then, toot! toot! back he'd scoot. There was quite a bunch of spectators. If the pigheaded German had shortened his range or changed his deflection he'd have gotten someone. But he just kept right on shootin' in the same place and everyone had a good time.

A Hun aeroplane observer fell down behind my battery yesterday and [the observer] sprained his ankle. The pilot wasn't hurt. The machine was wrecked. The French and Americans proceeded to pick them [over] for souvenirs, even taking the boots of the one with the sprained ankle. I guess they'd have carried the plane away piece by piece if they hadn't put a guard over it. Someone said the other day that Germany was fighting for territory,

England for the sea, France for patriotism, and Americans for souvenirs, and I guess it's so.

I took a walk out to my new O.P. the other day, about 7 kilometers (4 miles in real distance) the way I had to go zigzag through the trenches, and, a way out, not far from the German lines, I found a little poppy coming up through the rocks. I am sending it to you. It certainly had its nerve to try to grow right under the frowning walls of Ft. Donaumont, the impregnable and most famous one of this war. But there it grew, and pretty it looked in that shell-torn place. (More sobsister stuff.) I thought you might like to have it. I sent Bess the other one.

Say people. If the censor opens this letter or you let the contents of it outside the family, I'll be jugged or jimmied or bobtailed, to say the least. But I'm hoping he won't open it, and I've nothing worth writing about if I don't tell you some of the things I've seen.

The Commanding General of the 35th Division wrote me a letter of Commendation (capital C) because I had the best taken-care-of guns in the brigade. He recommended that the twelve other 75-mm batteries follow my good example, etc. etc. etc. ad lib. I don't ta [portion cut out by censor] my chief mechanic is to blame for it. He knows more about a 75 than the manufacturer but as usual in such cases the C. O. gets the credit. I'm going to endorse it and give him the credit and file the copy. I think I shall keep the original because it kind of gave me the swell-head.

I hope I haven't bored you with this long-drawn-out epistle, but you write me such good letters that I thought I'd try and tell you some of the things I see and do every day.

Give my best love to all the family and my very best for yourself.

Sincerely,
Your Cousin Harry

VII

"No One Wants to Be a Professional Soldier . . ."

At 5 AM on November 11, 1918, Captain Truman's field phone rang and the voice instructed him to cease firing at 11 AM. Battery D belched its last volley upon a tiny village northeast of Verdun.

The war over, Harry took a seven-day leave for some sightseeing. That accomplished, and with Christmas approaching, he and his men longed for home and civilian life.

Camp La Boholle
Near Verdun
December 18, 1918

My Dear Cousin [Ethel]:
Your letter of November 18 enclosing a beautiful silk handkerchief (just what I need) and six sticks of gum which tasted like the nectar of the gods was received today, and I am most happy to get it and to hear from you. Evidently you had not yet received my spasm from my last battery emplacement above Verdun in which I told you of my pleasant neighbors and my unpleasant ones too.

You've no idea how happy we all were to have

the war end. You know that the continual and promiscuous dropping of shells around you will eventually get on your nerves considerably and mine were pretty tightly strung by 11 o'clock Nov. 11. It was the most agreeable sigh of relief I ever hove when word came to cease firing. I stayed in the position about a week and then they moved me down to a camp in the woods south and east of Verdun. Except for copious gobs of mud everywhere, it's not a bad place to stay and is very healthy. None of my outfit [is] sick or have been since we've been here.

I have had a leave since I last wrote you and have been to Paris, Marseilles, and Nice. I was only in Paris for 24 hours going and 36 coming back but I managed to see some of the famous places; Notre Dame, Napoleon's tomb, Arc de Triomphe, Champs Elysées, Palace of the Invalides, the Louvre and the Tuileries, the Folies-Bergère, Casino de Paris and Grand Opera. That's going some, isn't it, in two days. I heard *Thaïs* at the Opera. The building is worth the price of admission to see. It was built by Napoleon III and is simply magnificent inside and out. It is the center of things in Paris, the Rue de l'Opéra being the Petticoat Lane of Paris. I also had dinner at Maxim's, the one mentioned in *The Merry Widow*. I saw the prettiest girl I've seen in France there and she was an American Red Cross girl with an American captain (native). *Thaïs* was beautifully sung and the scenery was everything that scenery can possibly be. The follies were the Follies and what you'd expect at the Gerty [in

Kansas City], only more so.

We stopped 24 hours in Marseilles and I saw Gaby Delys in her own theatre, the Casino de Marseilles, in a perfectly gorgeous show. She threw me a bunch of violets—I got 'em anyway whether they were intended for me or not. Marseilles is just about as gay as Paris and Paris is as wild as any place I ever saw.

Nice is an ideal place for a vacation. The blue Mediterranean on one side and the Alps on the other and sunshine and expense until you are completely satisfied or busted. I went to Monte Carlo and saw the finest gambling hall in the world but they wouldn't let me play because I had on a uniform.

Major Gates and I bought an interest in an auto and went over the Italian border at Menton and drove back to Nice by way [of] the Grande Corniche, which is Napoleon's road to Italy. It was a most beautiful drive, in fact the most beautiful I ever had. It runs right on top of the foothills of the Alps and you can see miles out to sea on one hand, the snowcapped Alps on the other. It is a very crooked road and around every turn is a more beautiful view than the last one.

The vacation was all too short and I did hate to come back to slavery again. I wanted to jump aboard one of the big steamers at Marseilles and come home. My, how I'd like to see you all Christmas Day as usual.

We have rumors of going home and rumors of g [portion cut out by censor] and rumors of staying where we are until peace is signed. I don't know what's correct, only I hope the home rumor's the right one. I've seen all of France and all the foreign scenery I care to, and as to being in the army in peacetime, well, I'd as soon be in jail. I want [to] follow a mule down a corn row all the rest of my days or be a congressman or something where I can cuss colonels and generals to my heart's content.

I wish you all a very Merry Christmas and wish I could send you a French spoon or something, but I can't. Please accept the thought for the deed, and I'll make up next time. Write when you can to—

Your cousin,
Harry

[P.S.] I got this letter kind of balled up and you may have to stand on your head to read it. H.S.T.

A month later, as President Woodrow Wilson negotiated peace in Paris and America's former wartime ally Russia endured the aftermath of a communist revolution, Truman, still camped in the mud, vented his frustrations to Ethel.

January 20, 1919

My Dear Cousin:

Your very interesting and highly appreciated letter arrived day before yesterday. I was most happy to hear from you, especially that you had outfought and conquered the flu. I only heard you had it about a week before I got your letter saying you were getting well. You've no idea how uneasy I've been with you and Mary and Bess all sick with the dreadful thing.

I guess I can somewhat appreciate how the home folks felt when we were a little under fire. Our risks do not seem to have been one half as great as those for whom we supposed we were taking them.

For my part, I've had a very enjoyable trip, have seen France—after dark mostly and on foot sometimes. Really got to see some pretty severe fighting (from a safe distance). Have collected a few souvenirs, been to Paris, Nice, and Marseilles, and, since I can't go to Jerusalem and Constantinople, I am very anxious that Woodie [Wilson] cease his gallivantin' around and send us home at once and quickly. As far as we're concerned, most of us don't give a whoop (to put it mildly) whether Russia has a Red government or no government, and if the King of the Lollipops wants to slaughter his subjects or his prime minister, it's all the same to us. The Hun is whipped and is fast killing and murdering himself, so why should we be kept over here to browbeat a peace conference that'll skin us anyway. . . .

You've no idea how disgusting peace soldiering is to most of us. When there was a great object to be obtained we'd study our heads off to accomplish it, work at night, march half across France, sleep in the mud, and do anything to get there. But now—well, some old general has gone horse-crazy and he sends around inspectors (mostly staff cols. and majs. who didn't get their feet off the desk during the argument) who tell us that the horses need currying morning, noon, and night, that they must be fed chaff out of the hay, and if they won't eat it, why salt it so they will! We haven't the salt most of the time. Then some other nut comes along and wants 'em to have oatmeal cooked, and we don't get started on that until another one comes along and says not [to] do it. The next bird is a work maniac on soft-soaping harness, and another one forces us to make the men sleep with only three blankets when they've been used to four. And so it goes from day to day.

You know, those fellows, half of 'em never saw a man until they inspected their first National Guard organization, and the other half never saw a man nor a horse. As to hearing any shells drop, well, staff headquarters is always in a nice safe place (emphasis on the safe). Most of 'em are West Pointers and old army men. You know, when a great many of those fellows were made, the Lord forgot to give 'em a good share of common sense. Next time they want a war fought I reckon the same kind of a bunch will fight it that fought this one, and, after it's over, they'll give the professional fighters nice staff jobs just as they've done now.

For my part, I don't care a hoot because I'm going to be happy following a mule down a corn row for the rest of my happy existence. No one wants to be a professional soldier who is not as the youth who answered (at West Point when they asked him why he wanted to go there) that the world was going to be divided into the oppressors and the oppressed, and he wanted to be among the former. I bet he was of German extraction. Enough of such foolishness.

It's some task to keep 190 men out of devilment now. I have to think up all sorts of tortures for delinquents. It's very very lucky that we are far from wine, women, and song or we'd have one h— of a time. Sometimes I have to soak a man with extra duty that I sure hate to punish. You know justice is an awful tyrant, and if I give one man a nice muddy wagon to wash on Sunday because he went to Verdun without asking me if he could, why I've got to give another one the same dose if he does the same thing even if he has the most plausible excuse.

I'm crazy about every one of 'em and I wouldn't trade my orneriest buck private for anybody's top sergeant. It very nearly breaks my heart sometimes to have to be mean as the dickens to some nice boy who has been a model soldier on the front and whose mail I've probably censored and I know he's plum crazy about some nice girl at home. But that makes no difference. I have to make 'em walk the chalk. You'd never recognize me when I'm acting Bty Commander.

I hope this won't bore you to death and that Aunt Ella and Uncle Joe, Nellie, Ruth and all the kids are well and happy and that you'll write me when you feel like it.

Most sincerely,
Harry

Expecting a letter but not getting one, and

angered over a Kansas City Star *interview with Henry J. Allen, governor of Kansas (wherein Allen criticized the 35th Division's artillery performance), HST quickly dispatched another letter to the sisters. His good humor, however, had not abandoned him.*

Rosières, France
Near Bar-le-Duc
[January 25, 1919]

My Dear Cousins:

It's in my mind that you are indebted to me to the extent of a letter or two. But since [Uncle] Sam's mail is somewhat uncertain, and you may have a good alibi for not having written, I'll write again.

I have moved since last you heard from me which was at La Boholle (synonym for La Mudhole). The regiment came down to a French billeting area near Bar-le-Duc. This town is noted for the height and frequency of its fertilizer piles (placed usually under the parlor windows), and for its various bad odors. I have a fine feather bed to sleep in, but most of my men have farm lofts.

American sanitation inspectors have marked the water "bad" but in canvassing the cemetery the other day I couldn't find anybody who'd died under 75 or 80. Most everybody in town seems to be about that age. There's one old man who's as spry as a kitten at 88; he has a son 65, a grandson 40, and a great-granddaughter 17. Now these people have been drinking this water right along for the last thousand years and growing old on it. The other morning an old woman came running down to the infirmary to get the medical sergeant to come and cure her daughter right quickly. He unlimbered his best bottle of pills and chased off to see a French miss, and when he got there she was 56 years old! It was quite a disappointment but the old woman who came after him was pretty spry to have a daughter so old.

Maybe they drink Vin Rouge instead of water. For safety's sake we chlorinate the water and satisfy the sanitary squad.

I guess we'll be coming home shortly in say two or three months. We're slated to sail April 20. But in order to do it, we've got to make the men fit their service records, pay all our debts—just and unjust—and do a lot of other necessary things [even] if it takes all the red ribbon the AEF has to do it. Battery commanders stand a show of getting yanked off the gangplank and left in sunny France indefinitely if they can't tell their money from the government's at first glance. You know that besides being responsible that every mother's son of 'em has shoes, caps, coats, pants and a full stomach, a battery commander has to be responsible that his battery has been properly paid since the war began, and see that they wash their teeth and comb their hair and write to their sweethearts, cousins, aunts, and mammas.

I had a letter from the Commanding General of the Second Army to [ask] if a bird in my aggregation was alive, and if so why didn't he write his ma.

I'd already had him up and made him write her because she's written me personally about it. He labored under the impression that he was getting even with the army by not writing his mother because he'd been fined and jugged when he went A.W.O.L. at Doniphan. Well, I made him write all night all right but he wound up his epistle by saying he was only doing it to keep out of the guardhouse. I let it go because that's exactly where he'd [have] gone if he hadn't written.

But they're not all like that. No, not 1 percent of 'em. I have the great majority who write their mothers regularly and their sweethearts doubly so, and some of the letters are masterpieces of thought and expression. Not for all their worries would I trade 'em for a $1,000,000. Why, I nearly had a fit when my clerk died of appendicitis in January. I felt exactly like I'd lost a boy of my very own. He was a loveable Irishman with a sweet tenor voice and one of my very best soldiers. He is only the second one I've lost in the whole battery in eight months. The other one died as a result of a wound in the Argonne drive. It's peculiar how you get to feel toward a bunch of men when they belong to a battery you are responsible for.

I reckon you've read some of the "Hon." Henry J. Allen's criticisms of the 35th Division artillery. I shouldn't be surprised if the "Hon." Henry J. and the [Kansas City] *Star* would get a good ride on a rail when the 129th Field Artillery and the rest of the 60th Field Artillery brigade get home. You know that [we have] been cited for excellence and efficiency by three division commanders, and to have a political fake like Allen who knows nothing about things military, who was only on the Meuse-Argonne front a couple of hours one afternoon (handing out candy and cigars to the Kansas boys and telling them he'd been elected governor), say that the 35th Division had no artillery support is positively ridiculous. In fact, it's a cussin' matter with us. We hate him and we hope he chokes and the *Star* along with him.

The 35th Division made a reputation on that drive that was not equaled by any division, even the much touted Rainbow and Marine Divisions. The 60th Artillery Brigade is one of the new National Guard artillery units that made good everywhere it went. We were received by General Pershing the other day and he told us we covered ourselves with glory and that no carping politician could take that satisfaction away from us. I'd rather have his opinion than any ex-YMCA Kansas governor's.

Well, I hope to see you before the summer is far advanced and I hope I have sense enough to stay in Jackson County, Missouri, the rest of my days. Write if you feel inclined to—

Your cousin,
Harry

His last letter from France found him sampling once again the sights of "Gay Paree."

March 24, 1919

Dearest Bess:

I am, as you can see by the stationery, in Paris again. It took a right good conversation and some maneuvering to land me here but I got to come and bring three of my sergeants along with me. All the officers who came over first have trunks at the American Express company. Someone had to come and get them.

I succeeded in getting my battery fund and my personal account balled up so that a Philadelphia lawyer couldn't tell which is my money and which is the battery's. You know French bookkeeping is a deep dark mystery, and they credited me with battery money and the battery with mine. Charged my checks to the battery and the battery's to me, and had done it without favor to either side. But it fixed the accounts so you could not tell head or tail. I had to come up here and draw the whole of both accounts and put my money in one pocket and the battery's in another. . . .

France has to do something to get American money after we're gone. I'm for the French anyway. They fought, bled and died more than all the rest of the world (except poor old Russia) and if they want to bleed a little money out of us, I'm for 'em. If you could see Verdun and Chemin des Dames where more Frenchmen were killed than we ever had men on the front, you'd sure be glad to help 'em any way you can.

They do say the Germans are treating our men so well that the whole Army of Occupation will go home German sympathizers. It's a peculiar human trait, I guess, to forget Belgium and ruined and devastated France, forget the *Lusitania* and the ruthless cruelty of the Huns, and remember only that they gave us feather beds when we went among them as conquerors and the French gave us barns, although we came to help them. The French gave their soldiers barns too. We'll remember that the French raised prices on us, yet our own patriotic citizens did us the same way at Lawton [Oklahoma] and in New York. For my part, I hope the great things of France will be remembered and the small ones forgotten, that the awful cruelties and atrocious treatment of Belgium and Northern France will be remembered, and the pie and feather beds forgotten in Germany's case.

Well, Paris is Paris, and a great place to be if you were only here too. But I wouldn't give a certain Jackson County, Missouri, farm I know of for the whole—town, with the rest of France thrown in for good measure.

We are going to sail about April 15th, nothing interfering, and I hope most sincerely that nothing does. I should see you about May 8th[1] or thereabouts. . . .

---

[1] His thirty-fifth birthday.

Write as often as you can to one who's pining for you daily.

I love you always,
Harry

HOBOKEN NJ 5PM APRIL 20 1919

MISS BESS WALLACE

219 DELAWAR[E] ST INDEPENDENCE MO

ARRIVED NEW YORK SAFE DESTINATION CAMP

MILLS WRITING HOPE SEE YOU SOON

HARRY S. TRUMAN

933 AM

VIII

"I Wanted to Go Home with You So Badly . . ."

[Diary]May 14, 1934

When we were discharged I went home but couldn't sit still or stand still. On June 28, 1919 I was married to my boyhood sweetheart. We are still married and always will be.

I finally decided to sell all my farm equipment, hogs, horses, cows, harness and whatnot and go into [a men's furnishings] business with my Jewish friend, my canteen sergeant, Edward Jacobson, on 12th Street in Kansas City. We opened up in December 1919 and for one whole year business was as everyone in business hopes it will be. We paid our clerks and ourselves good salaries and then the squeeze of 1921 came and completely eliminated us and our business.

Harry's haberdashery—called Truman-Jacobson Haberdashery—folded in 1922. Beforehand, while his company still looked solvent, he dabbled in veterans' affairs. The newly organized American Legion held its Missouri convention in Saint Joseph, and it exposed a future President to the hurly-burly of politics.

The legionnaires, Harry said, were "the cream of the country, every one of them, a man's man. They can do anything from fight a battle (not bottle) to spark a lady." He predicted, "The next twenty years will see them running the country, and it will be in safe hands."

He shared a room at the convention with James Pendergast, "a nice boy—and as smart as the old man he's named for." After Truman's furnishings store went under, the nice boy had a talk with his old man, Mike Pendergast. Mike headed a Democratic Party faction in eastern Jackson County, and he introduced Harry to his younger brother Tom. Tom Pendergast was the "Big Boss" of Kansas City's political machine that, like so many urban political organizations, ruled through favoritism and payoffs. But it ruled. And if the down-and-out haberdasher from Independence wanted to hold public office as a Democrat in Jackson County, he had to go along—at least up to a point.

Harry ran for a seat on the Jackson County Court (an administrative position, not a judicial one), and following his election victory, his cousin Ralph wired congratulations. Ralph and Harry were as close as brothers.

Independence, Mo.
August 6, 1922

Dear Ralph:

Thanks for the telegram. I won the dirtiest and hardest fought campaign eastern Jackson Co. has ever seen without money or promises. I received 4,230 votes and Mr. Montgomery, my nearest competitor in the race, got 3,951. He spent somewhere near $15,000, it is said, and his gang made me every kind of S.O.B. the army or civil life either ever produced, but I beat him anyway with a clean campaign.

Best wishes to the wife and kids.

Sincerely,
Harry

Working as a county judge kept Truman close to home. But because he joined the army reserves (with a promotion to major), he spent two weeks during most summers "playing war" over in Kansas, heading up an artillery unit.

His first reserve encampment was at Fort Leavenworth, and while he liked being a soldier again, Harry longed for Bess. He complained to her after his first night in camp that, while his cot was okay, and the tent air was fine, "I wanted someone to keep me covered up and to hug." Thinking he might look dapper sporting a mustache, the judge skipped shaving his upper lip for a few days.

[Fort Leavenworth, Kans.]
July 24, 1923

My Dear Bess:

We are still fighting the war. I was up at 5:15 this AM, had a bath, a shave and then some cream of wheat and milk with blackberries and plums for breakfast. I decided to cut out the ham and eggs because my belt is getting rather tight.

You should see my eyebrow on my upper lip or toothbrush as someone called it. You won't be able to approach me very closely if I leave it on. . . .

Hope to see you Thursday. The whistle's blown.

Yours,
Harry

Sure was good to hear your sweet voice over the phone.

He did see her Thursday; Bess paid a short visit to camp. But she was feeling sickly. Her worried husband, not realizing she was two months pregnant, thought she needed an appointment with the dentist!

Ft. Leavenworth, Kans.
July 27, 1923

Dear Bess:

I wanted to go home with you so badly last night, I could hardly stand it. You just looked as if you needed a shoulder to put your head on, and I, of course, acted like a mean brute usually does. I am dead sure you didn't feel a bit good, and that bumping [en route] did not make you any better. Well, it won't be but a couple of days more. I'll bet you'll feel fine though when all those teeth are fixed as they should be.

Well, yesterday you know was turnip day, and the instructions are to sow them wet or dry. If they'd been sown, they'd have been up tomorrow.

We had a trash mover[1] about 12:30 last night and I got up and loosened the ropes of our tent with assistance of Groves and Bliss to keep it from pulling the pegs out and falling down. There was more racket and chasing around in Avenue A about that time than there is on the real one. (Our street is A.)

We had a game of leapfrog this morning across the lot and back, and it was a circus. All the short-legged men got bumped or thrown, and it was almost a riot. Then double time and the usual light breakfast of prunes, oatmeal, fried eggs, milk, and oranges. We go on a communication problem today.

I hope you are feeling well.
Lots of love. Yours, Harry

The blessed event came in February, when Mary Margaret was born. Then another event, this one traumatic, visited the Truman household—Harry lost his job. In the only political contest he ever lost, Harry Truman was defeated for reelection to the county court.

Unemployed, with an expanded family and still paying off his defunct clothing store's creditors, he

---

[1]Evidently slang for a fierce Kansas wind.

went to work selling memberships for the Kansas City Automobile Club. He did well at it, and soon his new job provided a decent living. It also heightened his interest in the need for roads.

Taking a motor trip, if only for a short distance, was risky business in those days, as Harry knew all too well. "James [Pendergast] and I had a very satisfactory trip and would have been here by nine o'clock had we not run into a small chuckhole and broken a front spring," he explained to Bess from Joplin, Missouri, where they had gone for an American Legion convention. "The hole was not half as large as forty or fifty we'd been over before, but the old spring broke right in the center just as completely as if it had been sawed with a hacksaw, every leaf."

The road between Independence and Fort Riley, Kansas, was better maintained. And, back in Kansas again for a summer encampment, Lt. Colonel Truman (he had gotten a promotion) fussed regarding baby Margaret. She had an eye infection, but something else worried him more. "I'm so afraid she won't know me when I get home, I don't know what to do." It bothered him so much that the following weekend he almost went A.W.O.L.

Ft. Riley, Kans.
Sunday A.M.
[July 12, 1925]

Dear Sweethearts:
Yesterday afternoon I was so homesick to see you I didn't know what to do. I drove to Manhattan and

it was all I could do to keep from just taking the road and going home. I hadn't signed out though, and the round trip would have made me so tired I couldn't have acted with any satisfaction on the firing. . . .

I went down and watched them unload a regiment of National Guard artillery this morning. The Missouri regiment—128th F.A.—is to train here this week and next. I saw some of my old men in the outfit and it was like seeing long-lost friends or kinfolk. They are a fine looking bunch of men. One of my sergeants is horse sergeant for the battery from Clinton, and one of my corporals is a Lt. in the battery from Marysville. One of the 129th Lts. is now a Major.

I'm glad I took my promotion. They can't high-tone me anyway.

I hope the baby's eyes are all right. I didn't get any letter today. It makes it seem very long. Be sure and write me every day.

Your
Harry

He claimed he sold a thousand new automobile club memberships during his stint with the Kansas City Automobile Club. But politics interested him more.

[Diary, 1931]

In 1926, I was put on the *Democratic ticket* by the Big Boss as a candidate for presiding judge

105

[of Jackson County]. I wanted to be county collector which pays a handsome profit to the holder but the money power in the party upset that ambition, much to the disgust of the brother of the Big Boss [Mike Pendergast], said brother being my political daddy and mentor. He's dead now—God rest his soul—I loved him as I did my daddy.

After the landslide which made me the key man in the county govt. I began to take my job seriously and to try [to] live up to my mother's good teaching and be a real public servant.

Before assuming his duties as presiding judge, Harry went on a speech-making trip that carried him far beyond Jackson County, Missouri. His interest in roads had gotten him involved in the National Old Trails Road Association, an organization pledged to lobby for construction of a national highway coast to coast. He had become O.T.R.A.'s president, and to garner regional support, Harry got in his car and visited towns along the intended highway's route.

Heading into western Kansas, he scrawled a postcard to Bess. "Ninety-five miles from Indep. The roads are as fine as there are," he assured her. "Just as smooth as a slab. Everything fine."

"You'd think I was the President of the U.S.," he wrote prophetically from Herington, Kansas. By the time he got to Great Bend, he could report "This is almost like campaigning for President except that the people are making promises to me in-

stead of the other way around."

The weather turned cold and threatening at Herington, so Harry garaged his car and hopped the train for Dodge City, stopping at towns along the way.

THE PALACE HOTEL
Lyons, Kansas

Nov. 8, [1926] 8:30 P.M.

Dear Bess:

We got on a train at Herington at 1:20 after Davis[2] and I had made speeches to the Rotary Club and went to McPherson, a beautiful little town right in the center of a county of the same name. We had an hour there between trains and a number of the prominent citizens, including the mayor, what would be the presiding judge of the county court in Mo. (they call him commissioner out here), and the chamber of commerce head, met us at the chamber of commerce and we had a very good meeting.

At five o'clock we caught a Santa Fe train for this place and got here for the regular meeting which they turned into a good roads boosters' meeting and Harry had to make a real speech, or try to. They've put us up at a good hotel, and we can't pay for anything. . . .

I hope Miss Marger is behaving herself. I wish I could see her.

[2]Frank A. Davis, secretary of the Kansas O.T.R.A. group.

Be sure and kiss her for her daddy. Lots of love to her mamma from

Your Harry.

Finding some of the city fathers feuding along the way (they had posted outside their rivals' town limits confusing road signs designed to lure motorists their way), the visitor from Missouri acted as peacemaker. He reported triumphantly from Dodge City, "We succeeded in getting Larned and Kinsley to let the wind dispose of their signboards tonight, and all the towns from Garden City to Herington have buried the hatchet and are now pulling hammer and tongs for the National Old Trails Road."

He hardly paused at Independence on his way east for more O.T.R.A. meetings.

DANIEL BOONE TAVERN
Columbia, Mo.

November 13, 1926

Dear Bess:

We had a very good trip to Marshall. Stopped at Higginsville by making a 5½-mile detour. . . .

It sure poured down rain, but has quit now. We ran into a football game, and . . . came very near having to sleep in the street.[3] The clerk told us he had only rooms with cots and sent us up to look at them. He made a mistake and sent us to one of his

[3]Columbia is home of the University of Missouri Tigers football team.

real rooms, which we immediately signed up for.

We'll leave here about 8 AM, stop in Fulton about 10, and aim to get to Greenville, Ill. at stopping time tomorrow.

I had such a terrible time getting out of Independence I never did call you because I couldn't. It was 10:30 before I shook off all the leeches, and on account of the detour at Higginsville, I couldn't get to Marshall on time if I stopped. I'm calling you tonight to make up for it.

Write me care of the Dayton Automobile Club, Dayton, Ohio.

I hope you and the young lady are all O.K. Kiss her for me.

Love to you from
Your Harry

HOTEL LINCOLN
Indianapolis, Ind.

10:30 P.M., Nov. 16, '26

Dear Bess:

This day turned out to be fine in every way except the weather. Your letter came, we had a fine and successful meeting, got our pictures in both evening Dayton papers, and got back as far as Indianapolis on the return trip. It was a grand and glorious feeling when your letter came this morning . . . I'd like to see both you and the young lady.

There were some very fine and intelligent men here to talk over the situation with us. . . . I dictated a plan of action to the Auto Club steno. and it was adopted verbatim. All that has to be done now is work out a financial plan and that is tentatively agreed on.

The National Old Trails is back on the map east of Indiana and is there to stay.

This is some city. We left Dayton in a snowstorm, but ran out of it about 40 miles this side and it is now clear with the moon shining. We ate supper in James Whitcomb Riley's town of Greenfield. The "old swimmin' hole" is just outside of town, but it was a little chilly to go try it.

We arrived here at eight and got settled, then went out and walked over the downtown section. It's a lot easier to walk over it than to find a place to park.

We'd expected to stay at the Washington Hotel, a copiously road-advertised house, but we couldn't find it anywhere, so we stopped here. This is a bigger and finer place we discovered after stumbling onto the Washington while walking around. We came across it right on the street we came in on, but after placarding the roads for a hundred miles in each direction, the sign wasn't big enough to see on the hotel itself.

The Claypool is right across the street from here. That is where all the Indiana politics is brewed. It covers a whole block and has been here for a long time. We hope to see some of the Indianapolis politicians tomorrow.

We have to see the pres. of the chamber of commerce, the auto club, and the mayor or manager, if they have one. Probably get our pictures in the Indianapolis papers too.

We'll go to St. Louis tomorrow night and be home Thursday night. I'm going to call you on the phone.

Kiss the baby and love to you,
From your Harry

IX

". . . Haven't Had a Headache Since I Arrived"

Upon becoming presiding judge of the county seat, Harry began suffering sinus headaches. Relief came when he packed his bags and went on another Old Trails Road Association trip, even though the Kansas state legislature had just defeated an O.T.R.A.-sponsored bill.

THE NATIONAL LIMITED
Baltimore & Ohio RR

En Route Feb. 11, 1927

Dear Bess:

Davis suggests that I inform you of all the tricks we are entitled to on this Limited whether we use them or not, such as maid, hairdresser, barber shop & bath, secretary, valet, tailor, etc. etc. ad infinitum.

We left St. Louis immediately after I called exactly at 12 noon, and have been moving along about sixty to the hour ever since. I could dictate this letter, but I don't like to dictate letters to my honey, even at the risk of being accused of inebriety. This train does not slow up for curves, towns or crossings, hence the wobbly writing.

We are evidently in for a fine meeting at Wheeling [West Virginia]. Davis had two telegrams and three letters from the interested parties. The N.O.T. is getting bigger every minute, even if we did pull a bloomer at Topeka. There's no alibi for that, we were simply licked.

I hope the baby is all right and you too. It would surprise you how well my brain pan is feeling, and apparently working.

Much love and a kiss for my girl and you.

Your Harry

The headaches also abated when Harry packed his bags to attend a reserve encampment, or, as happened his first year as presiding judge, to stay at a remote lakeside cottage in the Ozarks.

The Ozarks weekend retreat was not a family affair, however. Made up of elected county officials responsible for spending the taxpayers' money, and hosted by a businessman who wanted a bigger slice of it, the outing mixed politics with pleasure. "You don't know how great a relief it is to be loose from that [court] responsibility," he wrote home. "I'm not going to think of anyone but my baby and come home without a headache."

Branson, Mo.
May [21], 1927 Saturday

Dear Bess:
I tried to get a letter off to you yesterday but the

mail boat went by before I got up and I found that there was no use in writing until today.

We were expecting to come home today but I am outranked. Boxley[1] just came in last night and the manager of the Prairie Pipe Line Co. and one of the Skelleys[2] came in, and our host won't let us depart until tomorrow, so it will be Sunday night before we get in.

Our host is Mr. Wheatley of the Wheatley Machine Works of K. C. & Tulsa. He has a brother who is a pitcher in the Western League and he is here too. They have a cottage on the lake. It is 15 miles from Branson by water and 10 by road and the road is impossible. Barr[3] is going to Springfield today to see his mother and I am getting him to mail this.

I am having a fine time and no expense and I haven't had a headache since I arrived. Boxley and the ball player have gone fishing. The Major and I shot up all the 45 shells without injuring anyone or hitting anything, so you won't have to worry about that.

Our telephones are all out down here or I'd have called you up. Be sure and kiss the young lady. I sure wish you were both here, everything would be right then.

Love to you both from
Your Harry

[1]Fred Boxley, Jackson County Counselor.
[2]Apparently a member of the Skelley Oil Company family.
[3]Robert W. Barr, fellow Jackson County judge.

As usual, July meant army reserve encampment. After a week there, Colonel Truman reported, ". . . have been horseback riding, watched the battery fire 9 problems, had a hour swim, a good meal, and am tired as I can be without any headache."

Next day, a father wrote his first letter to his daughter, three-year-old Mary Margaret.

Ft. Riley, Kans.
Saturday 16 July '27

Dear Little Daughter:

I received your letter this noon along with your mother's and it was very fine. I was glad to get it because another gentleman at my table had just received one just like it from his little girl.

There are two little yellow-haired girls in this same barrack. One of them is four and the other is two, and they have a fine time playing together. The four-year-old one ran across the porch yesterday and fell down. She bumped her nose just like you do when you fall, and she cried just like you do.

Her father is a nice looking cavalry captain. He picked her up and swore at the government for having him live where the boards in his front porch are loose so his little girl would fall. I told him that my little girl always picked a gravel road to fall on. These little girls have dolls and tea tables and scooters. You'd have a fine time with them.

Kiss your mother and write me again.
Your daddy

A few weeks later, back in Kansas on Old Trails Association business, Harry had some news for Bess and some advice for Margaret.

SWEET HOTELS

[Topeka, Kans.]
[Aug. 29, 1927]

Dear Bess:

I didn't get started until afternoon. I had to hold court up town until ten o'clock and then have a session with Boxley and then with the Sells-Floto [carnival] show man, and by the way, he gave me a hand full of passes, but I told him to give them to Barr and Buck.[4] Then I came up here on a dirt road to see how it was. Thought if it wasn't all right, I would come home and go on the train, but I found [the roads] like blvds. . . .

I hope your daughter is feeling fine by now, and that she will keep on doing it.

Margaret: you let your mother have a night's sleep or two while I'm gone and I'll bring you a pair of moccasins or a tomahawk or some other Indian curio.

Kiss your mamma and tell her to kiss you.

Your daddy & sweetie
Harry

Besides rallying support for a transcontinental

_____

[4]His fellow county judges, Robert Barr and Eugene "Buck" Purcell.

116

highway, the Old Trails Road Association determined what towns along the route could erect a state monument laying claim to the road's original pioneer trail.

With pride and tourist trade at stake, communities competed for the monument and, as O.T.R.A. president, Harry found himself in the thick of it.

[Council Grove, Kans.]
September 30, 1927

Dear Bess:

We left the Muehlebach [Hotel] on time, arrived in Olathe at 9:30, looked at their site, and then went home with ex [Kansas] Gov. Hodges to coffee and toast served by the good-looking daughters of the Hodges Bros. They each have one about eighteen.

We then made a canvass of the situation and had to wait until 11:45 for the cars from Baldwin to arrive. Got to Baldwin at 1:30 where they gave us lunch and the president of Baker University told us why we should put the monument on the campus. It is a very remarkable school, having been founded in the fifties, and was coeducational from its founding. It is one of Kansas' three accredited universities, has about 600 students. About four hundred couples have married from the university, and there is only one divorce, happened last year. Some record, I'd say.

We had supper in Burlingame where we listened to a plea for the monument by a commissioned officer in the federal army, and a man who had been over all the trails seventy years ago. He is 87 years

117

old, had all his faculties, and made us the best speech we've heard.

We came on to Council Grove where the band met us at 9:30 PM, marched down the street in front of the cars, and delivered us at the city hall where the D.A.R. women were in session. They read us the history of the town, showed us the site, and then I called you. . . .

I haven't spent a nickle, and I can't. They won't let me. Even the phone call was free.

Hope I see a letter at Dodge or somewhere. We'll be in Dodge at noon Saturday, Saturday night at La Hunta [Colorado] at the Harvey House.

Kiss my baby and look at my sweetie for me in your mirror.

Your Harry

From Dodge City he reported: "The Kansas situation is settled. Council Grove won."

Then the judge and his group went on to Albuquerque for a meeting to decide monument locations for New Mexico and Arizona. It was as rowdy as a national political convention. Springerville won for Arizona, and those boosting Albuquerque for New Mexico "backed me into a corner and tried to force me to promise to vote for this town for the monument. Then a Santa Fe outfit did me the same way, and then Albuquerque started all over. Santa [Fe] followed us to the hotel and wouldn't let us loose. . ."

Albuquerque won the monument.

X

"Am I a Fool or an Ethical Giant?"

On the judge's forty-fourth birthday, May 8, 1928, Jackson County voters approved funding for new roads, a hospital, a courthouse for Kansas City, and the remodeling of an existing one in Independence. "After the [bond] issues carried my troubles began," Harry recalled.

But before his troubles got too bad, he enjoyed his usual summer outing with the reserves. As these letters show, however, his mood vacillated depending on whether he got letters from home.

Ft. Riley, Kans.
July 16, 1928

Dear Bess:
After I got your special yesterday, I got another one in the regular way about noon with a nice letter from Marger enclosed. That is the only reason you are getting this one because here is another morning without any letter. You'll probably get gypped tomorrow because we go to Manhattan to stay all day and practice on the G.P.F. long gun up there. . . .

Has Margaret been a good girl? I hope she has,

because if she has she'll be glad, if she hasn't she'll be sorry when I get home.

Don't miss any more days. Please write.

Kiss my baby and a load of love to you.

Yours, Harry

Ft. Riley, Kans.
July 17, 1928

My Dear Little Daughter:

I am so very pleased that you are writing your daddy every day. I hope you keep up the habit when you are a big girl.

I am glad you haven't had to have Doctor Allen for any of your doll family. That certainly was a nice ride with Uncle Daw and Aunt Mea[1] and I wish I could have taken it with you.

There are still a lot of nice little girls out here, and they all go swimming in the cold pool every day. Little Eddie McKim was here Sunday and took his first horseback ride. He had a fine time and didn't fall off. He is seven years old, and looks exactly like his daddy.[2]

We had to put on our policeman caps and our high collars and our leather belts and go over and shake hands with the Assistant Secretary of War. It was very hot and I was glad to get mine off and take a great big glass of ice tea.

[1]Nicknames for Bess's brother George and his wife May.
[2]Edward McKim later became postmaster of Independence.

Be a very good girl, and kiss your mother three times for

Your loving
Daddy

The next summer found him in the same camp and writing again to Margaret.

Ft. Riley, Kans.
July 16, 1929

Dear Daughter:

I received your very nice letter when I came in this evening. I have been gone all day. I think it is about time I am coming home myself and I'll see you Saturday or Sunday.

I am glad Mrs. Cox took you to Zoo's Park, and I hope you saw all the lions and tigers and elephants and camels and the rest of the animals.

Yesterday afternoon a pretty little yellow-haired girl came in to see me while I was lying down. She said her name was Patsie Vance and that she was two years old. She had a stuffed rabbit in her arms and she wanted me to be sure and look at him. She had him all wrapped up in a blanket because she didn't want him to take cold.

She made me think of you and I wished, oh so much, that I had you here and could give you a good hug and kiss.

You tell your mother to be a good girl, and you

be sure and be one and write to your dad whenever you can.

Your loving
Daddy

Harry stood for reelection to the court in 1930, and had no problems winning. But barely into his second term as presiding judge, the pressures got to him. Just before Bess's birthday, he abruptly left home for an inspection tour of municipal buildings in southern cities. True, he wanted to find the best design for Kansas City's new courthouse, but as he explained to Bess from Little Rock, "I was becoming so keyed up that I either had to run away or go on a big drunk."

The county's finances were in terrible shape, and he blamed it upon two judges who had just left the court. They were, he said, "just full of anxiety to obtain any funds that they could because of their positions."[3] Then too, he worried over refinancing the mortgage on his mother's farm. It was hard times in America. It was the Great Depression, and Harry feared that if Mamma lost the farm "that good old woman who made me an honest man would pass on."

About this same time, Truman also committed to paper "some deep and conscientious thinking" about his relationship with "Boss" Tom Pendergast

[3]Truman claimed in his diary that they would "shoot craps while court was in session down behind the bench while I conducted business."

*and the graft he confronted increasingly in govern-
ment.*

[Diary, 1931]

I am obligated to the Big Boss, a man of his
word; but he gives it very seldom and usually
on a sure thing. But he's not a trimmer. He, in
times past, owned a bawdy house, a saloon and
gambling establishment, [and] was raised in that
environment. But he's all man. I wonder who is
worth more in the sight of the Lord?

I'm only a small duck in a very large puddle
but I am interested very deeply in local or municipal government. Who is to blame for present conditions but sniveling church members
who weep on Sunday, play with whores on
Monday, drink on Tuesday, sell out to the Boss
on Wednesday, repent about Friday and start
over on Sunday. I think maybe the Boss is
nearer heaven than the snivelers. . . .

After the [bond] issues carried, my troubles
began. The Boss wanted me to give a lot of
crooked contractors the inside and I couldn't.
He got awful angry at me but decided that my
way was best for the public and the party. But I
had to compromise with him. . . . I gave away
about a million to satisfy the politicians. But if I
hadn't done that the crooks would have had
half the seven million.

I wonder if I did right to put a lot of no account sons of bitches on the payroll and pay

123

other sons of bitches more money for supplies than they were worth in order to satisfy the political powers and save $3,500,000. I believe I did do right. Anyway I'm not a partner of any of them and I'll go out poorer in every way than when I came into office.

But the bleak prospect also bothered Harry Truman. "We've spent $7,000,000 in [county] bonds and $700,000 in [city] revenue in my administration," he confided to his diary. "I could have had [for myself] $1,500,000. I haven't $150. Am I a fool or an ethical giant?"

The more turbulent county politics became, the more the embattled judge looked forward to occasional trips like the one he took to Detroit to view road construction equipment.

Detroit, Mich.
[Jan. 13, 1932]

Dear Daughter:

I am sending you a picture of the hotel where mother and dad first stayed on their wedding trip. You ask mother if she can recognize it.

I have been out to see the road show. It is a great big airdome just full of trucks, tractors, rock crushers and pictures of roads all over the country.

Today I am going to see the place where they keep little girls and boys who don't mind their mothers, and who don't like to go to school. We are going to build a place like it in Kansas City. . . .

Tell mother to be a good girl just as you are, and

you keep on being one. Tell Grandmother and Uncle Fred and Miss Hanson hello, and kiss your mother for me.

Your loving
Dad

On another occasion, Margaret learned all about trains.

THE NATIONAL LIMITED

(En route)
Friday, Oct. 20, '33

My Dear Daughter:

I am enclosing you a little folder showing what this fine train has on it for its customers. It is exactly like the one we went through at Chicago. There are coaches up in front and then a club car which I'm in now, and then come the pullmans, followed by an observation car. The train is air-cooled or I should say air-conditioned by motors underneath the cars, so that no smoke or dust can get in. Everything is just as clean as it is at home.

They serve the meals on specially made blue china, with pictures of all the old engines we saw at the fair around the border [of the plates], and scenes along the road in the center. I am bringing you a book that tells all about it.

I hope you are practicing the "Military March," so we can play it when we get home. I also hope you will know all about long division and what to do with the "left overs."

The train is going so fast I can hardly write. We just passed Vincennes [Indiana]. You remember, we drove through it last spring.

Be sure and be a very good young lady and tell your mother to be a good girl too. I am hoping to be home Monday morning.

Lots of love and a kiss apiece for you and mother.

Dad

Now a full colonel in the reserves, in the summer of 1932 he spent two weeks of welcome diversion at Camp Ripley (Camp "Believe It or Not" the reservists called it) in Minnesota. But he couldn't forget completely about things he had left behind. On his way north, he wrote Bess asking that she send him a forgotten raincoat, and also to "look in my right-hand top drawer and get one of those full packages of razor blades and mail it to me."

Once settled in camp, he fussed more than usual about Bess's writing habits. "Since your mother hasn't written me today, I am going to write to you," he told Margaret, And at the end of his short letter, he instructed her to "Tell your mother I'd like to hear from her and that yesterday was a dull day when I didn't. You may give her only one kiss for me, but take a lot for yourself."

"I got even with you when your letter didn't come yesterday," he lectured Bess. "I just refused to write, so you'll skip one too."

The following spring, Margaret got strep throat, and the doctor feared her heart might be affected.

He advised that she be moved to a warmer climate. So Bess took her down to Biloxi, Mississippi, where the two stayed in a rented cottage for several months.

Harry meanwhile grappled at home with the county budget. It needed cutting, and his solution, not easily arrived at, was to fire two hundred job holders, all fellow Democrats. "Please be careful about eating anything that comes in the mail," he cautioned Bess. "Someone sent me a cake the other day and I threw it away. With these discharges coming off, you can't tell what they'll do."

Samplings from letters Harry wrote to Mississippi the first week in May 1933 show a mixture of humor and stress.

How are we going to tell which is Margaret and which is Nanny when you come home? I guess we'll have to tie a pink ribbon around Margaret's arm and then we can tell. I hope she stands still long enough to gain ten pounds. Please don't get homesick, I am counting on [soon] staying with you down there at least ten days.

Don't worry about me. I have gotten by in first-class condition. No one seems to be so very mad at me. They have taken it rather philosophically because they have been looking for it right along. . . .

We had the usual court session and the papers tried to start a row between me and the sheriff.

I don't want any row, but I am going to finish one. He is out on a limb, and I am going to saw it off a little at a time. They are looking for me now, but I told Tom Bourke[4] to tell no one where I am, and he won't. . . . I'm going to the farm and stay all night. I'll be at Independence as usual tomorrow looking for a letter, and then for the architects, the courthouse, and ten more days of hell and then Mississippi and heaven.

The sheriff has kicked over the traces now and closed the Independence jail. He thinks he'll cripple the road work. I'm not sorry he closed the jail because we don't need two, and it will give me an excuse to cut some more expense. He has a Hoover head (the sheriff), and Horse Doc Johnson for an advisor. It's a real combination. You can remember the time I had with him on the court. But he'll come around. I'm getting things all set and the papers are giving me a better break now. Things will work around right. Be sure and *watch* the baby. I'll be down just as soon as I can get there, but I must put things in shape so I can't be rolled before I leave.

I got two letters today and it made things a lot brighter although I am uneasy about the Kinaman woman's leaving. I wonder what [that nurse] expected anyway, but you always bet that

[4]Bourke remains unidentified. He apparently worked for the court.

you get what you pay for—no more, no less; and when you pay nothing, you get nothing. She evidently thought she was conferring a favor on us by being along, but I'd feel a lot easier if someone was with you. . . . If you get scared, go to the Markhorn and stay till I come and then we'll go back to the house. If I leave here now, we'll never build the courthouse and my budget will blow higher than a kite. . . . Please be careful. If I don't hear from you regularly, you'll get a charge phone call. When I didn't get a letter yesterday, your mother nearly stewed her head off and wanted to send a wire. Be as good as you can, and don't spank the baby too much.

I have been cutting salaries, and having an interview with Bash & Dr. Johnson.[5] I think I've got all difficulties ironed out. Bash is a contrary boy, but will come in I hope. . . . Please don't fail to write me every day because I am in so much hot water I just can't stand it to worry about what is closest to me.

I am glad you are happier without the nurse. I never did think she would be a success, but I knew I'd never get you there if we didn't take her, so she served her purpose. It would not have been possible for me to stay away as long as was necessary to accomplish the result we want. If the young lady comes home sound and

[5]The troublesome sheriff and his advisor.

well, I guess we can stand it, although I've never
been so lonesome since I was a boy.

*Years later, talking about the pressures of public
life, the feisty Missourian would boast, "If you
can't stand the heat, get out of the kitchen,"
implying that he never got out. But that spring of
1933, Harry hid out a great deal from irate unemployed Democrats, sometimes on his mother's
farm, sometimes in a Kansas City hotel, and once,
on the eve of his forty-ninth birthday, in Saint Joseph.*

*For what he had accomplished in life, "the forty
might as well be left off," he ruminated. Still, he
confessed, "I'd like to do it again."*

*"Politics," he figured, "should make a thief, a
roué, and a pessimist of anyone, but I don't believe
I'm any of them and if I can get the Kansas City
courthouse done without scandal, no other judge
will have done as much."*

*Pondering his political future with corruption
rampant all around him, Truman lamented:*

[Diary, 1933]

Why oh why can't we get some old Romans
who are fundamentally honest and clean up this
mess? It will take a revolution to do it and it is
coming in about ten generations. That, or a real
race will appear and take charge.

We teach our boys to worship the dollar and
to get it how they can. . . . Some day we'll

130

awake, have a reformation of the heart, teach our kids honor, and kill a few sex psychologists, put boys in high schools to themselves with *men* teachers (not sissies), close all the girls' finishing schools, shoot all the efficiency experts, and become a nation of God's people once more.

XI

"If the Almighty God Decides That I Go There . . ."

While Bess and Margaret were in Biloxi, Mississippi, the judge had a talk with Tom Pendergast. The boss told him that in 1934 he could run for either Congress or county tax collector. "Think of that a while," Harry wrote Bess. "Congressman pays $7,500 and has to live in Washington six months a year. Collector will pay $10,000 and stay at home." He opted to become tax collector, but the boss reversed himself and said no. Harry Truman, Big Tom decreed, would run for the United States Senate.

The night before he announced his candidacy, Harry, unable to sleep, sat pen in hand at 4 A.M. "I have come to the place where all men strive to be at my age," he wrote in his diary, "and I thought two weeks ago that retirement on a virtual pension in some minor county office was all that was in store for me." With the scratch of his pen breaking the stillness of the night, he reviewed his life, its twists and turns, its successes and failures. "And now I am a candidate for the United States Senate," he concluded with the sunrise. "If the Al-

mighty God decides that I go there, I am going to pray as King Solomon did for wisdom to do the job."

"He took Jackson County out of the mud!" his supporters cheered, hailing the new roads he'd built. One afternoon in May, their candidate backed his Dodge roadster out of the garage, and rumbled out across those roads to garner votes in the Democratic primary.

As he crisscrossed Missouri, he kept a meticulous record of his mileage, his expenses, and who was for him and who was against him. He talked to farmers. He talked to veterans. He talked to anyone who'd listen. Being acquainted with the state's county judges and their clerks helped. So, too, did his connection with Tom Pendergast's gang. In August, Truman won the Democratic primary by an impressive plurality. In November, he overwhelmed the Republican incumbent.

Missouri's new senator, his wife, and daughter moved into a furnished apartment in Washington, D.C. But not for long. In June, Bess returned with Margaret to the big house in Independence, and Harry, left behind, never felt so lonesome. He wrote home that when he walked into their empty apartment, "I thought I heard Margaret say 'Hello dad,' and I asked well where is mother as usual and then I walked all around to make sure I wasn't dreaming . . . Every time I'd hear that young lady in the next apartment I would be sure my family was coming in. We'll never do it again."

They would, however. Many times. Bess hated

the social whirl required of a senator's wife, and she escaped to home whenever she could. Besides, there wasn't enough money to maintain two full-time residences. Once the family returned to Independence, Harry could move into a cheaper place.

Sitting at his desk in Congress's upper chamber, Harry wrote his first letter to his daughter as a United States Senator.

Washington, D.C.
June 17, 1935

My Dear Margar:
I have been listening to the "King fish"[1] make a talk on the bill to give old people pensions and laboring people insurance. There was a time limit set, so he could talk for [only] forty-five minutes. . . .

I hope you are having a nice time, but your daddy sure misses you. When I went to our apartment last night, I was sure I could hear you talking to me several times, and I hoped I'd find you were there, but you weren't.

You must take care of your mother and not let her do things for you that you can do for yourself. Be a good girl and practice every day on the piano. I listened to you play when we got home, and I think you have musical talent. That means that you should work harder than ever to develop it. Lazy people never get anywhere in anything. . . .

[1] Senator Huey Long of Louisiana.

Kiss your mamma for me and take several for yourself.

Your loving
Dad

Having gotten a letter from Bess saying that after sixteen years of married life she had no regrets, Harry wrote "Just for that, I'll have to talk sordid things." There were bills to pay, and he listed them. And he calculated what he needed for room rent, laundry, and meals. He hoped they could "get enough ahead to get furniture and fixtures for next year." "I guess," he concluded, "we ought to be happy we have no doctor bills and all of us are well. If I made everybody I've gotten a job for since 1927 pay me by the month . . . we'd have a nice tidy sum to the leeward every month, but I'm just a d.f. I guess. I can't take it that way."

The Senate recessed for a long Fourth of July weekend, so Truman studied up on the Civil War battle at Gettysburg. Then, armed with maps sent him by the War College, he set out to relive history, and afterward wrote Margaret about it.

Washington, D.C.
July 9, 1935

My dear Young Lady:

I have been waiting patiently for a nice long letter from you. In fact I go through the mail every morning, hoping for two letters—one from you and one from Mudder. This morning I didn't get one from either of you.

Sunday, I went up to Gettysburg and went all over the battlefield. You know it is one of the great military contests of history. I stood on the spot where General Robert E. Lee stood while the famous immortal Pickett made his charge. The charge that was to win or lose the third day's battle. It lost and I wondered what "Marse Robert"[2] thought when the remnants of those brave battalions came straggling back across the field.

I picked two little flowers from the foot of the Virginia Monument which stands on the spot where Lee stood and I am sending them to you. They will remind you of how a great man takes a terrible defeat.

Lee didn't blame anybody. He accepted the responsibility and stated that if there was any fault it was his, although two of his principal leaders had been remiss in their duties. Longstreet did not come up and Ewell wouldn't move forward. Yet Lee blamed no one.

The Secretary of the Senate gave me a picture of him and I am hanging it under [George] Washington and over Margaret.

I am still going to look for that letter. Kiss mamma and practice every day.

Your loving
Dad

He also attended a July Fourth office picnic, and afterward Bess heard that Harry had enjoyed the

[2]Robert E. Lee.

ladies a little too much. "You shouldn't take a piece of idle gossip and try to twist it into something unpleasant," he urged defensively. And lest she be "curious" about his evenings, he detailed for her a typical night's activities of studying bills and reading. "I'll be glad when this damned session is over," he said. "I think maybe we'd better get a flat and stay here summer & winter."

Next day, the senator received two letters and wrote two letters.

Washington, D.C.
July 10, 1935

Dear Bess:

When I got back over to the office after the Senate quit, I found a fine letter from Margey and one just as nice from you . . .

We had quite a session yesterday. Wheeler[3] and the Senator from Ill., Mr. Dietrich, almost came to blows. The young upstart from West Va.[4] had to make a speech too. I'm afraid he has ambitions to be a second Huey [Long]. I don't know what we'll do with two of them. He had a very good audience, however, and I'll have to admit made a good speech.

I went out to Bud's to dinner last night. Johnnie[5] and his girl were there and the five of us played a

---

[3]Burton K. Wheeler, senator from Montana.
[4]Senator Rush D. Holt.
[5]Bud and Johnnie were Truman senatorial staff members.

137

card game called Dynamite. I got home about eleven o'clock.

I am going to dinner with the new Senators tonight at the expense of the Junior Senator from Calif. Mr. Wm Gibbs McAdoo. There are to be no *ladies,* for which I'm right thankful.

You don't know how I look for the letters and how I wish I were home. Please send at least one every day. Lots of love and remember me to all the family. Kiss Margey.

Harry

Washington, D.C.
July 10, 1935

My Dear Margey:

When I came back over to the office after the Senate recessed last night I found a very, very fine letter from you and one from Mudder. So you'll get two letters in this one [envelope].

I am very anxious to hear about "The Capture of the Clever One." I am sure it is a great success, and that it will have to be put on several times.[6] The Congress is a slow motion affair, but the paper said this morning we might be home by August.

I miss my daughter just as badly as she misses me. I should like very much to see that [hair] permanent. If you get one every week, you'll be in debt the rest of your life, won't you? . . .

I shall be looking for a nice long letter very soon.

[6]Reference is to a school play that Margaret was in.

Give mother a big kiss, and keep practicing.

Your loving
Dad

and lots of kisses in return X X X X.

Truman arrived in the Senate as President Franklin Roosevelt's Depression-fighting New Deal program reached high tide. "I was a New Dealer from the start," he boasted, and the Junior Senator from Missouri voted down the line for Roosevelt-requested economic and social reform programs.

His interest in transportation got him a seat on the Interstate Commerce Committee, and the first bill he introduced was one to promote highway safety. Had it passed, it would have required all states to use a uniform, more rigid driver's license examination.

It was all very rewarding but, separated from his family, Harry couldn't wait for his first Senate session to end.

Wash. D.C.
July 18, 1935

My dear little, or should I say Big Girl:
You don't know how much your daddy appreciated your very good letter.

That must have been a very good show. I wish I could have seen it. You surely worked hard at it because I see you have lost a pound since you wrote me before.

I'll be glad to take you to the Plantation Grill

when I get home, if I ever do. The session stretches out longer and longer. It looks now like Sept. before we get through. There seems to be something new coming up every day.

I have to go to Ft. Meade, Md. today to review the C.M.T.C. troops over there. You know, I have a couple of boys at work over there, and I think perhaps they got me into it.

I am sending you the funny papers every Monday, and I'm glad you enjoy them. Have you spent any more of your allowance to get your hair curled? Don't spend too much of it for that, but I hope to see you with one when I get home.

Don't play too hard, and practice a lot, for I want you to be the fine pianist I wanted to be. I hope you can put on another show when I get home.

The office force all want to be remembered to you. They all say they'd like to see you very much.

Tell your mother she can have the *Star* sent to me for another month, if she will. I'm lost without it.

I shall be looking for another letter now until I get it. Lots of love and kisses from

Your Daddy

Kiss Mamma for me.

With September approaching, and with the session's end finally near, Harry longed for home and a vacation trip. "Which way do you want to go?" he asked Bess. "North, West, or South? East is out. We won't go that direction."

He also wrote again to eleven-year-old Margaret.

Wash. D.C.
Aug. 16, 1935

My Dear Daughter:
I almost said dear little daughter, and then I thought she's now my big daughter. But your dad and your mother can only think of you as a sweet baby girl, learning to use your hands, learning to walk and kicking out a pair of shoes every week, learning to talk—to say "dada" which I said meant daddy; learning to read by picking out letters on the Kansas City *Star* headlines; learning to write, to add, subtract, divide, and finally to play the piano and be a great actress.

So you see you will always be my dear little girl and I'll always think of you that way no matter how big or how great you may be. . . .

Kiss mudder and grand mudder and tell Uncle Freddie and Aunt Christie hello, as well as Nat & Frank & May & Daw. Lots of love from

Your dad

Wash. D. C.
Aug. 22, 1935

Dear Miss Margey:
I am so sorry to hear about the sprained arm of yours. It must be very painful. I had a sprained foot once, and it hurt me as much as the broken leg did afterwards. I hope the young lady you fell over was not seriously injured.

It is my hope to be in Independence on next Monday or Tuesday if I can. You and mother must have your clothes all packed so we can go on a ten-day vacation. Then you can start to school and everyone will be happy.

Kiss mamma for me, and tell all uncles and aunts and the young nephew hello.

Love from
Dad

As Harry packed to join his family in Independence, humorist Will Rogers died in an Alaskan plane crash. "We can't see the why," Harry wrote home. "But I'd rather be put out at the top of my career than to come down the ladder and die of remorse." Rogers was, he judged, "almost a second Mark Twain. The world is better for having produced him. I'm glad his mother didn't believe in birth control."

XII

"I'm Going to Finish the Job or Die . . ."

My Dear Daughter:

You don't know how much your daddy appreciated that nice letter. It came just as I was getting ready to go out to look at pictures of me that Bud's father painted. I haven't seen [them] yet. It will have to wait until I get your letter off.

Here is your ten dollars. I hope it will be enough. You and Christie can have a nice time looking anyway.

I'm glad you had a nice time with Mr. and Mrs. Peters, but don't you think that 12:30 is a little late for a young lady twelve years old to stay out? My mamma wouldn't let me stay out that late until I was at least fifteen.

The apartment has a kitchen about like our other one and a dining room about ten by ten feet. The living room is about twelve by eighteen and has a nice porch at the east end. One bedroom opens from the west end of the living room, and the other one opens from the east end; the doors are on the north side of the living room. There are two full bathrooms with tubs and showers. One room has twin beds—corkscrew beds, and the other one has a double bed. There's a crazy mirror like your grandmother has in her living room, and a big fox hunt picture, lots of chairs and couches, etc.

I sent you some stamps in your mother's letter. I'd like a big kiss for Christmas.

Love from Dad

The cycle repeated itself. Harry found an apartment, went home at Christmastime, packed up the family, and drove them back to Washington. In June, when school was out, Bess and Margaret returned to Missouri.

After they left, the senator went to Philadelphia to attend the Democratic national convention.

Philadelphia, Pa.
June 21, 1936

My Dear Daughter:
You will never know how much your dad appreciated your telegram. I get telegrams and telephone messages by the hundred, but when I arrived in the City of Brotherly Love and had a telegram from my daughter handed to me by the clerk, I just had to stop and read it, and appreciate it more than anything that comes to me except, of course, your mother's letters. You know, of course, that your mother and your dad have been sweethearts since they were six years old. That makes quite a difference in what happens.

You are the nicest young lady I know, and you always will be no matter what happens. I wish you would write your old dad a letter once in a while. Please kiss Mamma for me. Love to my sweetest daughter.

Dad

Democrats gathered in convention that summer knowing that Franklin Roosevelt, after one term in the White House, would again head their presidential ticket that year. Indeed, there wouldn't even be a contest over the second spot; Vice President John Nance Garner was a shoo-in. Ritual, rather than political skirmish, would prevail in Philadelphia.

So, the Junior Senator from Missouri relaxed and enjoyed the show. "The convention was like all such gatherings, just one grand yell from start to finish," he told Bess.

Then he packed his grips and drove home. But he didn't stay long. Reserve encampment beckoned, and as Harry explained beforehand, "I must be out of reach as nearly as I can until after the primary." He didn't want to get involved in Missouri Democratic intraparty squabbles that summer.

Of course, he campaigned during the fall general elections, although Roosevelt didn't much need his help. The President took Missouri easily, and also triumphed in every other state but Maine and Vermont over his Republican opponent, Alf Landon from Kansas.

Following the Roosevelt landslide, a father, back

*in the nation's capital, and going on fifty-three
years old, shared some intimate thoughts about
schooling and mature love with his little girl.*

Washington, D.C.
Dec. 10, 1936

My Dear Daughter:

It was a very, very great pleasure for your dad to
get such a nice letter. I am glad to know what
Mother wants for Christmas, and I'll look around
downtown and see what I can see. I'll also see if I
can find you a pretty piece of music. I'd like very
much to see that red dress with puff sleeves and
everything. . . .

I am glad you made so many E's. Your mamma
made lots of 100's when she was your age and 100's
were E's then. I am sorry you don't like geography.
It is necessary to know if you expect to talk intelligently to educated people and you'll certainly
have to do that.

I stopped at a filling station coming over here and
a young man in the station wanted to know of me
if I had to go all the way to Washington in order to
turn off for Missouri. He thought Missouri was
south of Washington, and that I was going home.
You don't want to be in that state [of ignorance],
do you? It seems hard now but some day when you
get interested in history you'll want a clear idea of
just where all those interesting places are or have
been, and then you'll be glad you studied geography.

It is too bad about King Edward.[1] I had hoped he would keep his throne and assume his responsibility after going to the point of succession. Now if he'd met some beautiful young commoner when he was in his twenties and had decided to give up the crown for her, I'd have been 100% for him. But he is forty-two and has had many a romance, as had his Mrs. Simpson.

I'd have done it for Mamma at twenty-five, and would yet because she is my only sweetheart and I am hers. I'm not no three or no fifty. Ponder over that.

Get more E's. Kiss your mamma and write your dad.

Love by the carload.
Daddy

With the presidential inauguration approaching, Margaret wrote her dad that she had the flu, but was feeling better. Harry, still looking for an apartment, gave her some advice on how to stay healthy.

Washington, D.C.
Jan. 18, 1937

Dear Margie:
Your good letter came this morning and you can

[1]King Edward VIII, proclaiming his love for American divorcée Mrs. Wallace Simpson, abdicated the British throne rather than force a constitutional crisis.

rest assured that your dad was most happy to get it.

I am so glad you are up and around again. I hope this will [be] your last attack. It is good for your mother to walk sometimes, and I believe everyone will live longer and be healthier if he takes at least one long walk every day. You remember that, will you, and you'll never have to diet and maybe never be sick either, I hope.

The weather here has been warm and for two days it has rained very nearly all the time. Everyone is hoping for Franklin [Roosevelt] to have a pleasant day. He wrote the Committee on Arrangements that because of the press of business he didn't believe he could attend the inauguration, and then put a little note at the bottom and said he'd try to arrange to be present. It wouldn't be much of a show without him, would it?

I am being pestered to death by Missourians who want to see the show, and, of course, there is nothing I can do about it. Twelve tickets can't be stretched any further. I wish I could give you and mother one apiece, but I can't.

I'm still looking for that apartment, and when I find it, I'm coming for you.

Kiss mother and lots of love and kisses to my Skinny-Fatty-Sweetchild.

From Dad

Was glad to talk to you last night.

He didn't get an apartment, and the family didn't come to Washington at all that winter. For the price

148

they could afford, Harry couldn't find a decent place for them to live.

In late January, the senator rode the train to Saint Louis to meet with Missouri's new governor, Democrat Lloyd Stark. Returning east aboard the Spirit of St. Louis, *he knew he was in the doghouse for not going the additional three hundred miles home to Independence.*

After pausing in the club car for a scotch and soda, he wrote Bess that maybe he was "a clown and a fool." But, he pleaded, "I'd rather lose a hand or have an eye pulled out than make you a moment's suffering or hurt—either mentally or physically. I've seen so much difficulty caused by sheer unthoughtfulness that I've tried all my life to be thoughtful and to make every person I come in contact with happier for having seen me. Maybe that's silly too. I don't know. I've never paid any attention to what people have said about me and very little to what they say to me, because most people only mean about half [of what] they say."

When it came to Margaret's practicing on the piano, however, her father insisted that his words be heeded. Thinking that with dedication and lots of practice she'd become a great pianist, Harry instructed Bess, "You tell Margaret she is not doing as I told her, and for every day she doesn't practice one hour you are to take something off her allowance. If she does the whole hour, nothing is to come off. If she does only a half hour, five-cent fine; three-quarters of an hour, a three-cent fine; no practice at all, a ten-cent fine, and that goes from now on. I hate to have to make a potentially great pianist work by fining her."

The money angle turned around, however, to where Dad was handing out bonuses for accomplishment. And, on the eve of Margaret's thirteenth birthday, a trip to France was offered as an inducement for learning French.

Washington, D.C.
February 5, 1937

Dear Daughter:

Such a nice letter came this morning and it has made a sunshiny day a lot brighter. You know sunny days are very scarce here. It snowed last night and then melted just enough to freeze into a coat of ice. The streets are just a sheet of ice, but the sun probably will cure it.

I surely wish I could play those duets with you. Maybe we can do it later. Whenever you play that *Rigandon* of Raff's[2] to my satisfaction I'll make a substantial addition to that bank account.

You must learn to speak French fluently too, because when we take that trip to Paris and Nice and all the battlefields, somebody must be able to tell the ornery French what we want when we order fish, so we won't get "poison." I'm afraid the A.E.F. variety of Parlez Vous wouldn't work now, and the French have probably forgotten all the American swear words too. . . .

[2]Nineteenth-century German composer Joachim Raff.

150

Here is a kiss for you and you pass it on to Mother.

Love from
Dad

A few weeks later, Dad had some more thoughts about schooling, as well as about the "game of politics."

Washington, D. C.
Feb. 23, 1937

My Dear Daughter:

I hope you passed all your tests with flying colors. You have to work very hard now trying to get a lot of information into your head so you can be perfectly at home with educated people and can be tolerant with the uneducated ones. It seems very hard while you are doing it, but you'll be very glad that you can play the piano, speak French, talk intelligently about Agrippa and Genghis Khan, and reasonably understand geography and math. So keep right at it and in six or eight years you'll have a fine foundation for a practical education.

Politics is a great game. Your dad has been playing at it for some twenty-five years. It is a game of people and how they act under certain conditions. You never can tell, but you can sometimes guess, and I've been a good guesser. You must be able to tell the facts too, and to believe them yourself.

I'm going to look for my next letter on time, and if I get it, then maybe I'll tell you something you want to hear when I write again.

The office force all say hello.
Lots of love to my sweet Margie.

Dad

By this time, Truman had become chairman of a Senate subcommittee investigating railroad finances. The railroads were in a mess. Many faced bankruptcy, and Truman, suspecting that corrupt financiers had caused the problems, subpoenaed witnesses and held hearings.

"I will finish my hearings tomorrow," he wrote Bess as the Senate approached its spring recess in March. The family planned a much-needed vacation, this time to Mississippi, where earlier, on doctor's orders, Bess had stayed with Margaret. "I never needed rest as badly in my life and ten days down there would just about fix me up," Harry judged. "It would do us all good."

Driving back to Washington afterward, he stayed overnight in Pennsylvania.

WHITE SWAN HOTEL

Uniontown, Penna
Tuesday, Mar. 30, [1937]

Dear Bess:
Well, I couldn't get started on time today. It made me late all the way. I took a walk in Decatur [Illinois] last night and saw a hat I wanted. Decided to get it this morning and the outfit wasn't open at 8:15 so I left and didn't get it. I guess I'll have to go to Baltimore Saturday and see what I can do.

The weather and the roads are fine. I'm hoping Pa. hasn't any more detours. There was one on each side of Washington last night, over typical Penna roads—narrrow blacktop. I'd forgotten about losing an hour so it was eleven instead of ten when I got here.

Kiss my baby. Love to you.

Harry

He attended his first White House reception, and his description of the event reveals that Harry Truman still held prejudiced attitudes about black people.

Washington, D.C.
Apr. 7, 1937

Dear Margey:

Your dad had dinner last night with the President and Mrs. Roosevelt. You and your mother should have been there. My card, as you can see, told me to go to the east gate of the White House.

Now your dad wouldn't give five bad pennies to attend any social function, but your mother said I had to go and that I mustn't wear a blue shirt. Well, I went down to Garfinckel's and bought me a new white tie and a collar to match—all my old ones were either cracked or yellow, so I had to do something about it and I really couldn't wear a blue shirt.

Well, when I got to the east door of the White House, a very black Negro bowed and scraped and took my coat and hat, then a gentleman in a very elaborate gold-braided uniform gave me a place card and showed me a map of the table. I was to take Mrs. Minton in to dinner.

Then various uniformed and gold-braided young men guided and directed us upstairs to the East Room where a more elaborately gold-braided gentleman sonorously remarked to all present, "Senator Truman." (If your mamma had been there, he'd have said, "and Mrs. Truman.") Then a gold-braided young man took me over to the head of the line where several other senators were standing—McAdoo, Guffey, Minton, Hennings, and Chavez, and their wives.

We stood around awhile, and then a couple of young men marched up to the west door of the room and announced, "The President and Mrs. Roosevelt." They smiled and bowed, and then we all passed by and shook hands with both of them. Soon as that was done, we lined up by twos, the senators behind the President and the congressmen behind the senators, and then the generals and admirals and the "common people." There [were] forty couples.

We then marched down the main hall to the dining room, which you've seen. The table was horseshoe-shaped, as you can see by my place card map. The President was in the center of the bow facing west on the outside [of] the shoe; Mrs. Roosevelt was exactly opposite him on the inside [of] the shoe. . . .

The table was all aglitter with cut glass and silver and beautiful White House china. There was a silver sailing ship about two feet long between the President and Mrs. Roosevelt filled with pink flowers, and then there were roses and similax all up and down the table.

They gave a real good meal at the taxpayers' expense—tomato soup, filet of flounder, roast turkey, string beans, pineapple salad, chocolate ice cream, and cake, candy, and a little café noir afterwards.

All these things were in courses, deftly placed, and removed by an army of coons. I suggested to Mrs. Minton that these Negroes were evidently the top of the black social set in Washington.

As soon as everyone was done with the meal, Mrs. Roosevelt and all the ladies went to the Blue Room while the President and all the men sat around in the dining room and smoked and drank coffee. After a little while the President got up and we all went down to the East Room where they had placed the chairs and set up a stage at the north end. The girls from Ky. sang beautifully and the dances were very interesting. The magician was a wonder. I never saw a better one. About 11:30 the President left and everybody went home.

I'm glad it's over, but it was very interesting and I am sure your mother would have enjoyed it. She probably would have had McAdoo for a partner. You can tell her all about it and make her wish she was here.

You be a nice girl, get your lesson, and write your dad.

Much love & kisses to you.

Dad

He also wrote his baby about a Sunday excursion he took to Williamsburg, Virginia, to look over some restored history.

Washington, D.C.
Apr. 12, 1937

My dear Baby:

I am very happy to get your nice letter and I hope you'll persuade your mamma that she ought to come to Washington about April 25 and stay until I quit Congress. You know, you always saw as much of your dad as you wanted to, and it can be arranged again. Nettie came in to see me today and she said she sure wanted to see you and Mamma "awful bad." I told her I thought maybe you'd be here sometime about May 1st.

I went down to Williamsburg yesterday and saw all the fixings that Mr. Rockefeller has put up there as part of the Colonial City. Personally, I very much doubt that it ever looked like that. It must have been very fine for the highups, but it was terrible on people in debt. They showed me a jail where a man who couldn't pay his debts had to sit in stocks and stand in pillories while the bad boys threw stones and ripe eggs and other things at [him]. Sometimes they lost eyes and teeth as a result—and there were very few who lived in the fine houses and sat as judges on the poor who had to sit in the stocks. I'm glad I don't live in the "good old days," because I might have been in the pillory.

Here is your check. You be sure and keep up with your lessons because I don't want my pretty daughter to be a dumbbell. Kiss Mamma and I'll see you Saturday or Friday night if you are up.

Love,
Dad
XXXXXXX by the hundred.

That summer, Harry got quite a scare. During a routine physical exam, the doctor suggested he might have heart trouble. To find out, he submitted to a thorough checkup at the U.S. Army and Navy Hospital in Hot Springs, Arkansas.

Beforehand, hoping that rest was all he needed, he spent the weekend relaxing in a Hot Springs hotel.

Hot Springs, Ark.
Sunday, Sept. 12, '37

Dear Bess:

Well, it was nice to talk to you last night.

You ought to be here. I got up at six this morning, put on my yellow shirt, and walked up the mountain and back. The sign says it is 1.5 miles up. I made a shortcut or two and judge I made it in a mile. Anyway, I made the round trip in 35 minutes.

No one was up except an old granddad sitting on a bench halfway up the hill and the Negro bellboy delivering papers to the rooms. The front door of the hotel was lock[ed] when I went out. I didn't know they ever locked 'em. It was a perfectly grand morning—cool and clear. All these people shivering like wintertime.

I came back, took a bath, another nap, and had

breakfast at 8:30. Wrote my St. Louis speech and sent it to Vic[3] to type and then *took another nap*. It was noon by then so I ate a light lunch and walked to the other end of town, looked over the shows, but didn't go in. Got in my car and drove up the mountain. I walked up and went to the top of the tower—in the elevator, and saw the whole country around here. It is a wonderful view on a clear day. Again, wish you and miss Marger were here.

Go to the hoss pistol in the morning and I'd as soon it was a pistol, but maybe it won't be so bad.

Kiss Margey. Love to you. Remember me to the family.

Harry.

How's that for coming out even?[4]

Hot Springs, Ark.
Sept. 14, 1937

My dear ~~Little~~ Big Daughter:

Anyway, I'll always think of you as my little bit of a girl. Your dad carried you night after night when you weren't over a foot and a half high and weighed about fifteen pounds. Your mamma was wondering if you'd have straight legs and curly hair, and I was hoping you'd have a good brain—which you have. Now you must use it and put everything useful you can into it while it is young and active. When you

---

[3]Vic Messall, his secretary.
[4]His last line, including signature, spanned the stationery's exact width.

have a head full of learning, no one can take it away from you. Money and property and position you can lose, but a well-developed brain, never.

Here is a check for last week, and I hope I never have to fine you again. I don't like it any better than you do. . . .

Your dad's in a hospital, but not sick—to keep from getting sick. They are taking me over the hurdles, though.

Kiss Mamma and you can write me at Army & Navy Hospital, Hot Springs.

Lots of love from
Dad

Hospital life was more pleasant than he had expected.

Hot Springs, Ark.
Sept. 16, 1937

Dear Bess:

Well, this is a gala day. I walked down to the hotel awhile ago and there were four letters from you, one from Marger and one from Mary. . . .

They photographed my teeth today, and finished my eye examination. This eye man is as good as I've had. The glasses needed a change. The heart photo was analyzed and found all right. One valve is smaller than it should be, but it isn't the one that gives trouble, so they say. The blood test isn't finished, but I've had enough to eat four days hand running anyway. Fred can tell you how grand I'm fixed up.[5] There are four doctors giving me special care, and I'm nearly rested. Will stay as long as I can, though. Wish you'd come down when the notion hits you.

Do you need any money?

Love to you both, Harry

The doctors found nothing wrong, and he soon resumed his hectic senatorial routine, holding hearings, studying pending legislation, and reading stacks of books about railroad finances that he checked out of the Library of Congress. He was determined to expose illicit financial practices that had bankrupted several major rail carriers.

An occasional quick trip for speechmaking punctuated his schedule. Returning to Washington from trips to Cape Girardeau and Saint Louis, Missouri, he wrote:

25 Oct. 1937
C & O Train at Charlottesville, Va.

Dear Bess:

If you and Margaret were with me this would be a perfect day. The sun shines out of the bluest sky I've seen this year, and the Va. mountains are painted every color of the rainbow by frost. Just passed the Farmington Country Club and it certainly looked good. We've been going through some high mountains and a lot of tunnels. The ce-

[5]Fred Canfil, a friend since his county judge days, had paid him a visit.

dars and pines make the oaks and elms stand out. The mountainsides look like patchwork quilt with dark green for the main color.

This is rather a slow-motion train. Left St. Louis at noon, stopped at Indianapolis fifty minutes, and stayed forty-five at Cincinnati. It will arrive in Washington at 12:45 if it is on time and it seems to be. It is a very fine train called "The Sportsman." They have one they name "Geo. Washington" too. Since I'm investigating 'em, I wanted to see what they were like. This is the road that the Van Swear-engins used as a backbone of all their rail empire. It is so rich they couldn't break it. It still pays dividends.

I'm going to open up [hearings] again tomorrow and really go to the bottom of the Missouri Pacific [Railroad]. Hope some good will come of it.

I'm also going to find a place to live and you all are going to come.

Fred [Canfil] said I stole the show at Cape Girardeau. I didn't intend to.

Kiss Margey. Love to you.

Harry

The next weekend found the senator stopping in New York City on his way to West Point for a football game. When he turned on his hotel room radio he noticed "a couple of kids were singing 'They'll Never Believe Me' from The Girl from Utah." *It took him back to a time when another couple of kids he knew had listened to "that beautiful melody and lovely sentiment." And it made him want so*

161

badly to see his love "that I had to write her to sort of dry my eyes."

Following his West Point excursion, he returned to New York for a meeting with Tom Pendergast, and again he wrote home.

HOTEL NEW YORKER

Sunday A.M.
Oct. 31, 1937

Dear Bess:

Well, I had a grand day yesterday. Got up [at] 6:30, and after the usual preliminaries walked down to the 42nd St. Ferry and caught the 8:30 West Shore train for West Point.

Col. Littlejohn[6] met me in the biggest car on the post, the superintendent's, and took me on a sightseeing trip over the post. Had a grand lunch at the Col.'s house and then went to the game. It was a real contest, although the Army beat V.M.I. 20 to 7.

I sat in the General's[7] box and had a grand time with his wife, a funny old lady who is proud of her mince pies which she serves at every game at the end of the half with coffee and doughnuts. I found out from Littlejohn that she is the Walgreen Drug Co., so I guess she can afford mince pies.

It was a beautiful day and I enjoyed it. It would

[6]Col. Robert M. Littlejohn, Quartermaster of West Point.
[7]Probably West Point Commandant Maj. General John L. DeWitt, although his wife was not an heiress to the Walgreen Drug Co.

162

have been nicer if you and Margey had been there. The Littlejohns are lovely people, and have a daughter just Marg's age.

I had all the boys there I am acquainted with come and see me after the game, and they are a fine-looking outfit. It seemed to please them very much.

I'm to see T. J. this afternoon, and then back to the grind tomorrow again.

Kiss Margey. Love to you.

Harry

How's that hand?[8]

Before he went to the game, he had told Bess. "I needed something to sort of relieve my nerves." His railroad hearings had so strained his patience, "I wanted to punch witnesses rather than question them because they'd robbed and abused a great [railroad] property, and a lot of 'widows & orphans' you hear so much about."

"I went into the R. R. business again today," he wrote as his committee hearings resumed. Wanting to spend a long Thanksgiving holiday with the family, he couldn't. "If I quit this thing now they'll say that Kemper[9] and the Boss pulled me off, and I'm going to go through with it if I don't get home at all."

[8]Bess had injured her hand in a domestic accident.
[9]William Kemper, along with Pendergast a Kansas City Democratic Party kingpin.

"I'm going to finish the job or die in the attempt," he vowed. He explained further to Margaret, "A hearing is really a dogfight from start to finish. It is like pulling teeth to get a straight answer. These people are trying to steal a great railroad and, of course, they don't want to get caught."

But he was determined he would not spend Christmas alone. He found an apartment, bought some furniture, and in mid-December told Bess to get ready to join him. He would be home to drive the family back to Washington. All the furniture might not be in place. But that would be all right. "I may put in the bedroom outfit, and you and Margey can sleep in the beds & I can sleep on the floor the first night."

XIII

"It Just Takes Work . . ."

Stuck in Washington as Christmas approached in 1937, Harry had never worked so hard. Margaret, although not a letter writer like Dad, wrote him frequently during that long month before he came home to fetch her and Mamma. And in return, a father replied. Here are excerpts:

[Washington, D.C.]
[November 24, 1937]

I want to see that play most awful bad. I'm sure you'll do your part creditably. It takes work to do anything well. Most people expect everything and do nothing to get it. That is why some people are leaders in society, in politics, in religion, on the stage, and elsewhere, and some just stand and cry that they haven't been treated fairly. It just takes work and more work to accomplish anything—and your dad knows it better than anyone. It's been my policy to do every job assigned to me just a little better than anyone else has done it. I want you to do the same thing, whether it's washing dishes or being a leading lady, and I know you will.

[November 26, 1937]

I am going to see Jeanette MacDonald if I can get around to it. Your mother & I saw Emma Trentiru in *The Firefly*. It is a very lovely operetta and Emma could certainly sing. But she was not beautiful—to put it mildly.

[December 17, 1937]

There is a great crowd downtown these days. I went down yesterday and bought you & your mamma some hair nets & perfume. I don't know whether you can wear hair nets or not, but if you can't you can have all the perfume & your mother the nets.

He drove the family back to Washington, and the ritual repeated itself. Bess and Margaret stayed until school was out, then returned to Independence. Harry soon followed, and, as usual, he attended summer reserve camp.

Ft. Riley, Kans.
July 5, 1938

Dear Bess:
Harry Vaughan[1] had some ink, so you'll get an

[1] Fellow reserve officer destined to serve Truman as military aide during his presidency.

ink letter today.

I called on Gen. Henry as Colonel of [Field Artillery] this morning on my way over to the canteen to get a strap for Margaret's watch. He was pleased as punch and said he was just starting out to see me. He is one of the real [Brigadier Generals] in the army—name is Henry. I thought McCoy was in command.

They offered me the Post Hqs for my use and a stenographer too. I told 'em I'm not dictating any letters for a few days.

Went to the hospital this morning and had my heart and blood pressure tested. Heart perfect, blood presure 110. He said I'd probably live to be 110 years old.

It is rather hot out here but I had to have a blanket over me last night. Have been teaching the boys angles, and line of sight and angle of site. Some of 'em are pretty good. Snyder[2] and I were listening to a young West Point second lieut. explain a new instrument for laying the guns this morning, and Snyder said, "Harry, to realize that boy was a babe in arms when you and I were shooting in France!" We are now the Gen. Berrys of our time, I guess.[3]

I'm getting as brown as an Indian, sleeping and eating much, and feeling fine. Kiss Margie. Hope

[2]John Snyder, Saint Louis banker who became Treasurer of the United States during Truman's presidency.
[3]Lucien G. Berry, 35th Division's Commanding General in 1918, had conducted Lieutenant Truman's grueling examination for promotion to captain.

for a letter tomorrow. Much love.

Harry

How do you like my paper?[4]

He didn't realize it, but he was experiencing his last summer reserve outing. The Julys of Harry Truman's future would afford new vistas, accompanied by greater challenge.

The colonel's final letter home from a reserve camp favored fourteen-year-old Margaret, who had written Dad a complaint.

Ft. Riley, Kans.
July 12, 1938

My Dear Daughter:
You don't know how happy I was to come in last night and find your good letter on my bunk.

It seems as if everyone was either lazy or overcome with the heat if you could find no one to do any of the things you wanted to. I rather think that you and I are going to have to start going to Sunday School and church. I'd like to go if someone would go with me. But you know nearly everybody wants to sleep on Sunday morning. As you know, sleep means much to me before six A.M.—but not much after that. We'll see about it when I get home.

Wish you would call your old country grandmother and tell her that her boy is all right. I haven't written her from here, which

---

[4]He wrote the letter on HOTEL JAYHAWK, Topeka, Kansas, stationery.

isn't a bit nice.

We'll try and go riding often when I get home. Kiss Mamma. Lots of love.

Dad

After he got home, in addition to horseback riding with Margaret, there was a political campaign to deal with. 1938 was a congressional election year, and, while Harry still had two years left in his own senatorial term, other Democrats needed his help.

Following the elections, the campaign-weary senator returned to the Army and Navy Hospital for a checkup.

THE PARK
Hot Springs, Ark.

[Nov. 17, 1938]

Dear Bess:

Hot Springs is all prosperous. Things are all pepped up here. Nearly all the stores on the avenue have new fronts, and some of the others are getting them. The Arlington garage seems to be full of Packards, Chrysler Eights, and Cadillacs. They've taken up the car tracks and the town looks fine. They're advertising the alligator and ostrich farms again. So, I guess the Northern Republicans are spending again.

I'm going up to the hospital tomorrow and I hope the damned thing's full. I am sleeping almost day & night and I'm sure I need no hospital treatment.

169

They treated me fine but I made more nuisance contacts than I've made in a long time and I know I'll make a lot more if I go over there. I also made some nice ones too—Littlejohn, and the two Smiths[5] were fine. But I also found a lot of would-be pensioners too.

They gave me the best room in the house here after the Negro bellboy recognized me going up in the elevator. The clerk didn't know me and I never told him.

Wish you and Skinny were here. We'd have a grand time. Keenan wanted Canfil's place and date of birth. They're going to appoint him.[6] They figure they'll need Harry next session.

Kiss Margie. Love to you.

Harry

According to Margaret's biography of her father, the family suffered an auto accident about this time. It happened in Hagerstown, Maryland, when Dad ran a stop sign, hidden, he claimed, by a parked car. Struck in the middle of an intersection, the car was demolished. But, except for a few cuts and bruises, no one was seriously injured.

The following spring, Harry almost experienced another accident, this time in an airplane. He had gone home, and the White House asked him to

[5]Unidentified acquaintances, probably military personnel.
[6]Truman was seeking a state job for his friend Fred Canfil, former Jackson County official. Mr. Keenan was apparently an assistant to Missouri's governor.

rush back to the capital to cast a vote on a contro-
versial measure giving the President greater power
in reorganizing the government. Angered, the sen-
ator obeyed, but then let the White House know
how he felt.

What follows is a transcript of his telephone con-
versation with White House aide Steven Early. It's
from a typed document (the only document quoted
in this book not originally handwritten), but Tru-
man, a stickler on preserving "all the facts," cer-
tified the memo's authenticity when he scratched
across it "Put in senatorial file. HST."[7]

March 22, 1939

SENATOR TRUMAN—Well, I'm here, at your request, and I damn near got killed getting here by plane in time to vote, as I did on another occasion. I don't think the bill amounts to a tinker's dam, and I expect to get kicked in the ——just as I always have in the past in return for my services.

MR. EARLY—Well, Senator, what is it you want?

SENATOR TRUMAN—I don't want a goddamned thing. My vote is not for sale. I vote my convictions, just as I always have, but I think the President ought to have the decency and respect to treat me like the Senator from Missouri, and not like a goddamned office boy, and you can tell him

[7]Truman's absence from the Senate prior to the day the bill successfully passed (with his support) also lends credence to the document's validity.

what I said. If he wants me to, I'll come down and tell him myself.

MR. EARLY—All right, Senator, I'll tell the President.

Harry's combative mood can be explained in part by events back home. Things had soured in Missouri Democratic politics. Tom Pendergast was under federal investigation, and Missouri Governor Lloyd Stark, whom the Pendergast organization had helped elect, had started attacking the boss. To Truman this meant that Stark would oppose him in the state's 1940 Democratic primary. "I'm going to lick that double-crossing lying gov. if I can keep my health," he wrote Bess.

In the Senate meantime, using what he'd learned from his probe into illicit railroad financing schemes, Harry co-sponsored a transportation bill to prevent similar abuses in the future. And while no one went to jail, Truman's hearings held up to public ridicule various Wall Street financiers who had profited by undermining the financial solvency of a number of railroads. He also helped draft the Civil Aeronautics Act, which placed the country's fledgling airlines under federal regulation.

For diversion, he drove south one weekend to experience more Civil War history.

Richmond, Va.
July 7, 1939

My Dear Daughter:
You can't imagine how very much I enjoyed your

very good letter. I'm certainly sorry you couldn't go to the picnic. I hope you are entirely well by this time.

Your old dad couldn't sleep much last night—woke up at 3 A.M. and read a long story in *Adventure* and then it was daylight, so I got up and walked all around the Supreme Court building and the Library of Congress, and finally ended up at B Street and Independence Ave over by the old House Office Bldg.

It was a quarter of six by that time and I went into the greasy spoon on the corner and had tomato juice, whole wheat toast, and milk, all for a quarter—at my hotel it would be fifty cents.

Got over to the office at 6:30, read all the mail, waited until Vic came, got your letter, and went for a drive. Started for Appomattox Court House where the immortal Lee surrendered to Lincoln's Gen. U. S. Grant. When I got here about noon I was so tired I went to bed instead and have been asleep ever since. Hope to get to the Court House tomorrow.

Sent your check in your mother's letter yesterday. Hope it arrived safely.

Every time I come here I find something new. Ran across a grand statue of Stonewall Jackson as I came in on a new street, and there is a beautiful marble statue of Thos. Jefferson in the lobby of this hotel. Sometimes I almost sympathize with these people for living in the past and forgetting the white trash who made the country great.

Kiss your mamma and take one for yourself and

write me when you can.

Dad

Truman wasn't in Washington long before he learned that a senator's life encompasses many functions, among them attendance at numerous funerals. "Seems as if I'm the regular funeral escort," he surmised en route to yet another funeral.

When Senator Nathan L. Bachman of Tennessee died, Truman, sitting alone in his hotel after Bachman's last rites, ruminated about what a great storyteller the senator had been. His remembrance began:

HOTEL PATTEN

Chattanooga, Tenn.
Apr. 25, '37

We had a sad trip today, taking the body of Sen. Nathan L. Bachman to his home city for burial. Most of the day was spent toasting Nath for a safe voyage to the beyond and recounting his many excellent stories.

A few days before he died he told one to Mr. Roosevelt which he said was the origin of the sit-down strike.[8]

He said that two aristocratic female dogs

---

[8]Some months before, CIO auto workers, in their struggle to win General Motors recognition of their fledgling union, had seized GM's plants in Flint, Michigan, calling their action a "sit-down strike."

were walking down the village street when one of them spied old man Jones' male dog coming up the street from the opposite direction. Said one of the females, "There comes that Jones dog. You know, he has the coldest nose of any dog in this town." The second female dog replied, "That's certainly so. The best thing we can do is to sit down."

On another funeral trip, again to Chattanooga, and again to honor the memory of a senator from Tennessee, he wrote Margaret.

On the Southern Ry. to
Sam McReynold's Funeral
July 13, '39

Dear Miss Margie:
It was a very great pleasure to get your nice letter just as I ran for the train to Chattanooga. Sens. Burke, Connally, Miller, Tom Stewart and Mc-Kellar, along with a dozen House members, are the party to attend Sam McReynold's funeral. We were very suddenly picked.

This pen of mine wants to put out all the ink at once for some reason. I am being thoroughly shaken up and I'm afraid if I start over won't get done before Sen. Miller gets shaved for breakfast. You must take this as an example of how not to send a letter. . . .

I went to see *Goodbye Mr. Chips* all by myself night before last. It was a good show. Went up in the balcony at the Palace, saw a seat in the front row, and when I got to it there was another one in the front row between a couple of men right in front of me. So I just step[ped] over and there was a man's coat in the seat. He said "Oh. I hope you haven't smashed my fountain pen." I told him I hoped not, and the show went right on. An usher came down and asked me if I was Congressman Patrick and another one asked me that on the way out.

Forgot my check book, but will send that one for five [dollars] soon as I get back. Won't be home this weekend.

Tell Grandmother, Fred & Chris hello. Kiss Mamma for me and as many [to you] as you sent for your Dad.

He bypassed his usual reserve encampment that summer, and stayed in Washington. So, Margaret, not seeing her dad for a long while, again did better than usual at letter writing. Each reply her father sent contained something of interest.

[Washington, D.C.]
[July 20, 1939]

I am so sorry for those poor knees. You just won't have any if you keep on bumping them. Be sure and take care that no infection sets in. How in the world can you be that beautiful singing stage star without knees? They are most essential adjuncts to that career, and they are almost necessary for any career unless you want to be a wheel-chair beggar. So you take good care of 'em. I'm glad that lightning didn't catch up with you—that's worse than knee bumps.

[July 22, 1939]

Your dad and Sens. Wheeler, Austin, and some congressmen have been working on a railroad bill all day long. We almost reached an agreement, and I hope we will Monday.

[July 28, 1939]

We just received a terrible beating in the Senate. I presided yesterday and the vote on an amendment by Harry Byrd to take all appropriations for roads out of [my] bill was beaten by a vote of 40 to 38. [But] they asked for a reconsideration today, and got it by a vote of 42 to 39. . . . Sen. Hayden of Arizona & I have thought out a way to get the job done, but it will take until next year.

[August 2, 1939]

W-I-C-H-I-T-A is the way to spell that Kansas town. Properly it is Ouichita and is said Washitaw and is the name of a tribe of Texas and Oklahoma Indians. There's a river and a mountain also named for them. There is also a forest reserve in Arkansas of that name. You don't really know how very interesting . . . the study and tracing of names [can be] if you like it. You take those two pretty names of my beautiful daughter Mary (Hebrew, Miriam—Greek, Maria), beautiful rebellious one; Margaret means pearl; so, you are my beautiful rebellious pearl, and your last name is pure English and means just what it says.

[September 24, 1939]

Here are your funnies & your check—but you have been a bad girl—running around with the boys & forgetting your dad. Hope you had a grand time at all the parties. You might send me a postcard.

[September 25, 1939]

I am taking it for granted you got E on those tests, and am sending you another $1.00. It is rather hard for a nice young lady to get along on a dollar and five cents a week—but your dad got along on nothing a week until he got a job washing windows in a drugstore at $3.00 a week after school. The Crown Drug Store is in the same location that Clinton's was when I worked there.

[September 30, 1939]

I hope you came out all right on King Louis the XIV in the test. He's the king whose cook com-

178

mitted suicide when the king put salt in one of his fine culinary concoctions. His grandpa was the greatest king France ever had, King Henry IV. There are more good stories about him than any other French king. Lizzie was Queen of England at the same time he reigned. It takes a long time to get interested in the personalities of history, but when you do there's nothing equals it and you see why senators and presidents act as they do sometimes.

Then—another funeral trip. "Old man Logan's heart quit on him last night," Harry explained, referring to Senator Marvel Logan of Kentucky. "As usual, on senatorial funerals, it's a gay party," he reported from his train.

Because attending the funeral was official Senate business, he didn't have to pay for the trip. So he saved some travel expenses for a speech he'd scheduled beforehand at a county fair in Caruthersville, a town in Missouri's boot-heel country. But before he got to Caruthersville, part of his savings had been stolen. While taking a walk, someone lifted $33 from his wallet, left in his hotel room. Fortunately he had put his train ticket and $4 in his pocket. "I nearly fell over when I went to pay the hotel bill & the wallet was empty," he wrote Bess. "It gives you a sinking sort of feeling."

Arriving back in Washington, he felt better when he found a special letter from home among his stack of mail.

My dear Sistie:

Your nice letter with all the kisses was here when I came in this morning. It was highly appreciated. I am most happy you got a par grade in Latin. I am anxious for you to get that pretty head of yours full of facts and information that will be useful to you when you don't have any dad. I won't leave you any money or other assets, except I hope a reputation that you may point to with pride. So, I want you to get all the education you can get. No one can take that from you.

I don't want you to be a Tallulah Bankhead, neither do I want you to be a Mary McElroy.[9] I just want you to be properly equipped mentally to hold your own in this great world and maybe someday be the lady senator from Missouri to succeed your pa.

Hope you get another history teacher you can like. He must have had ability, or the church wouldn't have taken him. It doesn't matter whether you are a Methodist, L.D.S., Catholic, Mormon, Jew or what you believe—if you believe it and live it. They all hope to get to the same place sometime. Judge men and women by what they are and how they act, not by their religious label. Personally, I'd like 'em all to be Baptists, but I'm not heaving any

[9]Daughter of Kansas City's first city manager. She was kidnapped by her father's political enemies, and, although rescued, she later committed suicide.

of them from heaven because they're not.

Hope I can get home and buy that sundae soon. Be a nice girl. Kiss Mamma, and call your country grandma sometimes.

XXXXXX Love by the bushel, Dad OOOOOO

Then, involved in school, Margaret wrote letters less frequently.

Washington, D.C.
Oct. 19, 1939

Margie Dear:

I was most happy to get your good letter, and I hope you made the "As You Like It Club." It will be nice to know all the girls, and it will be an association you'll enjoy. . . .

Wish I could have seen the old slapstick comedy. I still like 'em. But the pictures have gone so high-hat, you can't see 'em anymore. Went to see *Mr. Smith Goes to Washington*. It makes senators look like goofs and crooks. I don't believe they are, though I'll admit I have a very prejudiced viewpoint.

Keep up those good grades. Remind me what my agreement was about those E's and I'll meet it.

You know, it is always fine to get things on merit and you should be proud to be elected on your grades. Then don't be snooty to those who can't be elected—treat them especially nice. But if you yourself can do the top things, then no one can be snooty to you. That's your dad's policy. In the Army, on the farm, in the Lodge, in politics, and in the Senate, your dad tries to do as well as anyone. Then nobody can find fault.

Kiss Mamma, and hundreds for you.

Dad

XIV

"Wouldn't That Be a Trip?"

"I am missing the greatest trip ever," Harry *complained to Bess. Members of his Senate military appropriations committee were going on an inspection trip to Central America. With war spreading across Europe following Hitler's attack on Poland in September 1939, American hemispheric defenses needed bolstering, and the committee needed to know by how much. "They leave here on [November] 10th, go to Ft. Knox, Ft. Sill, San Antonio, Brownsville, Tx., Vera Cruz, Guatemala, Nicaragua, Panama, San Salvador, Mexico City, San Diego, Seattle, Denver and back to Washington on Dec. 10."*

"Wouldn't that be a trip?" he asked Bess. "I don't suppose you'd let me go, and I shouldn't anyway."

Unable to wait for Bess's reply, he called her that same night, and she gave him her okay.

Aboard Bomber 09 over Va.
Nov. 9, '39

Dear Bess:
It was good to talk seven dollars' worth with you

183

last night for two-fifty. I succeeded in getting a lot of clothes into three suitcases. Two tuxedos (white & black), two wool suits, and three white ones.

Harry, Vic, and Fred came in after you called, or after I called, and so did Minton's secretary. We had a pleasant evening and went to bed at 9:30. Up at 5:30 this morning. Vic came by at seven, we had breakfast, and went to Bolling Field. Sen. Thomas & I were first to arrive. Then Swartz and Gurney.[1] Some of the congressmen were late. One never did show up.

We left at 8:35 (supposed to leave at 8) and are now over the Skyline Drive. The mountains are covered with snow and the trees are a beautiful color. The day is bright and beautifully clear. A most propitious start and I am sure we'll have a grand time.

Mrs. Swartz came to the plane with the sen[ator] and said she had to argue with herself for two nights before she'd let him go. She came to the same conclusion you did that the ride this way is as safe as forty [over] Wyoming roads covered with ice. . . .

They are going to send me your letters to Ft. Sill. You should have the revised schedule today. So I'll look for letters right along. Will mail this one in Louisville.

[1]Senators Harry Swartz (D. Wyo.) and Chan Gurney (R. S. Dak.).

Love to you. Kiss the baby.

Harry

How about those teeth?[2]

Shreveport, La.
Nov. 10, '39

[Margie]:
This is where we landed about 5 P.M. today in a big rain storm. We have grand pilots, and they think they have precious freight.

Dad

He had to say that because an engine on his airplane had caught fire a few hours earlier in Montgomery, Alabama. "Some slouchy soldier left the cap off the oil pressure feed tank," he told Bess later. Fortunately, the plane was on the ground when it caught fire.

Flying out of Camp Sill, Oklahoma, he got sentimental, and recalled for Margaret his days there at Camp Doniphan. He told her about how he had run the soldiers' canteen, and how now as a senator he had helped make his C. O. at Doniphan the commanding general of field artillery.

He ended his epistle by consoling her for not getting a perfect score on a recent history exam. He wished, he said, that "King Louis had signed

---

[2]Bess needed dental work. But she procrastinated and Harry kept reminding her.

the Magna Carta so you could have gotten a hundred."

During their stop at Fort Sill, the senators were issued packs "with a .45, a machete, emergency rations, and a parachute for use over the Central American and Mexican jungles." Harry added as his plane droned southward, "Hope we won't need 'em."

"We are now flying over the Gulf of Mexico, but the land is only about five miles away on our right—and we have life preservers aboard, so I'm sure it's safe," he assured Margaret. "Hope you and your mamma can take this trip with me some time. . . . We are wined and dined everywhere we stop. Of course, they are after some big appropriation, but it's nice just the same."

From San Salvador, he sent his brother Vivian a picture postcard.

[November 15, 1939]

Having a fine trip. Saw all this from a plane this A.M. Came about 600 miles from Vera Cruz in 3 ½ hours. Will write from Panama. H.S.T.

Stopping at San José, Costa Rica, he wrote in turn to Cousin Nellie. He wanted to send her a schoolhouse, but couldn't.

[November 17, 1939]

Could find no picture representing a temple of

186

education so had to send you my domicile while I'm here. This is a lovely country. People seem happy and contented. Harry

But a letter handed him by the American representative there showed that back home Bess wasn't very happy and contented. "I am sorry I didn't call [you] at Ft. Sill," her delinquent mate apologized. Now, safely out of the States, he confessed to her why. "I was afraid you might want details on the [airplane] fire at Montgomery, and might want me to get off the plane just as Vic [Messall] did."
Winging toward Panama, he favored Margaret.

Aboard Transport
San José, Costa Rica, to Panama
Nov. 17, 1939

Dear Margie:
You are going to get a plane letter today because I wrote Mother one last night.

This city is the most beautiful we've seen. It is in a valley entirely surrounded by mountains. To the southeast is a real live volcano belching steam and smoke as we go by. It is a very beautiful sight. We are now up 9,000 ft. and the other two planes look just like a couple of big fish standing still in a bowl of green with white clouds all around the edge of it. We can now see out over the great Pacific to the west and south, and on the other side are the Cordillera de Talamana Mountains, a continuation of the Sierra Madre from Old Mexico. They are perfectly lovely, with green forest below and fleecy white clouds around their summits, and once in a while a pillar of smoke from an active volcano.

The American minister to Costa Rica is a very pleasant man by the name of Horribrook. He had a reception for us at the American legation, which is a very beautiful white stone mansion owned by Uncle Sam. The President came and all the diplomatic corps. A grand time was had by all. Mr. Horribrook said the Italians celebrated their fascist birthday with a reception not long ago and no one went. He was much pleased at the turnout for ours.

The legation had some of the prettiest rugs and furniture I've seen. If your mamma had been here she'd certainly have wanted a Duncan Phyfe sofa and dining room table.

I hope you are still winning grades and honors, and I wish you were with me, you and mother. Give her a big kiss for me, and here are a lot for you.

XXXXXXXXXXXX Dad
OOOOOOOOOOOOOOOOOOOOOOOOOO

He spent three days in Panama, and wrote Bess about it. Here are some excerpts:

[Hotel Tivoli, Panama Canal Zone]
[Nov. 18, 1939]

I arrived at eleven o'clock yesterday, and have had review after review, and salute after salute. They fired one when we stepped off the planes, fired one when we called on the general in the

188

afternoon, and fired one this morning when we inspected the coast artillery post. They've shown us the big guns, 16 in., the little guns, the machine guns, and the new loch sites, and have told [us] why we should buy the Galápagos Islands from Peru or Ecuador, and Cocos Island from Costa Rica.

I went out riding with four congressmen and saw Old Panama. They are just now digging it out of the jungle after about 250 years. Morgan the buccaneer destroyed it in 1671. I was surprised by the immensity of the cathedral and the other ruins. I sent Margaret a card with a picture of the tower on it, and it was a tower, not a spire. Trees 3 ft. in diameter had grown up through the walls.

[November 19, 1939]

We have had two very strenuous days. Inspected three forts, a lot of artillery emplacements, and had a dinner party with the commanding general last night. It was a grand party at the "High Hat" Union Club in Panama City.

I bought a watch for Margaret today, so don't buy her one. It is an American watch, but sells half price down here. I thought it would be a good opportunity to get her one.

In addition to the watch, he also bought Margaret a local newspaper. "Thought you might like to study this out," he suggested in a letter, enclosing for her the colored funny paper section printed in Spanish.

From Panama, the senators flew north for stops at Managua, Nicaragua, and Guatemala. Airborne, Truman again took up his pen.

> Aboard the Transport
> Managua to Guatemala
> Nov. 21, '39

Dear Margie:

We had the grandest time in Managua we've had yet. The President himself personally entertained us at his house and at a very swank dinner. He signed his place card for you, and also gave me a stamp collection for you. He is a regular fellow and everyone left there this morning with a very friendly feeling for Nicaragua.

The country is beautiful, the soil very rich, but the people are very poor. They still use ox carts just like the ones that the Babylonians used 4,000 years ago. The wheels are all in one piece hewn from big trees. Some of them [are] as much as six feet in diameter. They squeak so you can hear them for blocks. The city was completely destroyed just a few years ago by an earthquake and it is not entirely rebuilt yet.

We are now passing one of the live volcanos that caused the quake. It is pouring out smoke and the President told us it glowed with fire at night.

Nearly everybody has malaria. We are hoping

our quinine will keep it from us. Besides, we saw no mosquitos.

I hope you passed your test in fine shape, and that there'll be another E. Aunt Mary saw one of your teachers the other night, and she told her what a fine student you'd become. That makes me very proud.

The plane is jumping around so I'll have to quit. We are over the volcano.

Kiss Mamma and take a lot for you.

D.A.D.
XXXXXXXXXXXXXXXXXXXX
OOOOOOOOOOOOOOOOOOOOOOOOO
XXXXXXXXX

Nov. 23, 1939
To Mexico City from Guatemala

Dear Bess:

Well, we're homeward bound again. One more day and we'll be in San Antonio, and I'm glad.

The American minister at Guatemala gave a grand party for us but the President didn't come. He looks like Napoleon and wants to act it, I guess. One of the young Cabots from Boston is secretary to the legation and after we got used to his Harvard accent, he wasn't a bad fellow, and his wife is a charming person. She was much more cordial to us than Madam la Minister.

Anyway, we're glad we're on our way. Nicaragua was the high spot of the trip, even if it was as hot as Hades. Guatemala is a beautiful place, though, and there are more things to see and to buy. If I'd stayed another day, I'd have had to wire home for money.

(We are up 9,500 ft. and the boat is rocking and the pen feeds too fast.) I have more ink on my hands than goes on the paper.

I'll say again that this is a most beautiful ride. The blue Pacific on the left, high mountains on the right, with now and then a smoking one, and a perfectly lovely plain under us.

I am anxious to get to Mexico City because I'm expecting a lot of mail. I'll wire you soon as we get to San Antonio.

There's not much to write about, and it is kind of rough up here, so I'll have to quit.

Love to you,
Harry

Once back in the States, he wrote Margaret his impressions of Mexico.

San Antonio, Tex.
Nov. 25, 1939

Dear Sistie:
It was a nice letter they handed me today—two, in fact, one from you and one from Mother. The pictures I sent you were taken by Cong. Shafer of Michigan, and he is going to give me a whole set when we get home.[3]

---

[3]If he did, they have not survived.

I am sending your mother a whole suitcase full of trinkets which you can help her unpack. Some of them are right pretty, and you may want one thing in particular. I think it is rather pretty.

Mexico City is a very fine place. I sent you a postcard picture. I think of old Popocatépetl, the Aztecs named him, and he is the "father of mountains." In the suitcase will be a painting of him which is very beautiful. We flew past him on both sides. Once, 13,700 feet up when all the land we could see was the top of Popo and Orizaba. We had to fly out over the Gulf of Mexico and come down through the clouds, and then land at Vera Cruz and wait awhile.

When we went up again, we had to go above the clouds again and after a half hour at 175 miles an hour we were over the beautiful valley of Mexico City. It is in a bowl surrounded by mountains, and the land is very rich. That is where the Spaniards first saw cotton, and the rugs I'm sending home are woven on an Indian loom by hand just as the Aztecs wove a thousand years ago. The Guatemala Indians are descendants of the Mayas and Aztecs. There is a very fine opera house in the City of Mexico, and the old Spanish cathedral is a marvel of beauty.

The shops make Paris and New York fade, and I've never seen so many automobiles, and they're all made up here in [the] U.S. It was a lot more dangerous to ride behind those Mexican police from the airport to the hotel than it was riding over jungle and mountain range from Guatemala.

Hope you had a nice party, and that you called Mamma on her birthday.[4] Kiss Mother for me, and here are a lot for you.

Dad

X X X X X X X X X X X X X X X X X X X

"We are grounded at Midland, Tx. It is halfway between Ft. Worth and El Paso. We go by train from here," a postcard informed Margaret.

Over the Arizona Desert
in a *rain storm*
Nov. 28, '39

Dear Bess:

Our planes finally came on to El Paso, and after some delay we left there with the sun still obscured. We'll never let Thomason live it down.[5]

We stopped at the Arizona Ft. Huachuca and let the Negro soldiers put on a review for us; and they really gave us one. Then went over to Tucson for gas, and are now over the desert where we run into showers every little bit. They make us rock around quite a bit, and you probably will have trouble reading this.

We never did see the sun in El Paso, and it was

[4]The senator's mother celebrated her eighty-seventh birthday on November 25th.
[5]The Thomasons, friends of Harry and Bess, lived in El Paso and boasted about its weather.

cold as it could be. The Thomasons took us over to a night club in Juarez called the Tivoli, same [name] as our hotel in Panama, where we met the gov. of Chihuahua and the commanding general of the northern Mexican army. They were very cordial to us and the club put on a good floor show. We were back in the hotel at 12:30 this morning, and up again at 5:30. Then we didn't get away until 11 A.M. on account of the clouds. . . .

The chamber of commerce of El Paso gave us a grand dinner where Minton made a good speech, and so did Costello of Calif. We've made it a rule that only one senator and one congressman may talk at banquets.

They gave us each a beautiful serape which we'll have to decide how to dispose of when I get home. Maybe I can cut it in two, and give each of you half.

We are now flying over the All American Canal and a lot of beautifully irrigated land. More water than we've seen since we crossed the old Mississip at Vicksburg. (Not counting the Gulf of Mexico and the Pacific Ocean.)

We're right over Yuma, and I'm going to have to quit until tonight. Kiss Margie. Love to you.

Harry

One of my bridges came out awhile ago, so I'll have a little teething to do myself when I get home.[6]

[6]Bess had just completed some dental work.

HOTEL DEL CORONADO

Between San Diego &
March Field, Calif.
Nov. 29, '39

Dear Bess:

On account of the weather, we were late at San Diego and the poor chamber of commerce could only half kill us instead of doing the whole job.

Inspected a big plane factory, and then went to the palace of the owner for cocktails, where sincere efforts were made to impress the country boys. Then a grand dinner at the above hotel where we all went to sleep at the table while Elmer [Thomas][7] was making a 55-minute speech. You know we got up at 5:30 Central Time or Mountain Time at El Paso and they kept us up on Pacific Time, so what could you expect. The place is beautiful, however, I had to admit it even to the Calif. congressman, who contributed to our sleepiness along with Elmer. . . .

Kiss Margie. Love to you
Harry

We stayed in this hotel for about 40 winks.

From Los Angeles, he wrote Bess two letters on Ambassador Hotel stationery. As these excerpts show, the first one was scolding, but both were informative.

[7]Senator from Utah

Well this day hasn't been so good—no letter at Ft. Huachuca, no letter at San Diego, no letter at March Field—and none here. Maybe I've been spoiled because I've had a chance to crow over everybody because at every port there was a letter, and sometimes two.

[In San Diego, we] were up at 6:30 again this morning to see a most beautiful sunshiny day on a blue Pacific just outside my sitting room window, with a battleship anchored in the distance. The Coronado is built around a court full of palm tress and all sorts of flowers in full bloom. We had a grand breakfast, visited some more plane factories, and then flew to March Field where I mailed you a letter. Inspected the lay out there, had a delicious lunch at the officers' club with hot biscuits and orange blossom honey for dessert, and then came to Long Beach in the planes. Inspected another fort, and two more plane factories, and came to this hotel. They gave us cocktails, and then took us to Earl Carroll's for dinner, where we saw a very fine show, and I am writing this at midnight. Tomorrow we start again—and I hope I get a *couple* of letters.

Nov. 30, '39

It was a grand and glorious feeling to talk to you just a little while ago. . . . We had quite a day today. They took us through the Douglas plant, Lockheed, Voultee plants, and then we inspected some flying cadets at Burbank. There were boys from Missouri. One from Fulton, one from Bowling Green, and two from Kansas City. They seemed very glad to see me. . . . Then we went to lunch at M.G.M. where Mr. Mayer himself presided. Will Hays was there, and the mayor of Los Angeles, and William Powell, Mickey Rooney, Mary Howard, Lana Turner, the O'Sullivan lady, Helen Gilbert, and Jeanette MacDonald. Miss MacDonald had to run for a set, so I didn't get her name on the card for Margaret, and I didn't see Mr. Powell until he was introduced, so I missed him too. Leni Lynn and Kathryn Grayson sang for us. They have beautiful voices, and are lovely children—one fourteen and the other seventeen. Mr. Mayer said that the Lynn child had a better voice than Deana Durban. She sang two beautiful songs and "The Last Rose of Summer" for an encore.

He especially liked San Francisco. At least parts of it. Sending Margaret a card showing Chinatown, he commented, "This is a lot nicer than the real things. It's cleaner, the paint is better, and you can't smell it."

Feeling he'd neglected writing Margaret, he shared with her his impressions of the West Coast, and sent her what autographs he'd collected. Of course, he also had some advice about schooling.

Dear Sistie:

You gave your dad a lot of pleasure with that nice letter they handed me when I stopped out of the plane here. I sincerely hope that suitcase will come right away so you won't have that case of nervous prostration. I'll have it myself if it gets lost after all the thinking I did to get those things together.

I am glad you got caught up on those government questions. You know, a beautiful young lady who is a senator's daughter is supposed to know all about how the federal government works, and also all about a lot of other things. You'll have to work hard to learn all the necessary things, and then there are millions of things you learn every day. It was always a handicap to your dad because he didn't know as much as he should. He's still trying to learn.

Yes, I saw the Coconut Grove, but I didn't go in. I only looked into the door. The Chamber of Commerce of Los Angeles took us to dinner at Earl Carroll's one night, and the next night I had dinner at the home of Mr. Geo Eastman, a supporter of moral rearmament, and went from his house to the broadcasting station.[8]

Los Angeles is a beautiful big country town made up of a lot of little settlements of people from all over the United States. There are enough Iowans to elect a congressman if they wanted to,

---

[8]Truman had spoken in behalf of moral rearmament.

same as Oklahoma, Kansas, and Nebraska.

San Francisco, San Diego, and Monterey are all individual cities with a background and a past of much interest. From the air San Diego was the most beautiful city we've seen. San José, Costa Rica, the next, and San Francisco the next. Los Angeles looked like about a dozen towns from the air, and that's what it is on the ground too.

San Diego is the first settlement by white men, and it's not as old as Santa Fe, N.M. Monterey has a historic background that is very interesting, and so has Sacramento. The gold rush of '49 was started from here. I am sending you a picture of Sutter's Fort which is in the center of town, and from which the gold came that caused the rush. He was quite a man. I am bringing you a book about him.

San Francisco is one of the world's great and famous cities. It has an atmosphere all its own, and it doesn't get it from Iowa, Kansas, and Oklahoma. It has a Chinatown, a Fisherman's Market, a grand waterfront, and the greatest harbor on the Pacific Ocean. It has more hills than any other city in the world, and they are hills. They still use cable cars because no other kind can climb the hills. Automobiles have to have special gears and brakes, and in some places if you fell down, you'd roll three blocks before you could get up. I wish I could have stayed a week and really seen the town.

I saw all [of] Los Angeles I wanted to see in one day's ride over it. If it weren't for the movie stars and the chamber of commerce, we'd never hear of

Los Angeles—well, Aimee McPherson and Old Doc Townsend help some, but none of them is much to be famous for.[9]

Hope you win some more E's. I have forgotten how many you have earned. Can you tell me? And have you gone below the deadline in anything?

We go from here to Seattle, and then to another famous individual city, Salt Lake City. Hope I can stay with the party long enough to see it.

Kiss Mamma for me, and here are a lot for you. . . .

X X X X X X Dad X X X X
O O O O O O O O O O O O O

His next stop—Fort Lewis, Washington. "We have had the same old thing here," he wrote home, "inspection, review, dinner. Only after dinner, there was a crap game. I won $20 and now am going to bed."

Washington State was the end of the line for the senator's month-long inspection tour. "Your old man is the only one who has been able to take it day in and day out without any complaint," he boasted to Bess.

His final letter home, posted from Seattle, shows he was as feisty as ever.

[9]Flamboyant evangelist Aimee Semple McPherson founded the Angelus Temple Church of Foursquare Gospel. Dr. Francis E. Townsend directed a movement seeking government pensions for all aged citizens.

Dec. 6, 1939

Dear Bess:

I didn't get the expected letter. . . .

I made my S. F. speech here instead of in the Calif. city. . . .

We stayed all night last night at Ft. Lewis at the Ft. Lewis Inn. They charged us $2.85 for lunch, bed, and breakfast. The Fairmont Hotel [in San Francisco] charged me $2.45 for laundry. I had four shirts, two suits of underwear, and a suit of pajamas in the bundle. Just the difference between an honest hostelry and a den of thieves.

We rode in cars from Ft. Lewis by way of Tacoma to Seattle. Mt. Ranier was in sight all the time, and next to Orizaba & Popocatépetl it is the most beautiful mountain I've seen. Rises to 14,392 ft. from sea level. Everybody I talked to gave me a different elevation for it—all the way from 14,500 to 15,000. The latter figure is the chamber of commerce one from Tacoma. But I'd seen the official flying map of the US Army, which was too bad for the boys. I was too polite, however, to display my information. . . .

Here is another card for Miss Margie, signed by the Mayor of Seattle. She'll have some collection. He sat beside me and believes in my sort of public morals—as old Taft said to Jay Lee,[10] a "rare bird."

[10]Author of *The Artilleryman*.

Kiss Margie for me & I hope I get to do the same to you tomorrow evening.

Love to you, Harry

XV

"I've Just Got to Win . . ."

Back in Washington, thinking about his chances to be reelected senator in 1940, Harry wrote home that "The terrible things done by the highups in K. C. will be a lead weight to me from now on." Tom Pendergast was in prison for income tax evasion, and the man who sent him there, U.S. District Attorney Maurice Milligan, announced he would oppose "Tom's Boy" in the 1940 Missouri Democratic primary. So too, would Missouri's governor, Lloyd Stark. There was no way the Pendergast-tainted senator could win. But their opponent, despite the odds, was a determined man. Long before the primary, he had decided "I've just got to win anyhow, and make 'em like it."

To make matters worse, Franklin Roosevelt started to waffle. The President suggested that maybe Harry might be interested in a job with the Interstate Commerce Commission. "Roosevelt was mad. I don't know why he was mad, but he was very vindictive if he got mad at anybody," Olive Truman, cousin Ralph's wife, recalls. She also remembers how her husband, a major general, ended up on the inactive service roster. As Olive tells it, FDR sent two men from the Inspector General's office down to a Louisiana army maneuvers to follow Ralph around. Their mission was to get some goods on him in order to embarrass him and Harry. "Ralph found out what they were doing there, so he took them on a merry chase, and lost them in the swamp. They were stranded in a swamp for three days and nights without anything to drink."

As Christmas 1939 approached, Harry wrote home, "It is a miserable state of affairs when a man dreads showing up in his hometown because all his friends are either in jail or about to go there." So, he quietly shifted his political headquarters to Saint Louis and, after a strategy meeting there in January, geared up for the campaign.

In March, however, he found things reversed from normal. Bess and Margaret had gone to Washington, and he was with his kinfolk back in Missouri.

Kansas City, Mo.
March 26, '40

My Dear Daughter:
I was a very happy daddy this morning when the big-voiced Mr. Canfil handed me your nice airmail letter from "Zinzinnatie." I also had a telegram from Vic, and your Independence grandma had a wire from your mother, while your farmer grandma had a card from you from the second largest city in Ohio. Take it altogether, it was a very nice day.

I saw Aunt Mat, and hauled her uptown to get a

package out of Mr. Hind's emporium at the corner of Osage and Maple.[1] I saw Uncle Daw at a precinct captain's meeting at the city hall, and then went to see my mamma, and eat a chicken dinner, which she'd fried herself.

She killed two of the chickens which hatched under her front porch on her birthday last fall. Out of nine, she'd raised six through all that zero weather. Now only four remain. She said if you'd come back, she'd cook 'em for you, but if you didn't, Vivian's boys would probably get 'em.

I hope you are a competent and capable [train] engineer now. If you like, I'll ask old man Willard, the president of the B & O, to give you a job. Which end of the run do you want—from St. Louis to Cincinnati, or from Washington to Grafton? I'll have to know that, of course.

Vic called me today, and told me I might have to fly to the Capitol City tomorrow to vote on the trade treaty bill. So, I may see you Thursday.

Kiss Mamma—love to you.

Dad

XXXXXX OOO OOO XXXXXX
OOOXXX XXX OOO OOOXXX

His primary campaign didn't officially begin until June 15th, but Harry didn't believe in wasting time. Crossing southern Missouri by rail, he wrote a letter—between the lines of his dining car's menu!

[1] The Independence post office.

My Dear Daughter:

Your "old" dad has had a most strenuous couple of days. Monday at 3:40 P.M. I left Washington D.C., and drove to Washington, Pa., stayed all night; got up at 4:30 A.M., left there at 5:15, and drove 760 miles to Chillicothe, Mo., and on the road [I] called you. It was nice to talk to you, and you did right to take the call. (Kiss Mamma, because she was not there.)

Spoke at Trenton to the railroad men & Canfil drove me at 80 mi. per hr (don't tell Ma) to St. Louis. Had eight phone calls, and Ralph DePugh flew to St.Louis to ask me to be for him for sheriff. I couldn't, but he left in good humor. They never did let me go to bed until way after 12 o'clock.

Got up at six, took this train at seven, and have made so many friends in St. Louis, I am inclined to believe I will carry St. Louis. Have been working all day on the St. Louis men, and I've helped I hope.

Kiss Mamma & try to get her to come to Sedalia on June 15 to help to open the campaign.

Hope you go & see your old country grandma, because she's crazy about your dad. Kiss Mamma & lots of them for you.

Dad

OOOOOOOOOOOOOOOO

The Truman women stood beside Harry that campaign kickoff day in Sedalia. "Both of you did yeoman service, and the more I think of that day's work, the more pleased I am," he thanked Bess and Margaret.

August 6th was primary election day, but Truman lost two weeks of campaigning because the Senate was still in session, and he felt obliged to be there. For one thing, he said, "I've got to try to pass a rail bill over the presidential veto tomorrow."

He took out after Stark and Milligan in July. When he'd finished, he had won a narrow primary victory. "Stark went fishing & forgot he lost. So did Mr. Roosevelt—and Mr. Milligan," Harry noted gleefully afterward.

He had a few additional comments about his adversaries, past and future, as he looked to November and his election contest with Manvel Davis, his Republican opponent.

Washington, D.C.
Aug. 11, 1940

Dear Bess:
Well, the letter came yesterday after I'd dropped mine down the shoot, so I couldn't get it back to tell you I was glad to get it and the enclosures, even my own telegram saying I'd arrived safely. I [now] know you received it. . . .

I got up at 8:10, had breakfast at the hotel, and have been opening letters of congratulation ever since. Must have been two or three hundred in this mail. Got one from Milligan's manager, Roy Williams, and one from Jack Stapleton, Stark's publicity man. None from the two principals. Probably won't hear from either one.

The *Star-Times* in St. Louis has decided that there is nothing to do, only go Republican. The *Globe* and the P[ost]-D[ispatch] of course feel the same way, and for the welfare of the country, the K. C. *Star* could do nothing else. There's one consolation, however; they can't say anything new about me, and they can't beat me. Manvel Davis is a pro-German, and a very poor campaigner. With all the Democrats together, we ought to get three or four hundred thousand majority and I believe we will. . . .

Hope there's a letter at the hotel when I get over there. Love to you both.

Harry.

Receiving a congratulatory message from Margaret, he replied:

Washington, D.C.
Aug. 12, 1940

My dear Sistie:
Such a nice letter deserves a prompt reply. . . .

I'm glad Uncle Frank & Geo. have finally decided that I won. I must have. Has Aunt May's pa ever admitted it?[2] The governor never has—nor has his mudpuddle helper, Mr. Milligan.

I had dinner with Sen. Barkley tonight, and told

[2]Aunt May's "pa" was William Southern, publisher of the Independence *Examiner.*

him what you said. He said he liked that kind of bacon & that I had a mighty pretty wife, and a very sweet and pretty daughter. I'll tell [Sen.] Hatch tomorrow.

The [victory] luncheon was grand. Almost your dad's become a stuffed shirt, they've been so interested in his welfare. Didn't know he counted for so much in the Senate. There have been no other senatorial primaries. Some come next month.

Haven't seen a picture [show] yet. Probably won't. Never saw so many letters to sign in my life. We've used $35 for stamps on congratulations acknowledgments—and piles yet unanswered.

Here are some Costa Rica stamps. Kiss your mamma for me & be a good girl. Lot of love from

Dad

X X X X X X X X X X X X X X X X

O O O O O O O O O O O O O O O O

In a vindictive mood, he described for Bess an encounter with a Stark supporter:

Aug. 21, 1940

Mr. Boyle Clark from Columbia came in to see me this morning. He is Mr. Stark's great friend— wanted to know if I had heard from the gov., and [I] told him I hadn't and didn't want to hear from the S.O.B. and that so far as I am concerned I didn't give a damn what he did or intended to do, and that I hoped he'd tell him just that. Then he wanted to know if I was angry at Stark's followers. I told him I wasn't, but they would all be in the bandwagon anyway [in November] for most of 'em hated the gov. as badly as I do. He said that is a fact and left in a good humor.

He wasn't much worried about his chances in the November general elections. But, busy in the Senate, it was always good to receive encouraging news from home.

Washington, D.C.
Aug. 27, 1940

Dear Bess:

Well, your letter came on time this morning, and so did the marked *Mo. Dem[ocrat]*. I was most glad to get the paper because I hadn't had the chance to look at it. It shows that the reaction of the country papers is good. I am of the opinion that we will not have very many disgruntled Democrats when November comes. I hope not anyway.

Just had to go out and put some people from Jeff. City into the [Senate] gallery. The people are lined up halfway to the House side waiting to get in. Never was it so bad even in the days of Huey's filibuster.

We had our first night session last night. I went uptown to the Carlton and had dinner with John Snyder & Mr. Deal and got back just in time to vote on an amendment by Sen. Wagner to give the nigs equal rights in the Air Corps. [Sen.] Jimmy Byrnes voted with us and explained to me afterward that he didn't want a majority of the Dems against it.

He was standing in the back of the chamber this morning talking to Mitchell, that Negro congressman from Chicago. When he went into the cloakroom, Schwellenbach[3] & I went out and told him that a candid camera fellow in the press gallery had taken his picture to send to So. Carolina with the statement that the congressman was congratulating him on his equality vote. Of course, no such picture was taken, but Jim didn't pay any attention to us anyway. . . .

Glad you had a good time at the party. Wish I'd been there . . . It looks like I won't get home. Kiss Margie. Love to you.

Harry

As the session wore on, Harry, sitting at his Senate desk, wrote Margaret, who had recently soloed in the family automobile.

Washington, D.C.
August 28, '40
2:30 P.M.

Dear Daughter:

Mother tells me you are a full-fledged driver now, and that you go to church, to town, and all around without a helper. I'm glad of that. Maybe you can be my chauffeur in the campaign.

She also tells me you are going to study Spanish.

---

[3]Lewis Schwellenbach, Democratic senator from Washington State.

That is a very useful language these days. Maybe I could get you an interpreter's position at Panama, Guatemala, or Santiago, Chile, someday. Anyway, I hope you'll be good at it & your music. . . .

Mr. Stark is a ham, whether it is governor, candidate, or judge.

I thought I'd be starting home tomorrow night, but I won't be able to make it. We'll probably finish this bill today, the big appropriations tomorrow, and then take up the transportation bill Saturday. That means no home for me this weekend. I'll have to miss the meeting in St. Louis, and the legion convention at Sedalia too.

I suppose you have started to school almost by now. Are you a junior this year?

Senator Burke is giving a party at the Army & Navy Club tomorrow to celebrate my victory. Five senators and five representatives. Nice of him, isn't it? Wish you & Mamma were here. I miss you terribly.

Kiss Mamma. Love to you.

Dad

X X X X X X X X X X X X X X X X X X X

O O O O O O O O O O O O O O O O O O O

"Don't throw Margie's congratulations away," Harry instructed Bess after learning she planned, following their daughter's sixteenth birthday, to do a little housecleaning. "Sixteen years are very short in retrospect. Remember how you cried because you thought I was displeased she wasn't a

boy? Well, I'm glad she's not, and there are nephews enough to continue the name anyway."

But that also concerned the household named Truman that autumn. Returning to Washington aboard an airliner, Dad experienced an engine failure. "I don't think you'd have been scared," he pacified Bess, "because the plane did not jump around much. I was looking out of the window when he turned around, but no one else knew it until they were told by the stewardess."

Then a few days later, Earnest Lundeen, a Senate colleague from Minnesota, was killed in a plane wreck. "I suppose they just gathered him up the best they could," Harry said. "Of course, I did [not] investigate. It might have made me a little leery about riding by air if I had."

But Bess and Margaret weren't so philosophical. They urged Dad not to fly, and returning east after a visit home, he yielded and took the train. He wrote Margaret afterward: "I can't promise not to fly any more. You never can tell when it will be essential for me to be somewhere on short notice, and I'm not afraid."

His last letter home before returning to Missouri to start his fall reelection campaign went to Bess. On his mind, in addition to politics, was his mother's forced eviction from the farm she'd lived on nearly all her eighty-eight years. A mortgage foreclosure (orchestrated by an anti-Truman magistrate) forced her and Mary Jane to sell off their belongings and move into a house Harry rented for them in Grandview.

Washington, D.C.
Oct. 2, 1940

Dear Bess:

Your good letters of yesterday and the day before came today. I was most happy to get 'em. The air mail seems to come in bunches.

Sorry you missed Mamma and Mary. Had a letter from Mary bemoaning the fact that they'd gone for a ride when you were there. She'd already sold the feather beds when we were talking. Vivian has three of the original grandmother beds, and said he'd give me one—so we are safe.

I've had a most hectic two days. Mr. McKittrick[4] almost ruined us by a crazy ruling. I got him to withdraw it, and hope that things are straight once more. All old-age pensions would have been stopped until the legislature meets in January if it had stood.

Joe Guffey[5] took me to dinner last night with Prentiss Brown[6] and Lew Schwellenbach on a Pennsylvania millionaire's yacht. It is 107 feet long, has two 300 h. p. diesel motors on it, and all the comforts of home. Had turkey and all the trimmings with champagne. The gentleman, whose name I believe is Touts, lives in York, and had just been awarded some millions of shell and gun contracts by the govt. We had a very pleasant evening, and I was in bed at ten P.M.

[4]Roy McKittrick, Missouri's attorney general.
[5]Senator Joseph F. Guffey, from Pennsylvania.
[6]Senator from Michigan.

The Senate has been on a rampage today over a wool bill. Thomas of Okla. talked all day and then we voted. Mr. Bridges had to make a speech, and just now at seven o'clock we quit. . . .

Had a session with the Mo. delegation today on campaign policy. . . . *some Delegation.* Kiss Margie. Glad she's going to church. Love to you.

Harry

In August, Truman had predicted he'd defeat his Republican opponent Manvel Davis by a "three hundred or four hundred thousand majority" in the November elections. He beat him by less than 50,000. Still, that was ample to assure Harry another six years on Capitol Hill, and even greater adventures to come.

XVI

"We Don't Need Old Stiffs Like You"

The United States drifted toward war following Truman's reelection, and he considered resigning his Senate seat to go on active duty with the Army. He talked about it with General George C. Marshall, Army Chief of Staff, and according to Truman, the general smiled, peered over his reading glasses, and asked "How old are you?" Fifty-six, Harry replied. "We don't need old stiffs like you," Marshall said. "This will be a young man's war."

With wounded pride, the senator decided he'd have to do something else for his country's defense. He got into his new '41 Chrysler club coupe (an election victory gift to himself) and drove down to Florida, over to Texas, up through Oklahoma to Michigan, and finally back to Washington. "The trip was an eye-opener." Visiting defense plants and military posts, he found lots of waste. The United States needed a watchdog committee to oversee defense spending, he told the Senate. His colleagues agreed, and Harry Truman became chairman of a new Senate committee.

As the senator organized his committee, Bess

and Margaret left Washington for Independence.

Washington, D.C.
Mar. 17, 1941

Dear Bess:

Well, it was a rather lonesome apartment when I returned to it. Had two glasses of buttermilk and some toast, read on the mystery story for awhile, and was asleep by eleven P.M. I woke up at 12 o'clock to tell Margaret to put out her light—and it was out.

Got up at six this morning, had breakfast at 6:45, and was down here at 7:30. It has been a dizzy day. Miss Caroline Ware from the consumers division, National Defense Comm., came down to tell me how to run my committee, and there have been some dozen or so in on the same suggestions. . . .

I'm glad you weren't on the Pa. RR. They had a terrible wreck west of Pittsburgh about 30 minutes before your 1:40 train would have come along. Hope you made the Mo. P.

Kiss my baby. Hope Christie is doing well and Mamma too. Love to you.

Lonesome Harry

Bess and Margaret had gone home earlier than usual, before school let out. Lest Margie miss some book learning, Dad wrote Mom to suggest "She might try going to high school three weeks.'

Whether Margaret did or not is unknown. But she did write Dad a letter, and he promptly replied.

Washington, D.C.
March 20, 1941

Dear Margie:

Your nice letter came this morning and that saved the girls their jobs for another day. I always tell them that if I get no letter from your mother or Aunt Mary I'll fire them before night. They know, of course, that I won't, but they are always glad when I get the letter, and so am I.

You tell your Aunt Chris to behave herself and do what the doctor tells her, that we can't afford to buy flowers. I am glad your old country grandma looks well. I wish I could see her. For some reason, which I can't understand, she seems always to be most happy to see your dad.

The girls seem to be very well pleased with the new office setup. But, my oh me, the work we are doing. . . . Your dad will make a speech Monday night, March 24, at 10:30 P.M. Washington time, 9:30 yours, over the Blue Network of NBC on national defense. That's the Wash. *Star's* radio forum. I guess WREN will have it. . . .

Kiss Mamma. Love to you. Dad OOOOOOOOO
X X X X X X X X X X X X X X X X X X

"I never was so lonesome in my life," Harry told Bess. "The flat looks like a tomb." Because he had just been appointed Masonic Grand Master in Missouri, however, he had an excuse to go home in April. But what with Masonic meetings and banquets to attend, he didn't see much of the family.

Nor did he get across the street to visit the No-lands. "I am very sorry," he apologized to Ethel afterward. Every time he started out the front door to see her "the porch was full again" of politicos.

When Ethel remembered his birthday in May, Harry explained why he hadn't come home that month.

Washington, D.C.
May 12, 1941

Dear Ethel:

I sure appreciated your card and birthday greeting. I am so happy Aunt Ella had a nice one. Wish we could have celebrated together.

I was intending to come home Thursday and stay until today, but between my investigating committee and the fact that the job hunters would have pulled me in two, I decided not to come. A Masonic lodge up at Albany was celebrating its 90th birthday on May 8th and asked me to officiate and celebrate mine at the same time. But I'd have had to stay for Lord Halifax today, and my committee had to meet, so I stayed in Washington and went over to Baltimore and watched Whirlaway win the Preakness and won $23 on him. Now you put that out to my Baptist constituents and make me some votes in 1946.

Hope you're all in good health. . . .

Sincerely,
Harry

On his next trip home, Harry committed the ultimate sin; he forgot to say goodbye to Bess's mother when he departed again for Washington. "The more I think of it, the worse it gets," his guilty conscience commanded.

After receiving a wire from Margaret, he also questioned his worth as a father.

Washington, D.C.
June 16, 1941

My Dear Daughter:
Your old dad was most highly pleased when he came in this morning and found your telegram. There was a note on the apartment door saying Mr. Vaughan had called me up to tell me it had arrived. You see, I went out there about two o'clock and went to bed, turned the phone on downstairs, and told Mrs. Rickets to take all calls—and she did it literally. So I didn't know about the nice wire until this morning.

I wish that I could be a real nice dad, but you know with all this terrible emergency and the awful political fights your dad has had to make ever since you were born, there hasn't been much chance to be the right kind of dad. I am most happy, however, with a sensible, beautiful young lady for a daughter—and that's because she had the right sort of mother.

Now you can help square me with your Independence grandmother. I went off without saying goodbye, an awful thing to do. See what she thinks about it and tell me.

Kiss your mamma for me. I'm sending you some funny papers.

Much love,
Dad

X X X X X X X X X X X X X X X X X X X X X X X X

Margaret followed up her telegram with two letters in quick succession. Her dad, although busy as could be, answered them just as quickly.

Letters he wrote to her and Bess over the next several weeks chronicle his hectic routine, his thoughts, and his travels.

Washington, D.C.
June 19, 1941

Dear Margie:

It was a nice letter, and I hope for many more like it.

This has been a most busy day. I was up at 6:30 in spite of a late hour to bed due to an entertainment my investigators gave me. There were letters to dictate as usual, a man who had the aluminum problem solved, so he said, who had to be interviewed; a meeting of a subcommittee in my office on the oil pipeline situation; an interview at the same time with the chief counsel of the American Association of Railroads; a conference with two feature writers from *Fortune* magazine; some people from Independence [and] Frank Monroe from

Sedalia; a look-in on a military committee presided over by the Hon. Bob Reynolds of No'th Ca'lina; and attendance on a subcommittee on military appropriations of the Appropriations Committee before which Mr. Knudsen was testifying; and then the Senate session considering the labor appropriations bill and the WPA appropriations bill; an interview with asst. counsel of my committee on aluminum—a couple of hundred letters to sign—in between times running over to the Senate to vote on various amendments; and then going to the Mayflower [Hotel] to meet Neil Helm, Cong. Zimmerman, Cong. Frank Boykin and Vic on some cotton legislation, and then back here to finish signing mail and to write to my sweet daughter.

That's only a sample day. I'll try to see that Navy picture. It sounds good.

Kiss Mamma for me, be a good girl.

X X X X X X X X X Dad X X X X X X X X X

Washington, D.C.
June 23, 1941

Dear Margie:

I appreciated your nice letter and the note sent with Mamma's letter. I am glad the greenbacks came in handy. They are usually pretty good things to have around. There usually isn't enough of them.

I can remember the first $3.00 I received from working a week—seven days from seven o'clock until school time, and from four o'clock until ten at night, all day Saturday and Sunday. I had to wipe off bottles, mop the floor every morning, make ice cream for sodas and wait on the customers. It was in Jim Clinton's drugstore—where the Crown is now. That three silver dollars looked like three million and meant a lot more. I bought a present for Mamma and tried to give the rest of it to my dad and he wouldn't take it. It was, as I say, a great day all around when I got that $3.00. I've never had as much or as big a payday since.

I am going to Gulfport tonight with the casket of the great Pat Harrison. He was a grand man—a magnificent orator, an able legislator, and a good friend. He was extremely nice to me when I first came to the Senate. I voted for him for floor leader against Barkley, and he never forgot it. I told Barkley what I intended to do, and he never has held it against me. You know he was only elected by one vote. Some distinguished solons told both men they'd vote for 'em. You can't make friends that way. . . .

Kiss Mamma, love to you.
XXXXXXXXXXXXX
Dad
OOOOOOOOOOOOOOOOOOO

Special Train en route
to Gulfport
June 24, '41

Dear Bess:
Well, they asked me to go to Pat's funeral and I'm on the way. Was most happy to get your special of

Sunday with [a] note from Margie in it before I left.

I sent the laundry, closed the windows, and put everything in order before I left. Stopped the *Star,* forgot the *Post,* and had never started the milk, so I guess we won't be so badly off.

I postponed the committee meetings and have arranged for Hatch to hold some hearings in July. Got the Interstate Commerce Committee straightened out, and I'm going to take that promised rest, I hope. Went to bed at ten last night and slept until eight this morning and feel better already.

It's the strain that does the damage. There's more than any one man can do. When we worry about not getting it done, then it is only worse. I'm hoping to get to Hot Springs Friday and stay there ten days, and then come by for you and be in Washington July 7th.

We have a special train, each one in a stateroom by himself. Guffey is on one side of me and Henning on the other. Had breakfast with the V. P. and Green of R.I. There are about 30 senators and as many house members and what's left of Pat and his family.

It's not as good a party as Joe Robinson's was. Garner's gone, so is Burke. Minton and Schwellenbach are judges. Tom Stewart couldn't come. There's no poker game—so it's a real funeral.

Will phone you from Biloxi. You'll like that, I know. Love to you & Margie.

Harry

Hope you found Mamma all right.

Dear Sistie:

This will be the first pencil letter from your dad. Can't use a pen, the ink all comes out at once since we are up in the air about 5,000 feet—maybe more. We went up to 7,000 between New Orleans and Memphis.

I walked up the Rue Royale [in New Orleans] this morning about 7:30 and looked in all the curio and antique shops and the fancy perfumerie places, and wished for you and Mamma. I stayed at the Monte Leon. They have put in a new lobby and have air-conditioned it. The rooms aren't air-conditioned except for a fan under the light—a big wooden one with four blades like a restaurant fan.

Had dinner at Antoine's last night. They gave me so much I couldn't enjoy it for thinking of the waste. And it is too late in the season for oysters Rockefeller, and I could not eat crepes suzette, so I had to make out with some black soup and steak with a whole bucketful of vegetables and mushrooms poured over it. . . .

You & Mother should have been with me. Saw Mrs. Luxich & Biloxi & Pass Christian.[1] They are just the same except for improvements—new roads & new houses.

Will be in Hot Sps. until July 6, I guess. Kiss Mamma, lots of love to you.

X X X X X X X X X X X X Dad O O O O O O

[1]Mrs. Luxich rented the cottage to Bess during her stay in Biloxi with Margaret.

Army & Navy Hospital
Hot Springs, Ark.
June 29, 1941

Dear Bess:

I thought I'd get a letter today either forwarded from the capital or directly from home, but the mail fell down on me.

I have had nothing to eat since breakfast. They are giving me that dye test in which Dr. Myers was so much interested.[2] I'm to have something to eat at 4:30—bread and crackers and fruit juice and tea and then at 5 o'clock another dose of dye. They took an X ray at 8 o'clock this morning, then I had my usual breakfast, cream of wheat—they don't have oatmeal—toast and milk with orange juice to start off.

After this so-called carbohydrate meal at 4:30 today, I won't get anything more to eat until noon tomorrow. They take some more X rays at 11 o'clock in the morning. They ought to know all about it when they get done. Fred says a perfectly sound and well man can be made a hopeless invalid in two days in this place.

I've been asleep nearly all the time. Just got up from a four-hour nap. I guess I was tired sure enough. By Saturday I ought to be caught up.

Hope I get a letter by tomorrow. I am uneasy about your mother.

Love to you & Margie.

Harry

[2]Harry had complained of stomach problems.

UNITED STATES SENATE
WASHINGTON

Army & Navy Hospital
Hot Springs, Ark.
July 1, 1941

Dear Bess:

I found this high-hat stationery in my bag and thought maybe you'd appreciate hearing from a United States Senator.

I don't know how that telegram came to be wrongly addressed—just thinking of you as Miss Lizzie, I suppose. . . .[3]

I am still on the merry-go-around. Had what they called a metabolism test this morning. They put a clothespin on my nose and stuck a rubber tube attached to an oxygen tank and an electric writing machine into my mouth, and I had to breathe that way for ten minutes while the pen made §§§ something like that on a piece of paper. Then I went up to another ward and had a tube stuck in the other end for some purpose best known to the doc. Tomorrow more stomach photos and nose and throat.

I feel so much better I may hop a train any minute. All I needed was to catch up on sleep. Just now woke up again. Had lunch at 12:30 and went to bed and slept until 3.

Been doing that every day and sleeping all night

[3]Wiring her a twenty-second wedding anniversary greeting, Harry had addressed it to "Mrs. *Bess* Truman," eliciting a complaint from his tradition-adhering wife.

too, and sometimes from ten until noon besides.

I would like to stay another week and get some [hot] baths, and I may do it. I guess Hatch, Mead, and Brewster could operate [the committee]. . . .

Hope our mothers continue to improve. Heat is not bad here at all. I have a cool room. Love to you & Margie.

Harry

Army & Navy Hosp.
Hot Springs, Ark.
July 2, 1941

Dear Margie:
I appreciated most highly your two nice notes. Your mother's letter came by airmail this morning, and yours arrived by regular mail this afternoon.

I want to hear you play the "Moonlight Sonata" by Beethoven. We have all the records by Paderewski and they are fine. I never heard him play it [in person], but I did hear him twice when he was in his prime. He had long bushy yellow hair and most powerful hands. He played his "Minuet" for one encore and the "Blue Danube Waltz" for another.

Then I heard Moriz Rosenthal play it—the "Danube," and in a short time Josef Lhévinne came along and also played it. Lhévinne was by far the best of them all. Paderewski was the best showman and one grand pianist, but Lhévinne was a musician too.

I heard old Vladimir de Pachmann play Mozart's Ninth Sonata, and play it as it should be. I think it was the most beautiful piano solo I ever heard. He was a very peculiar old man. He'd talk all the time he was playing, explaining the beauties of the piece. Lhévinne played that little "March" by Poldini, which I have, for an encore. It is very beautiful too. Hope you'll learn them all.

I hope you are having a good time. I may be home next week—but I'm not sure. Glad your country grandma is O.K. Hope the town one is too. Lots of love & kiss Mamma.

XXXXXXXXXX Dad OOO

[Army & Navy Hospital]
July 3, 1941

Dear Bess:
It was fine to get your letter yesterday just now. I'm glad it cooled off.

I am finished up with examinations & X rays and started in on a special course of [hot] baths this morning. They are very anxious for me to stay next week and take at least seven of them. I haven't made up my mind yet about it.

I feel so much better and have nearly caught up on sleep, so I don't know whether to let my special committee dangle another week and get into fighting trim, or just go back to work by way of home Saturday. I am sorely tempted to stay, but I'm afraid that the time for action on the committee may go by too. . . .

Wish we could go to Colorado for a month and forget everything, but I guess that's clear out. I'll call you when I decide what to do. I'm waiting to hear from Fulton & Harry about the [committee] situation.

I know Margie must have sung very well. Hope your mother is better. Love to you—kiss Margie,

Harry

His medical report showed nothing wrong but fatigue. He did need new glasses, however, and he was given "some pills to balance lack of hydrochloric acid in the stomach caused by fatigue."

So, he made plans to get on the road again, this time with Bess, leaving Margaret at home.

Army & Navy Hosp.
Hot Springs, Ark.
July 9, 1941

My Dear Daughter:
Glad to get your nice note of Tuesday, along with one from your mother.

I will be most happy to see you this weekend, but I very much doubt if we'll get to a show. I must be in Washington Monday morning, and I've told Mamma to make a reservation for us on the Penn's Gotham Limited which leaves St. Louis at 6 P.M. Saturday and gets to Washington on Sunday 4:45.

We are leaving you the car. You must take nice care of it—see that it is properly greased and oiled—the battery kept full of filtered water and that it doesn't run into a ditch or another car.

I think it would be a proper thing for you to buy a bond. Maybe you can buy two. They only cost

$18.75 apiece and grow into $25 after so long a time.

Be a nice girl, and tell your mother to be one too. Hope your grandmothers are well. Lots of love.
XXXXXXXXXXXXXXXXXXX Dad XXXXXXX
OOOOOOOOOOOOOOOOOOOOOOOOOOOOO

XVII

"My, What a Difference . . ."

Aboard plane over
Riverside, Calif.
Sunday, Aug. 17, '41

Dear Bess:

We've just come through the pass east of Los A. at 10,000 feet. It has been a pleasant day except that we've done some rocking around on account of air currents off the desert. There have also been some showers on each side of us. But it is a most monotonous ride. Country all looks alike except where there's a little water.

We passed over Salome, where Dick Wick Hall said "She danced." Had lunch at Tucson, gave Phoenix the go-by, and will soon land in Los Angeles.

Hope to call you later. Kiss Margie.

Love to you. Harry

He was on his first inspection tour as chairman of the Truman Committee. And while busy as ever, the senator's accommodations, paid for by the commitee, were now far more commodious. "This

233

is the hotel, a part of which I have leased," he in-formed Margaret on a picture postcard showing L.A.'s Biltmore Hotel.

From the hotel's "presidential suite," Harry gave Bess and Margaret a rundown on what he'd learned. At a San Diego airplane factory, he had to question lots of people about production, be-cause individually "the managers are all such liars you can't tell anything about the facts." Looking over Los Angeles harbor by Coast Guard cutter, he found it "a mess." "Oil, lumber, ship yards, docks and everything a hopeless jumble. What a fire it would make."

Of course, movie stars and their autographs in-terested teenager Margaret more, and on this trip Dad wasn't too encouraging.

THE BILTMORE HOTEL
Los Angeles

Aug. 21, '41

My Dear Daughter:
It was a nice letter . . . I'm glad you liked the ring.

I hope I can see that show you recommend, but I know I can't. The customers are as bad here as at home. All the Missourians in this part of the world are trying to see me, and so are the California crackpots. But that's part of the game. . . .

I don't think I'll get to see any picture artists, but if I do, I'll get you some autographs. I have thought of having the whole [movie] colony arrested and brought before the committee, but I don't know what I could charge 'em with on national defense except rotten acting and draft dodging, and I'm very doubtful if I have that authority.

Will be at St. Francis Hotel in San Francisco Saturday. Tell your mamma. I forgot to tell her where I'd stop. Be a nice girl.

Here's some soda money. XXXXXX Dad
OOOOOOOOOOOOOOOOOOOOOOOOO

THE ST. FRANCIS
San Francisco

Aug 23, 1941

My Dear Margie:

I was just as sorry as you were not to get to talk with you Sunday, but your mother said you were asleep, and I always hate to wake anyone up when he's resting.

Be all right to buy your record, especially that one. It is very beautiful. I am glad it has a piano in it.

You and your mamma should be along with me. I held hearings in Los Angeles yesterday morning and ran out a lot of crackpots. I had more calls and callers than I have at home.

We boarded a Navy plane and flew up the San Joaquin Valley between two mountain ranges—a most beautiful sight. We landed at 4:15 P.M. and came to this tall hot hotel. The manager, the asst. manager, the general in command of the 9th Corps Area, the admiral in command of the naval district, and a lot of blue- and tan-uniformed officers met us. They gave me a bedroom about 20 x 40 in size, connected with a parlor and two more bedrooms for the senator from N.Y., and an army man who is with us. . . .

I'm going down to Chinatown after awhile and see if I can find you some earrings and anklets. Shall I get Mamma some too? Kiss her for me.

Lots of love.

Dad OOOOOOO

XXXXXXXXXXXXXXXXXXXXXXXXXXXX

From the Pacific Northwest, Margaret got a picture of what a sea battle looks like.

OLYMPIC HOTEL

Seattle, Wash.
Aug. 27, 1941

Dear Margie:

Your good letter was in the box when I returned from the Bremerton Navy Yard, and it was a most happy surprise to receive it. I'm glad you got the record you wanted. I am anxious to hear it. Hope you and young Tommy had a nice time at the show. I am glad you have all those clothes. I hope you have enough of a coat to keep warm this winter. Maybe it won't be very cold. You can let me wear the sweater if you think it's big enough.

I inspected a British battleship today that was being repaired at our navy yard. Lord somebody or other met me at the gangplank with bugles, pipes,

236

salutes, etc., and then a nice tall Englishman, a Lt. Commander in His Majesty's Royal Navy, showed me the hole a Nazi bomb made at the Battle of Crete. He said it killed fifty men and knocked four guns into the sea. Another bomb exploded alongside and made a big dent in the hull. He said the Stuka bombers came over in waves every half hour and just kept dropping bombs; that they shot down some seventeen of them, and some of them fell into the sea before they could come out of the dive.

He said one battleship was sunk, as were several destroyers, that many more of them were hit just as he was. They were under terrific fire for four days. He said the Italians would not come near the fight; they dropped their bombs from two to six miles away and left as fast as they could. This ship came through the Suez Canal and across the Pacific on its own power.

It was an interesting trip. I looked over the new construction, had lunch with all the navy officers, and came back here. Had dinner with Mr. Veatch[1] and am getting ready to go to bed. . . .

Kiss Mamma. Love to you

XXXXXXXXXXXXXXX Dad XXX
OOOOOOOOOOOOOOOOOOOO
XXXXXXXXXXXXXXXXXXXXXXXX
OOOOOOOOOOOOOOOOOOOO

Mamma heard about the tail end of the trip.

[1] M. T. Veatch, a friend from his county court days.

237

Dear Bess:

We had a most pleasant ride yesterday from Seattle over here in a car furnished by one of Sen. Wallgren's friends. Stopped in Ellenburg for lunch after crossing the Cascade Mts. The pass is only 3,004 feet up and not nearly as full of trees as are those in Md. On the west side of the range they have an abundance of rain, on the east it requires irrigation.

We ate at a Chinese restaurant run by a family of Chinamen who started it 50 years ago. They give customers more and better food for less money than is obtainable anywhere I've ever been [to] out here.

When we left Ellenburg we crossed the Columbia River and then went on over the high bench on the other side of which is the valley in which the river is supposed to have run before the Ice Age. It is a perfectly dry valley except for brackish lakes now and then supposedly left when the river decided to go around a longer way. The highest dry fall in the world is one of the wonders.

We stopped at Grand Coulee Dam—the largest of its kind in the world. It backs the river up beyond the Canadian border some hundred miles away and creates a perfectly enormous amount of power. They expect to use some of that power to pump the river over into its old valley and irrigate it, still leaving more than enough water in its present course for use in that valley too.

I called Lew Schwellenbach as soon as I arrived,

and he came down to see us all, and then we went out to see his house. Mrs. S. wanted to be remembered. I am going to stay all night with them tonight and then fly to Salt Lake City Saturday where I [am] hoping to get a rest over a quiet weekend. Utah is dry in two ways and does not countenance shows or anything else on Sunday. So maybe I can get some rest. . . .

Still cool and nice out here. Had heat [on] and overcoats in Seattle.

Love to you. Harry

Salt Lake City, Utah
Aug. 31, 1941

Dear Bess:

It was sure a pleasure to talk with you and it made me so homesick I almost cried when we quit talking. I haven't had any pleasure on this damned trip. It's been work and worry ever since I left. The meetings on the west coast were seemingly successful, and I did enjoy my stay with Lew Schwellenbach, but I find that O'Mahoney and Murdock[2] have been here and held exactly duplicate hearings with the public lands committee, and unless I can find some misplaced contracts, there will be no reason for my hearings on Tuesday. . . .

As long as I stay in the Senate, there will never be another trip across the country where I am responsible for a lot of senators. They have been as

[2]Senators Joseph C. O'Mahoney (Dem. Wyo.) and Abe Murdock (Dem. Utah).

fine a lot as can be gotten together, but it takes so much work to make a two-hour hearing, and then you never know what you've done. Mead, Brewster, Fulton and Wilson went [on] to Alaska.[3] They got to Sitka all right, but had to stay there after taking a fourteen hundred mile trip over water the next day . . . . Then Mead and Fulton came back to Vancouver and Brewster and Wilson stayed in Alaska. Mead and Fulton haven't been heard from since they landed in Vancouver, and I suppose Wilson and Brewster are still flying around Alaska. So, I have to wait for the congregation to arrive and then we'll go on to Washington. I can't get away until I would have if I'd held the hearings [here].

If O'Mahoney and Murdock had been anywhere near senatorial courtesy, they would have waited and we could have worked all together and everything would have been lovely.

Your yesterday's letter just came up. I am sure Margie has a voice, and I know there has been improvement, but I'm prejudiced. It would be perfect to me no matter how it is to other people—so we must have unbiased advice which may make us mad—but I'm very sure we won't get that kind.

This is a most beautiful city from the air and this hotel is the grandest I've seen. The [Mormon] Temple is across the street and as soon as I've had a

[3]Senators James Mead (Dem. N.Y.) and Owen Brewster (R. Maine) were committee members. Hugh Fulton was committee counsel, while Lt. Col. Arthur R. Wilson was a War Department liaison officer.

nap, I shall go and see it.

I hope you don't attempt to wear yourself out on that trip [back to Washington]. Take plenty of time. Your mother can't stand too much, and what difference does it make if you don't arrive until Sunday P.M. If you'll tell me, I'll order what you want, and if there are hotels and restaurants still running in Washington—we'll eat all right.

Kiss Margie—Love to you.

Harry

The senator, who the year before dreaded showing up in Kansas City because all his friends were going to jail, now found a far different atmosphere there. With Bess back in Washington, he wrote her about his sumptuous accommodations and his new image.

HOTEL MUEHLEBACH
Kansas City, Mo.

Sept. 24, 1941

Dear Bess:
Got two letters today. What a day that made it. I mean I got two yesterday, because it is now 12:10 A.M., Sept. 24.

I held court all day yesterday (Monday) and saw everybody who had the nerve and the patience to wait. This suite has a dining room with a living room off of it with double doors between them, then there is a hallway and a twin bedroom. There are two bathrooms and an extra toilet. I sat in the

241

dining room at the head of the table so everybody in the living room could see me, and then I put the customer with his back to the double doors, both open, and occasionally, while he was telling me his tale of woe, I'd smile and nod to someone waiting, and you'd be surprised how fast they went through. I must have seen a thousand people counting Friday, yesterday and today. . . .

My, what a difference from last year at this time, and what a kick there is in it. They all cuss [Bennett] Clark[4] and wonder what I am going to do for the poor old *"Party."* What should I do? . . .

Archie Lodge had a nice meeting Monday night. . . . There was an old hillbilly by the name of Goodrich who was the master of ceremonies and Sec. of the Lodge. He looked like old Prof. Blackburn, our county supt. of schools for so long, only his head was size 7 ⅜ . . . In introducing me [he] said that he'd been discouraged by the brethren when he suggested inviting me. They told him I was too busy and too big a man to come to Archie—"but my friends and brethren, he's bigger than I thought he was—he came."

Well, I had a grand time and got back to the Muehlebach (that's the way they actually spell it, because I'm writing this over one of their ads) at eleven o'clock.

After lunch today (Tuesday) I went to Independence to pay Dan Deets for overhauling the car

[4]Missouri's senior United States senator.

yesterday (Monday). It cost $16 but it was needed. . . .

I came back over here, picked up my nigger preacher suit, and went out to Mamma's. Vivian came in while we were eating dinner and we had a family reunion. They are all in good health, and so is Aunt Ella—saw her, Ethel & Nellie Monday evening going through the alley to get the car. Had it greased.

Grandview really put on a district meeting for me tonight. Every lodge in [the] district represented but two. Hall full to overflowing and they gave me a grand reception. I pinned a fifty-year-old button on an old man 85 years old and he made a speech a senator could have been proud to make.

Ed McKim is asleep in one of my twin beds and I guess I ought to be. But instead of driving to Columbia, I'm writing this and will sleep all the way to Fulton tomorrow morning. . . .

You should see Geo. Morgan's biography of your old man for the Gr. Lodge proceedings. You'd be like the old lady at the funeral of her husband; you'd have someone check to be sure it is the right corpse.

Hello to Mrs. W. Kiss Margie. Love to you. Harry

XVIII

"I Have Been Afraid It Would Come . . ."

Washington, D.C.
December 14, 1941

Dear Ethel:

. . . . Well, there's been a lot of happenings since I was calling you on my daddy's birthday. I have been afraid it would come, but not just the way it did. We're always surprised, of course, even when the expected happens—if it's war anyway.

I [had] left Saturday [Dec. 6th] for Columbia to get a good night's sleep over the weekend before Monday at Jeff City. In fact, I was hoping for two. Went to bed at the Pennant Hotel outside of town about seven o'clock Saturday night and had breakfast Sunday at 8:00. Called the madam and went back to bed. The boy who drove me down left about noon, and at about three o'clock called me from Cross Timbers (I bet you never heard of it) and told me the Japs had bombed Honolulu. . . .

Well, I phoned the St. Louis office of T.W.A. and told 'em I had to be in Washington the next morning, and about that time Bess called and said the Sec. of the Senate had called to say there'd be a joint session Monday and that I should be there. I had no car and no dinner, so I called the little airport at Columbia right across the road from the hotel and the manager said he had a plane and would take me to St. Louis. We left at 4:50 and I was on the ground and in the station of the St. Louis airport at 5:35. It took us just 40 minutes to fly 130 miles.

Then my trouble began. I tried to go to Chicago and then tried Memphis and finally I think T.W.A. dumped somebody off and I got on the 11 P.M. plane for Pittsburgh. Sat up all night and listened to the radio. Got to Pittsburgh at 3:30 where I met Sen. Chavez of N. Mex. who came from Chicago, Sen. Davis of Pa. who lives there, and Curley Brooks, the great Republican isolationist from Chicago. He's a new senator from Ill., [a] legionnaire, fat, curly haired, has a synthetic blond wife, and is a most important Chicago *Tribune* senator. He looked as if he'd swallowed a hot stove, and that's the way all those anti-preparedness boys looked the next day. It wasn't because they'd been up all night getting there either.

I went home (we got here at 5:30 A.M.), found Bess up getting breakfast. My new secretary, Harry Vaughan, [had been] at the airport with my car and I was at home by 6 o'clock. Went to bed and slept until ten and then came to the Senate. It was quite an occasion. Guess you heard it over the radio. Then, on the 11th, we had to accept another invitation from Germany and Italy.

Goodness knows where it will end. I wish I was

30 and in command of a battery. It would be a lot easier. They may let me run a regiment yet, although they say not.

An old lady in Philadelphia wants to sell me a crest—for $50. I'll send you her letter & my reply.[1] It's terrible how important a senator is when he gets some pubicity for doing what he ought to.

Hope you are all well, and that you stay that way. Bess & Marg will be home Dec. 18th on the train. Hope I can come later.

My very best to all of you,

Harry

The United States was at war. Like chips in a mosaic, excerpts from Harry Truman's letters home portray his continued devotion to family and friends, and provide a running description of life in wartime Washington and elsewhere.

[To Bess, Washington, D.C.]
[Dec. 18, 1941]

You ought to be settled by the time you get this. Right now if the train is on time you should be just outside of Cincinnati. It's a rather dull place in that flat without Miss Margie to raise sand with about going to bed and her mamma to be begged not to get up. The breakfast was as usual,

[1]Ethel Noland had become the Truman family historian, and handled questions of genealogy for Cousin Harry.

246

only an hour earlier, and not so good as when *someone* else gets it.

Mrs. Vaughan had a nice chicken dinner with pumpkin pie [last night]. Harry told her it was tough, but it wasn't. I told him he was tough, but not the chicken.

[To Margaret, Washington, D.C.]
[Jan. 3, 1942]

Yes, we are going to, and did lose Manila—due to our peace at any price policy and to brass hats in charge of strategy who thought more of social engagements and booze than of the career and the country for which they had been educated. Educated at the taxpayer's expense to be useful in the very emergency that came and found them asleep. Read the Parable of the Virgins. Manila fell because the attack on Hawaii demobilized the fleet and our air force, and we couldn't get help to the able and brave defenders. Abbott & Costello have not been here in *Keep 'Em Flying*. Hope to get to see it. . . . I went to dinner at the Shoreham . . . They had a right good floor show—some girl tumblers and some South American dancers. The orchestra played "Vienna Woods" and the "Emperor Waltzes," and the pianist played a Chopin Nocturne and a couple of other classics which I didn't recognize in the intermission.

247

[To Margaret, Washington, D.C.]
[June 17, 1942]

[Uncle] Frank ought to make a good air raid warden. He can holler as loud as anybody and he's big enough to make 'em get under cover. I hope he'll never have to do it. We are going to have an all-night blackout here tonight beginning at 10 o'clock. Millie is having all the office force out to her house for dinner, but I hope we can get home before the blackout.

Hope you have a nice time and enjoy the summer. Be sure and go see your old country grandmother as often as you can because it may be her last summer.

[To Bess, Washington, D.C.]
[June 23, 1942]

The rug cleaned up fine. Had to iron some tonight—the d——d laundry sent some wet clothes back, two pajamas, underwear, and some handkerchiefs.

[June 25, 1942]

Now what have you done about those treatments you agreed to take? I've seen no reference to them in any of your letters. Get it done, and get those teeth X-rayed. It'll save you misery later and perhaps a tour in a hospital. You can take those two worries off my mind if you want to. And I'll still have plenty left to keep me out of mischief. . . . Get that important job done now & let me know you have.

[June 26, 1942]

It is . . . seven o'clock instead of six—but I'm at the office. You see, my bread all spoiled. It had the prettiest growth of mold on it you ever saw. So I am eating at the Senate restaurant as soon as it opens. . . . It's not very happy at the apt. when you're gone—but I'm still afraid of that [enemy air] raid.

[June 29, 1942]

The milk didn't come yesterday, but I guess I'll get two today. I'm going to stop it and the papers too before I leave so we won't have anything on hand to worry about. . . . Tell Margie I forgot to enclose her movie magazine with the Sunday papers, but I'll send it today.

[July 1, 1942]

I sent Margie the pictures and magazines, put in both powders, and the only slip I could find was one that came back with the washing last week, so I'm bringing it. I put the porch furniture in the dining room, the rug in the dinette, and the two plants at the office. . . . I packed up, and

249

straightened up. . . . [Will] probably stay at Wheeling and should be home on Friday night. It's like getting out of jail—but I expect to get into the pentitentiary by comparison when I get home. It'll be a change of scenery anyway.

[Washington, D.C.]
[July 25, 1942]

I cancelled my date with Mrs. Atwell.[2] Had Millie tell her I was going out of town. Also told Mrs. McLean[3] I'd be away the night of her dinner. Too much society to suit me. Maybe I'm nutty, but I can't see anything to those people but a bunch of drunks and parasites, most of whom would be better off in some institution. And they are not conferring any favor on me by asking me out as one of the animals for display purposes. I've got a job to do, and I'm going to work my head off to do it, and maybe it'll help save the country for our grandchildren—if we have any, and that's all I care about.

[July 26, 1942]

If you have any turnip seed, they should be sown today—I forgot to tell you over the phone. This also is Nellie Noland's birthday. She must be

[2]An unidentified Washington hostess.
[3]Evelyn McLean, heiress to a mining fortune.

sixty-two or thereabouts, but I guess she won't tell you.

I've been listening to the newscasters and reading the editorials and columnist comment on the war and it gives me the dumps sure enough. The country would be better off if all the column writers were in jail and all the broadcasters were shot, but I guess we can't do it. There ought to be a smart government man who could give out facts in a series of one paragraph for each fact and the papers should use that instead of columnist comment. The Pres. told Lister Hill[4] and me that's what he intended to do—but you know the Pres.

[Aug. 22, 1942]

When is [your brother] Fred coming? All I have to do is put the clean laundry away and there'll be a place for him to sleep. There are clean sheets and pillow slips on the bed. I'll just leave the bar shut up. There won't be any reason to open it or go in the kitchen because there is no food there. Only some butter and peaches and a ham and some bacon and Seven-Up. I'll try and clean the place up this afternoon so it will be presentable.

[4]Senator from Alabama.

251

You know, I've almost looked my eyes out for a letter from my lovely daughter, and for some reason that good-for-nothing mailman hasn't come through with one.

You know, your old dad is lonesome for a look at you and your mother. Nearly every place I've been, I've seen some nice looking young lady who made me think of Margaret. But always there was something missing. The sweet smile wasn't there, couldn't sing, or she couldn't be the right color, or she was round-shouldered or something was not there that my good looking daughter had—but I always thought I could see Margie anyway.

Your dad is trying very hard to do something for his country. I don't want the young men twenty-five years from now doing what I did twenty-five years ago and what our young men are doing now. You know, if we could only learn to harness this great machine age of ours for constructive instead of destructive purposes, every family in the world could have a high standard of living. I want you to study and find out how to do that because your dad can't live long enough to help get it done.

[June 24, 1943]

Well, the clothes got a thorough going over. Leighton Shields did it, and what I mean, it was done. He found a moth in one of your coats, and it was well we went over them. Wish I was home or you were here. I know you'll be better off in Colorado though. This is the hottest June in 50 years, so the paper says.

[June 27, 1943]

Well, tomorrow will be somewhat different from June 28, 1919—won't it? Remember how pretty you looked and how my gray checkered suit showed up? The Blackstone, Port Huron, and home. Well, would you do it over?

[July 11, 1943]

I imagine that feeding the family in [Colorado] high altitude is really something. I am extremely hopeful you can have a rest before you have to come back here for the grind. It is my intention to take the coupe home and try to sell it. But I won't make too big an effort if you and Margie want to use it. I can have it sold after you come back here. Some fellow called me this morning and wanted to buy it.

Well, my younger brother has had quite a week-end. I took [Vivian] to dinner with the Busches on Friday, to a party for Jim Beatty last night, and to Joe Guffey's for dinner today. He made a hit with all of 'em. There were about 50 at Beatty's party, and he sat next to an engineer from the general accounting office. They had place cards all around, and this fellow said to him, "Why, you spell your name just like the Senator does." He told him that he usually did as he happens to be my younger brother.

[To Bess, Hot Springs, Ark.]
[Sept. 6, 1943]

Had a most pleasant drive down here and didn't get at all tired. The old car slips along like a new one—the only trouble is the speedometer—it's always going up for some unknown reason.

[Sept. 7, 1943]

Went to the hospital this morning and had a visit with *Gen*. Goldthwaite. He took me to the nose expert who poked around in the upper reaches of my head through the nose, and made me shed about a half pint of tears. He said there was some inflammation, ordered me to the X-ray room where they took four pictures of my head. I'm to go back in the morning and find out if I have a clogged brain pan. From what the nice looking young captain said, there won't be much to do except probably put drops up my nose. He put some stuff up in my head on cotton and left it awhile, and things feel and look better even now.

[To Bess (in Washington), Kansas City, Mo.]
[Sept. 30, 1943]

I went out to Grandview. Mamma was very sick on Saturday and Tuesday. Mary said she passed out in the bathroom Tuesday and it was a job to get her into bed. Dr. Greene says she has fully recovered, and so does she say so, but I can't help but be uneasy. I stayed for lunch, and I'm going back tomorrow. Left the car in Independence to get those oil drive points changed to another bearing, and to get the windows fixed. As soon as it is done, I'll go to Grandview again.

[To Bess (in Washington), Hot Springs, Ark.]
[Oct. 13, 1943]

I'm so glad that Margie's good sorority is making her understand that the best part of the day is before noon. Maybe I'll come in and say those organizations can do some good beyond dating, [and furthering] a social standing if that one teaches her to get up on time.

I almost got in the car and started for Washington after talking to you last night. I felt like a deserter. If I hadn't started on the teeth, I'd surely have done it. The tooth man is still probing and still says he can save it. He's a nice fellow from Oregon State, but a career man in the Army. The help around the hospital tell me he has made some excellent contributions to dental surgery, so I guess I'm in proper hands.

[Regarding the] keynote speech which I have to make in St. Louis to the secretaries of state of all the states. Thought I'd make it postwar and inform the states that instead of coming to Washington for handouts, they must prepare to help meet that terrible situation. I am just as certain as I can be that the struggle to maintain what we are fighting for after we win the war will be much harder than the war itself.

[To Ethel Noland, Washington, D.C.]
[Dec. 5, 1943]

I wrote Mr. Hailey and told him I would arrive at Independence on the evening of Dec. 22 at six P.M. if the train between here and there didn't do any gyrations and ran substantially on time, and if he wanted a meeting on the 23rd, I'd be agreeable. I can't see, though, why anybody would want to listen to me speak, especially a bunch of educated people as schoolmasters are.

I'm glad Mamma had a nice birthday. Wish I could have been there. Hope Aunt Ella is well. This is Pappa's birthday. He'd be 92 if he were still with us. Saw Uncle Will's great grandson at

West Point the other day. His name is Jim Sumner, Grace's grandson. His dad was crawling on the floor when I was in Texas with Ralph in 1901.

I was chaperone for my 19-year-old daughter and her pal at the Thanksgiving dance, only I didn't get to the dance. Had to make a broadcast over the NBC. Corbie[5] was Margie's host.

[To Bess (in Washington), Kansas City, Mo.]
[Feb. 22, 1944]

It was a sore disappointment when I called last night and didn't get to talk to you. But your mother and brothers and sisters-in-law had a very grand time and that was some recompense. They're all fine and Natalie gave me a most excellent steak dinner with thawed out strawberries she'd picked herself at Shelton's last June. Frank seemed in a much happier mood, and, of course, George, May and Spot were as exuberant as usual (that's a bad word, and I don't know how to spell it). Aunt Ella is very feeble. She had a sick spell last Sunday a week ago, and became unconscious, but Dr. Greene brought her out of it. She talked all right to me when I just went in, but forgot whether I was Vivian or myself before the evening was over. J. C. has quit his job and joined the Army—that makes three [boys] for Vivian, and the other boy goes in July. It really is

[5]Cousin Ralph Truman's youngest son.

257

getting close to home. Mamma & Mary are fine. Mary looks better than she has in months.

[May 2, 1944]

Went by to see Mamma and Mary. Mamma was sitting up in a rocking chair, and she looked as smartly at me as some kid, as if daring me to object. She sat up a little while and then said she thought I'd better help her into bed, which I did. I believe she's going to get up. When we went to leave she asked me to take that little radio to town and have it fixed. It's the one I used in the 1940 campaign when I was going around so I could hear the campaign speeches at night.

Well, the efficient Mr. Canfil grabbed it and took it to the car—and then he couldn't find his keys. We looked everywhere for them, where he sat, where he laid his hat, down by the grapevine, and all around, but couldn't find 'em. He had an extra set in his glove box, but it was locked. One of my keys happened to fit it, and we got out the extra set. I happened to look around at the radio in the back seat, and there were the keys alongside it. So you see, we are both absent-minded.

[July 12, 1944]

Mr. Canfil met me in St. Louis and we went to see the tire man. He is Mr. Hannegan's next-door neighbor. They are close personal friends.

258

You know about his finding three of my tires no good and not up to specifications a year ago. The restrictions on tubes has been taken off and he was able, by some maneuvering, to get me four Goodyear puncture-proof tubes and one new tire. We are good for the duration. I think I can get four retreads for your car—and then we will be fixed up. We'll take the tires off your car and have them retreaded. Mr. Mandle says that his retreads run 30,000 miles.

Concerning political campaigns, Truman's growing stature as a national figure put him in demand by Democrats seeking office in states other than Missouri. "If Illinois wants me, they'd better come across quick, and I don't care whether they do or not," the senator told his secretary as the '42 congressional elections neared.

[To Bess, Caruthersville, Mo.]
[October 2, 1942]

Pulled into the [county] fair grounds at 2 P.M.—mighty slow time for Mr. Canfil. We saw a lot of people and watched five horse races, two of which were won by a woman jockey. I met an old woman by the name of Eliza Jane who said she'd been racing horses for fifty-seven years and that she just couldn't quit. She owned a horse in nearly every race. . . . My speech goes on about mid-afternoon tomorrow, and then Fred will take me to St. Louis.

Had a fine meeting at Lexington last night and saw a lot of good Democrats—none of the leaders were my friends in previous years and I told them the Josh Billings story about being nice to your poor relatives because you could never tell when they might become suddenly rich, and then it is hard to explain. They seemed to understand. . . . My speech [in Columbia] came off before the truckers in great shape. They gave me an ovation. I have two speeches tonight, one downtown and one out in the country. . . . I'll be in Jefferson City, Thursday; Joplin, Friday; Springfield, Saturday, and St. Joe on Monday. . . . I am billed at Belleville, Ill. on Wednesday the 28th, and Canton, Ill. on the 29th. I am saving the 30th for Clyde Henning in Des Moines, but I haven't heard from him.

[To Bess, Springfield, Mo.]
[October 24, 1942]

Last night was a banner night on the trip. All the civic organizations gave me a testimonial dinner. Not a politician or candidate for office present. The mayors of Joplin & Webb City, the presidents of all the banks and the head of all the civic organizations, the editor of the Joplin *Globe* made up the party. They preached my funeral but didn't bury me. I was really embarrassed.

[To Bess, St. Louis, Mo.]
[October 29, 1942]

Well, my Ilinois engagements are completed and I am even up and one to carry with Scott Lucas.[6] You know he opened my campaign in 1940 at Moberly and did it in a masterly manner. We finally got over to Illinois. Had the most enthusiastic meeting at Carlinville that you can imagine in these terrible times. I took the hide off Curley Brooks and Stephan Ray and salted the pelts down for keeps. It took my Democratic audience out of their seats. Even the pessimistic Mr. Canfil said we made a lot of votes.

Concerning the hard-hitting Truman Committee on Defense Spending, which brought him national acclaim:

[To Bess, Washington, D.C.]
[December 19, 1941]

Had a Jewish gentleman named Cohen on the stand. He's the Empire Ordinance Co. and he's run up a shoestring into $7,000,000 worth of assets. Mostly at British expense, and by softening certain people in the war Dept. by ways "that are dark—and peculiar" to say the least.

I have to appear before the Education and Labor

[6]Senator from Illinois.

261

Committee today and talk about defense housing. It's a mess too.

[December 20, 1941]

I had quite a fight in the Senate yesterday, but got the job done. Appeared before the Education and Labor Committee on the defense housing bill and then before the Appropriations Committee on the appropriation, and finally forced the last amendment on the floor. It seems that the majority of both sides of the aisle have some confidence in your old man. That's worth more than all the money in the world.

[January 7, 1942]

I am to lose my secretary right away. They just ordered him up for a final physical and duty at Camp Roberts, California, and I guess I'll have to let him go—but it'll be a blow. Bill Boyle will pinch-hit for him, and I'm sure will do a good job. But Harry [Salisbury] is just getting on to the ropes right. We can't say a word though. The only fly in the ointment is that the senator has to stay on the job.

[April 3, 1942]

I've sat and listened to so much dirt since I've been back here that I'm in a perfect whirl. Hennings went on a rampage and resigned from the subcommittee because I let Mead preside the day I was gone. But I talked him out of it. It is almost as bad as running the county court, only these are real showgirls and require more careful technique in handling.

As Truman gained political clout, radio commentators and other news analysts increasingly took notice. The country's corporate elite paraded before his committee, and the senators' questions about production snags or faulty aircraft parts aroused controversy. Conflict also developed between Truman and Roosevelt appointee Donald Nelson, head of the government's War Production Board. Nelson's agency oversaw war production quotas, and Harry and his colleagues decided that Nelson had surrounded himself with too many dollar-a-year corporate types. In a committee report, the senators charged that conversion to war production had lagged following Pearl Harbor because the W.P.B. crowd had been too sympathetic toward the needs and concerns of big business.
The day before Truman released the report, he apprised Bess of the situation:

[June 17, 1942]

I didn't hear [Drew] Pearson & [Robert S.] Allen Sunday, but someone told me they were needling me [on their radio programs]. I postponed the date of the release [of the committee's report] out of courtesy to Nelson, expecting him to come and talk to me—but he talked to Tom Connally and Tom called him [to tell him] to see me. He came down at 9:30 . . . Nelson really told me how I'd ruin his [War Production Board] setup and stop the war if I made the report. He'd sent me a nasty letter, and when he got through, I told [him] just what I thought, and what I expected to do. I told him what I thought of his help and what would happen to him if he continued with some of his most outstanding S.O.B.'s, that the report would be made as agreed on by the whole committee and that I wasn't running the committee for the W.P.B. but for the Senate & in the public interest as the committee & I saw it.

How's that for handling Prima Donnas? Wheeler says we all are, so I guess it's no insult. So she goes in tomorrow and I'll be skinned by the "kept press," but it [is] right.

Now wherever he ventured, whether it was to inspect a steel plant, an aircraft factory, or a hotel converted to house soldiers, journalists kept close tabs on the senator. So, too, did the military's top brass.

[To Bess, Chicago, Ill.]
[February 19, 1943]

We were met by a horde of reporters and photographers in Columbus. They asked me everything that could be asked and had all of us pose for picture after picture. Had to step on one smart aleck reporter and the others showed that they were embarrassed by his action. He wanted a conclusion by the committee which could not be given until we had all the facts. At the conference after our trip through the Columbus plant on which Uncle Samuel has expended $86,000,000, I told Sen. Wallgren to preside. . . . I also asked the Curtis-Wright management to listen. It was an unusual procedure, and it looks as if there will be an improvement all along the line.

[To Bess, en route by train]
[February 22, 1943]

I spent a very pleasant day in Chicago. Sen. Kilgore & I had breakfast at 9:30 and then went over and inspected the Stevens Hotel. It is a mess. They have taken out the beds and put in Army cots and bunks, left the carpets down and the dressers in the rooms. They are housing 13,000 soldiers at the two hotels, the Congress & the Stevens. They work 'em in three shifts, marching them down to the Coliseum for classes. There are classes in the ballrooms at the hotels too. They feed 'em in shifts of 800 in about a dozen dining rooms. It makes you sick to see what they have done to some of the beautiful rooms. We gave the Army an awful scare when we walked in. I never thought I'd ever make a B[rigadier] G[eneral] step around like that one did.

During the summer of '43, Truman's defense spending investigations yielded momentarily to his determination to defeat a congressional move to liquidate the National Youth Administration. The N.Y.A. had been created in the '30s as a depression-fighting New Deal agency to help unemployed youth stay in school, and now during wartime it provided vocational training. The House voted for liquidation, and Senate conservatives rallied to follow suit. Truman, arguing that the N.Y.A. was a great asset to wartime industry, led the floor fight against the agency's demise, but to no avail.

[To Bess, Washington, D.C.]
[July 2, 1943]

I'm in for another floor fight today, and I don't suppose there is much chance of my winning this one. As I told you, we're in a snail [pace], and I'll bet we miss the recess. The Pres. is mad and so is everybody else, and they simply cut off their own noses, all of 'em.

[To Margaret, Chicago, Ill.]
[July 4, 1943]

I had another terrific fight on the Senate floor and was unmercifully trounced by a vote of 39 to 33. . . . I sure hated to lose because it's my first real knock-down fight in the Senate. . . . Wish I were there, but I can't come right away. Must close up the Senate & my committee.

Once Congress recessed, Harry again took to the road, and that's where he spent a great deal of time his last year in the United States senate.

[To Bess, Des Moines, Ia.]
[July 30, 1943]

Had breakfast at Indianola at Simpson College. . . We went to the church, which was full of students and citizens. Dr. Judd made a grand speech and took 'em with him. Then I wound up with a few facts and the kids proceeded to ask questions. One young man who evidently thought he was very brilliant (smart aleck) began a long involved question for me. I asked [him] to be specific, and he said the State Department hadn't been efficient in No. Africa. I told him it was the least costly landing in history including everything from Bill of Normandy to date, and that was the best answer. The rest of the kids nearly tore the roof off, and he shut up.

[To Bess, Salt Lake City, Utah]
[August 16, 1943]

Sen. [Elmer] Thomas came to see us while [we] were having dinner on the roof of this hotel. He acted as if we were long-lost relations from a desert island. But he can't go with us on the plant inspection. It is certainly some plant. It will cost $213,000,000 and won't make steel until October. It looks like it might be another Curtis-Wright

Columbus orgy with gov't funds. Maybe it won't be. I hope not anyway.

[To Bess, Northern California]
[March 29, 1944]

We are progressing down the Southern Pacific at a pace which would land us in Washington in about two weeks if we were eastbound instead of southbound. Left Seattle at 4:30 yesterday and now we are approaching Sacramento at about the same time today. I was supposed to fly to Los Angeles yesterday morning so I could make a speech to 1200 Democrats who had paid $25 a plate for the privilege of being present. I felt I couldn't leave the [Seattle] committee hearing to make a political speech . . . But I'm going to address the same sort of a meeting in San Francisco tomorrow night. I don't care whether they like it or not. I'm not going to be completely muzzled just because the special committee has made good.

[To Bess, Los Angeles, Ca.]
[April 2, 1944]

Friday morning [in San Francisco] we went on an inspection tour aboard a naval vessel around the Bay. We saw freighters by the score, injured plane carriers being repaired, troop ships loading, went through a naval repair base and wound up at Mare Island where 44,000 people are em-ployed building submarines, destroyers, and other types of naval vessels. Had a nice lunch and then inspected an artificial limb setup at the hospital. They are making the limbs on a new basis and they are so successful that a man can use them almost as well as the real thing.

[April 3, 1944]

We inspected the harbor of L.A. yesterday from a Coast Guard boat and then took a converted yacht that they use for patrol and went to Catalina where we had a grand lunch at Coast Guard hdqs. Donald Douglas is commodore of the volunteer patrols. He went along and we talked planes and improvements for manpower in this district. Wallgren, Jackson, and I came back on one of the fast rescue boats at 30 knots an hour. It was some ride. I was supposed to go to dinner with Howard Hughes but put him off and went to bed.

[To Bess, Ogden, Utah]
[April 5, 1944]

My train landed on time and nobody to meet me, so I just went up to the hotel and had started out to get a handle fixed on my grip when in came a photographer. Said he'd met a train from Spokane, Wash. at seven o'clock and so had all the public officials. Some mix-up in information. He took my picture and took me to the grip fixer who sewed the handle on and wouldn't take any pay. You'd never meet an outfit like that east of the Allegheny Mtns. He didn't know me and only remarked it wasn't enough work to be paid for.

[To Margaret, Kansas City, Mo.]
[Easter, April 9, 1944]

My transportation was delayed today, so I didn't get to have dinner with [your grandmother and Mary] today as I had planned. Spoke in Lubbock, Texas to about 500 people after the usual runaround to air fields and defense plants, receptions and press conferences. They ran a special car all the way out there from Dallas with reporters from Dallas & Ft. Worth papers, as well as Associated Press. Then they had a press conference in the afternoon with about 20 country editors. If you don't think your dad caught it, you are mistaken. On top of all that, they broadcast the speech all over west Texas. Then they put me in a car and had a Negro named Sambo drive me to Amarillo. Got there at 1 A.M. and went to bed at the Herring Hotel.

My plane was due to leave at 8:22, and I went to the airport and found that the plane was still in Burbank, Calif., a thousand miles away, so I laid down on a bench and took a good nap.

XIX

"Oh Harry, You Mustn't Fly!"

Running for an unprecedented fourth term in the White House, Franklin Roosevelt needed someone on the ticket with him in 1944 who could help unite a divided Democratic Party. Vice President Henry Wallace, too liberal for southern Democrats, had to go. Missouri was a border state, and Harry Truman had made a lot of friends in the Senate among the party's southern wing.

At first Harry wasn't interested. The day before he left for the Democratic convention in Chicago, he gave "a tough interview" to Roy Roberts of the Kansas City Star. *He didn't want to be Vice President, Truman told Roberts, and, as he explained to Bess afterward, "Also told the West Va. and Okla. delegations to go for Barkley.[1] Also told Downey I didn't want the California delegation. Mr. Roberts says I have it in the bag if I don't say no—and I've said it as tough as I can."*

But he couldn't say it tough enough. "That darn committee got me in a lot of trouble," Truman

[1]Alben W. Barkley, Senate majority leader from Kentucky.

271

*jested to a college group years later. "They made
me take the Vice Presidency and I ended up in a
lot more trouble."*

*He also told the students how he and FDR
planned their campaign.*

[Editor's Notes, Truman Library]
[November 29, 1962]

I remember one day back in '44 when the President and I went out onto the back lawn—it's the front lawn of the White House now—and sat under the trees that [Andrew] Jackson had planted. He asked me if I wouldn't go around the country and talk to the people and help in the campaign. I said, "Oh sure. I've already made reservations with the airlines and railroads." Then he leaned over and said in all earnestness—"Oh Harry. You mustn't fly! It's too dangerous, and we both must be careful." (Laughing) So I told him I'd go by train, and I did. I went out to the west coast and back across the east.

Before the campaign began against the Republican ticket headed by New York Governor Thomas E. Dewey, Harry, choking back tears, informed his defense committee he was resigning as their chairman. But never one to leave a job undone, during his final weeks on Capitol Hill, the senator gave his all.

[To Bess, Washington, D.C.]
[August 8, 1944]

Went over to the Senate, made the speech, had lunch on John Overton, went to a [legislative] steering committee meeting in Barkley's office—No. 1 in my 9 ½ years in the Senate. It was on reconversion [after the war]—whether we'd take a dose of Walter George and Dr. Vandenberg, or a bottle of Dr. Kilgore's prescription, with a pinch of No. 7 by [Phil] Murray, a drop of No. 8 by H.S.T., some coal smoke by RR labor, and some castor oil by [the] C.I.O.[2] They decided to let the river take its course. Maybe we will get a bill—I hope, I hope, I hope. Went back to the office and discuss[ed] V.P. policy with *Time* [magazine]. Signed 500 letters and brought 500 more home and [have] a thousand to read.

[August 11, 1944]

I'm almost on top of all the mail now, and I hope will stay that way. . . . I've signed and put foot-notes on at least 6,000 letters of congratulation acknowledgements and just signed that many more. I'm still trying to get the warring factions in the Senate to meet on common ground. They can if we can keep out personal bitterness.

[2]Reference is to senators, labor leaders, and unions who held divergent views regarding postwar economic policy.

Well, the sabotage sheets are after me. The *Chicago Tribune* had what they were very sure was a mean editorial, the main base of which was that I tried to get [Sidney] Hillman and [Phil] Murray into line with Byrnes and the solid South.[3] The Washington echo sheet, the *Times Herald,* had a whole editorial column devoted to the subject "Truman vs Truman" in which they were endeavoring to show that in my [committee] reports and in the *American Magazine* article I had viciously attacked the administration, therefore I'd attacked myself now. They are surely desperate for an issue.

The committee met and passed a resolution that almost makes me a close relative of Christ. Arthur Walsh said he intended to give a party and sell seats to the pool across from the Lincoln Memorial so they could watch me walk on it. (That's awful.)

With Fred Canfil at the wheel, Truman drove south in October to board his campaign train in New Orleans to begin a "whistle-stop" trek to the west coast. They paused beforehand in Gulfport, Mississippi, where Bess had stayed with Margaret. "Let's retire here when I get done—right here," he wrote Bess.

---

[3]Hillman and Murray, C.I.O. leaders, were usually at odds with Southern democrats.

New Orleans, La.
Oct. 12, '44

Dear Bess:

It's six A.M. and I've got to make a broadcast at 7:30 to the farms of the river system over the Columbia stations in the valley—54 of 'em. Then make another flood control speech to the lunch customers at noon.

We leave here at 11 P.M. tonight for L.A. I dread seeing all those crackpots—they'll be worse now that Aimee [Semple McPherson] is gone to her brand of heaven.

Wish you and Margie could have been along when we went to see the Luxiches [in Gulfport]. They have built the tool shed over into a house and have moved into it and rented the one where we lived. . . . They had us in and opened a prewar bottle and gave us all a drink and asked at least a hundred questions about you and Margie. . . .

Well, I hope you'll send me at least three letters to L.A. I stood in the lobby and read the two I received here—made the bellboy wait—and then read 'em again just now. So—don't fail me.

Must go for that broadcast. Kiss Margie. Lots & lots of love.

Harry

The "crackpots" gave him "the most strenuous two days in all my campaigning history." When he got to Seattle, he had the biggest reception of all. "There were 10,000 in the same hall where Dewey spoke to 5,000, and were they enthusiastic!"

Saturday, Oct. 21, '44
Butte, Mont.

Dear Bess:

You don't know how badly I felt when I didn't get to talk to you from Seattle. They simply had me so full of appointments and time was so short there that I couldn't even eat any dinner. It was so necessary to help Mon [Wallgren][4] all I could that I didn't dare take a chance of insulting anyone. . . .

We had quite a day yesterday. Everywhere the train stops for a minute there are big crowds and back platform appearances are in order. At two Idaho towns they dismissed the schools and all the kids were at the station. I am very popular, at least with the kids in those towns.

I've made 26 speeches since leaving New Orleans and I was only supposed to make three up to this point. But we knocked 'em over in Los Angeles and San Francisco, and even *Time* is coming out with a special edition with me on the cover Nov. 6. "Ain't that sompin'." It's a satisfaction to make 'em like it. . . .

Here is the new schedule. It's a dinger. They seem to think I'm cast iron, and I am in a campaign I guess.

Kiss my baby. Love. Lots of it. Harry
Read the schedule to the office [staff]. It is your business too to tell me what goes on at the office. Very much I'd say.

[4]Wallgren was running for Washington State's gubernatorial seat.

The Democratic ticket won big. Harry Truman soon languished in the ceremonial position of Vice President, ignored by Roosevelt, cut off from the hurly-burly life of a senator. But he still looked for chances to get on the road, even if it required cancellation of a doctor's appointment or two. "Don't tell anybody where H is unless it has been broadcast," Bess wrote Ethel Noland. "He will be in K. C. on the 29th. Some silly Eastern Star performance—and he has no business breaking into the treatments he is taking."

Writing Ethel again in the springtime, Bess told her about a visit to New York City she and Harry and Margaret had taken. "It was too brief a trip," she complained, "but it was a relief to get out of this town even for twenty-four hours. And it was the first time in ages we three had had time all to ourselves all winter.

Having learned that a Boston Globe *journalist had just come to Independence to gather material on Harry "just in case" ailing, gaunt-looking Franklin Roosevelt might die, Bess added: "I hope the Boston* Globe *man is a mighty bad prognosticator. F. D. looks fine to me. I sat by him at a W. H. dinner last week and had a good chance for close observation. He's a little deaf, but that's not going to wreck him."*

But Franklin Roosevelt suffered from more than deafness. Less than two weeks later, Harry Truman, Vice President for only eighty-one days, took a fateful trip up Pennsylvania Avenue. Summoned to rush to the White House, they ushered him to the upstairs living quarters. Eleanor Roosevelt put her hand on his shoulder and said "Harry, the President is dead." "It was the only time in my life, I think, that I ever felt like I'd had a real shock," he told his mother and sister.

XX

". . . Just Look Where It Landed Me!"

The man who carried Franklin Roosevelt's fallen torch gently told Mrs. Roosevelt to take her time in moving out of the White House. The Trumans moved in three weeks after FDR's funeral, and on his sixty-first birthday, the new President awoke from his first night's sleep in the Executive Mansion. "Dear Mamma and Mary," he began a letter that morning. They were to come to Washington on Mother's Day, and to fetch them he promised "the finest plane, and all kinds of help. So please don't disappoint me."

His mother didn't. Franklin Roosevelt may have feared flying, but ninety-two-year-old Martha Truman boarded the presidential airplane, the Sacred Cow, *and took her first plane ride. Her only complaint, whispered to Harry as photographers clustered around them at the airport, was that if she'd known there'd be all the fuss, she'd have stayed home!*

Fuss there'd be from now on for all the Trumans. When, in June, Bess and Margaret escaped as usual to Independence, Dad wrote his first letter to his daughter as President of the United States.

THE WHITE HOUSE

June 11, 1945

My Dear Daughter:

Your letter was most welcome. I read it with a lot of appreciation. You evidently are just finding out what a terrible situation the President's daughter is facing. That was the main reason for my not wanting to be Vice President. I knew what it would mean to you and your mother—to your aunts and uncles and grandmothers and cousins, particularly those named Truman, if what has happened came about.

But you will have to try and bear it as best you can because it is a reality, and as old Cleveland said, you are facing a condition—not a theory. So, you must face it, keep your balance and go along just as your dad is trying to go.

People will be trying to find something in your conduct and in mine to talk about and criticize. If they really have something to find fault with, then, of course, it is too bad. But if there is no truth in what they say, we must go along, doing right, and paying no attention to the dirt which is thrown at us. That has been my policy since I was a little boy—and just look where it landed me! Maybe it was wrong.

I am sending you a tissue of lies put out by Drew Pearson, which brought on this philosophical discourse. Had a lot of fun with Reathal about it. It is funny when you consider that your dad not only didn't chase you out of town, but that he felt like weeping when you did leave—even in spite of that spell of bad humor.

I've always known that Washington is a hick town—in fact, I don't know of a so-called hick town that isn't a better and more friendly place—but I could never make you and your mamma believe it.[1]

Hope [your cat] Michael Joseph Casey has a grand summer, and finally gets his private lodging properly placed. What does the fat Mr. Spot Wallace think of this interloper named Mike? I'll wager his opinion is not printable—if it could be expressed.

I hope you have a nice time at home, and I'll count the days until you return. I'm not going to San Francisco until next week. Had a nice boat ride Sunday with the newsmen who went the rounds with me on the V. P. campaign last fall.

Glad you went to see Aunt Mary and Mamma.

Write your dad when you have time—kiss your mamma for me.

Lots & lots of love,
Dad

"Looks like our summer cruise has gone a glimmer," he wrote Mon Wallgren, now Washington

---

[1] In light of Bess's dislike for the Washington scene, and her frequent flights from it, this is a perplexing statement.

State's new governor. "You should see me work now!"

Still, because his first decision as President concerned giving the go-ahead for a scheduled United Nations charter meeting in San Francisco, Truman saw his friend after all. He thought he'd fly up to see Mon for a quick visit en route to the UN meeting, but a procedural delay at the conference allowed him to linger a while in the Pacific Northwest.

Bess knew Harry would have a good time with Wallgren. In fact, she thought she detected a little too much levity in his voice when he called her the night he arrived.

[Olympia, Wash.]
June 20, '45

Dear Bess:

It was nice to talk to you last night. I'm of the opinion that because my bronchial tubes were on the rampage as a result of some 13,000 feet up for a period of six hours, you were sure that Gov. Mon and I were right "high" for other reasons. We had a nice mixed drink before dinner and not one thing afterward.

Mon and Mrs. Wallgren met me at McChord Field . . . They have a most beautiful Capitol Hill. . . . Looking out of [my] window on the north I can see up [Puget] Sound a mountain range on the Olympia Peninsula. Mt. Olympus is the highest peak all covered with snow. But I haven't seen Ju-

282

piter or Juno nor have I witnessed any feasts or nectar. Some early explorer undoubtedly was a student of the Greek classics. To the east is Mt. Rainier, a most beautiful mountain . . . It looks like a big ice cream cone upside down, or more like the ice cream out of one of the old conical dippers we had long ago. Mon is sending us over there to get a closeup view on Friday.

We took a most beautiful drive in an open Chrysler car this afternoon up the west side of the Sound. I was the driver of the open car—the first time I've been at the wheel but a time or two since I became V. P., Jan. 20th. But we had a carload of state police in front of us, a carload of Secret Servicemen behind us, and a carload of newsmen behind the Secret Service. At that, I had a big kick out of driving once more. . . .

[Word came that Mon's brother-in-law had died suddenly of a heart attack.]

Seems to me that is a good way to go. No hospital bills, no worry about getting well, no doctor bills—all the shock at once and have it over with. I told Mon and Mrs. Wallgren we'd leave right away and they seemed to feel as badly about that as they did about the sudden death—so I am staying until Monday. . . .

We are going up the Sound in a boat tomorrow and try to catch a 40-pound salmon. But I'm sure we won't catch one. . . .

Well, I'm counting the days until I see you. Kiss Margie. Lots of love to you.

Harry

Truman later recounted his fun-filled fishing trip on Puget Sound in a speech draft.

Seattle, Washington
Nov. 26, 1955

. . . We fished and fished and the fish were aware of too much rank in our fishing boat and just would not accept our lures and our bait. Finally Senator Magnuson spied a couple of gentlemen of Swedish descent in a small boat who were pulling them out almost as fast as a line could be thrown in the water. . . . He consulted with them, and when they found that he was Senator Magnuson, they offered to give him as many of their catch as he needed.

The senator came back to our boat with three of the finest specimens Puget Sound can produce. He put one on my line and you all remember the picture of me with a big fish on the end of my fishing equipment. . . .

Well, my friends, there is a sad sequel to this good story . . . It seems that the good man from whom the senator obtained my fish went home to a scolding that evening because he'd gone fishing and had laid off from work. It seems that the good lady who oversees his household was violently opposed to his visits to a place where he could obtain copious amounts of good Swedish schnapps. She accused him of visiting this place, and, of course, he denied it and told her that he'd been fishing and had given the President of the United States and Senator Magnuson one. And she knew positively that he'd spent the afternoon in the tavern.

Other high jinks took place during Truman's interlude in Olympia. Finding part of his wardrobe missing afterward, Harry wired Mon, his friend of Swedish ancestry:

WE ARE SHORT ONE SUIT TAN PAJAMAS BEARING INITIALS HST WHEN LAST SEEN THEY WERE BEING WORN BY A FAT SWEDE   HST

Mon Wallgren wired back:

SWEDE IN CUSTODY PAJAMAS BEING HELD FOR SCREENING WILL SHIP SHORTLY FURTHER SURVEY WILL REVEAL PLAID SLACKS MISSING BEST REGARDS

"You'll never know what a grand time I had, even if you did filch my pajamas and slacks," Truman thanked Wallgren. "I'd give nine suits of each to be out there again."

His attendance at the United Nations meeting in San Francisco capped months of sparring with the Soviet Union over the UN's organizational setup. Truman had earlier recorded some very private opinions on the matter.

... I've no faith in any totalitarian state, be it Russian, German, Spanish, Argentinian, Dago, or Japanese. They all start with a wrong premise—that lies are justified and that the old, disproven Jesuit formula, the end justifies the means, is right and necessary to maintain the power of government. I don't agree, nor do I believe that either formula can help humanity to the long hoped for millennium. Honest Communism, as set out in the "Acts of the Apostles," would work. But Russian Godless Pervert Systems won't work.

Anyway, the human animal can't be trusted for anything *good* except en masse. The combined thought and action of the whole people of any race, creed, or nationality will always point in the Right Direction—"As ye would others should do unto you do ye also unto them." Confucius, Buddha, Christ, and all moralists come to the same conclusion.

XXI

"Wish I Didn't Have to Go . . ."

"I am getting ready to go see Stalin and Churchill, and it is a chore," Harry wrote Mamma and Mary. *"I have to take my tuxedo, tails, Negro preacher coat, high hat, low hat, and hard hat, as well as sundry other things."* Hitler's Germany lay in rubble, and Truman's destination was the unbombed village of Potsdam near Berlin. *"Wish I didn't have to go, but I do, and it can't be stopped now."*

As the U.S. Navy's heavy cruiser *Augusta* plied its way toward Europe, its distinguished passenger surely thought back to when another President, after another war, had tried and failed to create a world safe for democracy. Woodrow Wilson's *"gallivantin' around"* a quarter of a century before had irritated Captain Harry Truman. Stuck in the mud outside Verdun, France, he had even predicted Wilson's defeat at Paris. *"Why should we be kept over here to browbeat a peace conference that'll skin us anyway?"* he'd complained to Cousin Ethel.

No, he vowed. This President would not repeat Wilson's mistakes. This President would seek less Utopian aims: to get Russia into the war against *still undefeated Japan, to hammer out an equitable German reparations settlement, to firm up agreements made by FDR at Yalta, and to set up a workable governing arrangement for postwar Germany.*

The Augusta *took eight days to reach her European destination, time enough to relax a tired and apprehensive Chief Executive.*

[Aboard the *Augusta*]
July 14, 1945

Dear Margie:

This has been a great voyage. I wish you and your mother could have come with me. For a great wonder, I haven't been sick a single day! But it has been a very smooth crossing. It seems to take two warships to get your pa across the pond. The cruisers *Augusta* and *Philadelphia,* with an admiral in command—he is a rear one.

I never could understand why admirals had to be rear. Seems to me that after you have started at the top, the ranks could come down—vice, lieutenant, captain—admiral, and you wouldn't have to put anybody in the back yard or porch to have him ranked. Things are very, very mysterious though when you are dealing with naval or military affairs.

We've eaten ourselves into larger waistlines, and have witnessed naval gunnery and catapult plane launchings, etc.

A British warship and six destroyers met us this morning and escorted us through the English Channel. I saw the white cliffs of Dover in the sunshine, very nice to look at. When the British fleet went to leave, I had to stand on the bridge and take three cheers from each vessel as it passed going back— wave my hat and grin my thanks for the courtesy.

We have an excellent band on board of thirty pieces. It plays every day and then sends an orchestra to play for dinner every evening. I'm sending you the programs, the last one signed by all the members of the band.

Hope you are having a nice time. Send any letters to the White House with your name on the outside and they'll come to me by air.

Kiss your mamma and here are some for you from

Dad

XXXXXXXXXXXXXXXXXXXXXXXXXXXXXXXXX
OOOOOOOOOOOOOOOOOOOOOOOOOOOOOOOOO

Truman later remembered for a White House assistant his first days at Potsdam.

Potsdam
Note for Mr. [Eben] Ayers
[September 1951]

Stalin was a day late in arriving. It was reported that he was not feeling up to par. He called on me as soon as he arrived. It was 11 A.M. He, Molotov, Vishinski, and Pavlov stayed for lunch. We had a most pleasant conference and Stalin assured me that Russia intended to carry out the Yalta agreements and to enter the war against Japan in August.

Mr. Churchill had arrived on time the day set for the conference. He had called on me as soon as he arrived in Berlin. He was very anxious that we keep strong forces in Germany, and that we should *not* move back to the line agreed to at Yalta. I told him we intended to keep our agreements.

While waiting for Stalin to arrive, the American President toured war-ravaged Berlin. "Hitler's folly," he called it in a diary he kept at Potsdam. Receiving word just then that the world's first atomic explosion had been detonated in a test in New Mexico, he also ruminated on whether it was too late for everlasting peace. "I fear machines are ahead of morals by some centuries," he wrote. Maybe when morals caught up it would be too late. "We are only termites on a planet," he judged, "and maybe when we bore too deeply into the planet, there'll be a reckoning—who knows?"

As the talks at Potsdam got under way, so too did the social whirl.

Berlin
July 22, 1945

Dear Margie:
It was nice to talk to you and your mamma yesterday morning. It made me very, very homesick. While I am nicely situated here and am waited upon by everybody, that doesn't fill the gap. . . .

You keep in touch with your old country grandma as much as you can, and pet Aunt Mary a little because she's worth all we can do for her—she's been so good to her mother.

You should have seen your Cousin Harry[1] when he came here. He was on the *Queen Elizabeth* at Glasgow, and they took him off and flew him here. His first plane ride. Fred Canfil and Gen. Vaughan showed him everything there was to see, and I sent him to N.Y. by plane. Should hear from him today if he lands safely.

Father Tiernan is here, and he looks fine. I am going to church twice this morning. At 10 o'clock to a Protestant service, and at 11:30 the Padre will put on a special mass for me.

Then Winnie[2] is coming to see me, maybe to stay for lunch, after which I'll have to work the rest of the day on the conference.

Mr. Stalin held his dinner last evening and was it a dandy. Started with caviar and vodka and mare's milk butter, then smoked herring, then white fish and vegetables, then venison and vegetables, then duck and chicken, and finally two desserts, ice cream and strawberries, and a wind-up of sliced watermelon. White wine, red wine, champagne and cognac in liberal quantities, and a toast every five minutes to somebody or something—to the United States and its great, magnifique Presidente, to me individually—to the U.S. Army, the U.S. Navy, the U.S. working people, and the same procedure

[1]Vivian's son, a field artillery sergeant on his way back to the States.
[2]Winston Churchill.

to the British & the Russians; to Molotov, Byrnes,[3] Eden, the American Ambassador, to Russia, the Russian Ambassador to [the] U.S.A., ditto for the British, to the interpreters, and finally Joe and I had to go shake hands with and toast the musicians. Two excellent pianists and two women violinists. They were as good as you've ever listened to (but they had dirty faces).

But it was one grand and glorious evening. I fooled 'em on the drinks, and there was so much getting up and down that I didn't have to eat much either. Got back to my boarding house (Berlin White House—it's yellow & red) at 11:30, and was in bed asleep at 12:30.

Kiss Mamma for me and take a dozen for yourself.

Loads of love,
OOOOOOOOOOOO Dad
XXXXXXXXXXXXXXXXXX

Berlin
July 25, 1945

Dear Margie:
We went to the British dinner night before last— and was *it* a showpiece too! Mr. Byrnes and I walked from the Berlin White House (it's still yellow, trimmed in dirty red—dirty yellow too) to Mr. Churchill's place about three blocks down the street or up (it's level so either one is all right).

[3]James F. Byrnes, former senator and supreme court justice, now secretary of state.

Churchill had phoned Gen. Vaughan, my *chief* of protocol, that he would greatly, very greatly appreciate it if I would arrive a few minutes late as I happened to be the senior guest and Uncle Joe should realize it.

Well, we arrived as directed and were received by the P.M. and his daughter, Mary. I had to shake hands with Marshal, now Generalissimo Stalin, General of the Army Antonov, Marshal Zhukov, Field Marshal Montgomery, Lord this & that, and a lot more Ruskies and Limies. We [then] went out to dinner.

It was a very colorful affair, as you can see. I am enclosing you the menu and the list of guests. The menu is signed to you by J. Stalin & Winston Churchill, and the guest list is signed by all the guests.

Stalin and Churchill paid your pop a most high compliment by saying that my presiding had been the ablest they'd ever seen. That's what Adm. Leahy and all the rest say, but it is hard to believe because I've had plenty of trouble.

Churchill and his crowd went home today to see how the vote in England came out. I am going to Frankfurt tomorrow and inspect some American divisions. Friday we resume sessions, and I believe we shall wind up Sunday so I should be out to sea on Tuesday, and home by Sunday August 14th.

Had a telegram saying Harry had safely landed at Washington Airport. He should be home by the time this letter gets to you.

I hope you and your mamma will be at the White

House when I get back to Washington. That old barn is terribly lonely for me alone. Especially since I'm so hemmed in.

Kiss Mamma & lots for you.

XXXXXXXXXXXXXXXX Dad
OOOOOOOOOOOOOOOOO

The Potsdam conference was prolonged because the British elections removed Winston Churchill as Prime Minister. A bountiful mail pouch and the arrival of Churchill's successor, Clement Attlee, prompted the President to write again to his daughter.

Berlin
July 29, 1945

Dear Margie:

It was sure nice to talk to you and Mamma night before last, or yesterday morning here. I had been sitting around all day waiting for the British to come. The pouch came in about 10 A.M., and there were letters in it! One from you, two from Mother, and one from Aunt Mary. So I had a field day. . . .

I have been able to help out a lot of soldiers since coming over here. The bread they were giving them was terrible. I sent Mr. Canfil to make an inspection and you should have seen it straighten out.

The British finally arrived at 9:30 P.M. yesterday. Mr. Attlee is not so keen as old fat Winston, and Mr. Bevin looks rather rotund to be a Foreign Minister. Seems Bevin is sort of the John L. Lewis type.[4] Eden[5] was a perfect striped pants boy. I wasn't fond of Eden—he is a much overrated man; and he didn't play fair with his boss.

I did like old Churchill. He was as windy as old Langer,[6] but he knew his English language, and after he'd talked half an hour, there'd be at least one gem of a sentence and two thoughts maybe, which could have been expressed in four minutes. But if we ever got him on record, which was seldom, he stayed put. Anyway, he is a likable person, and these two are sourpusses.

Attlee is an Oxford graduate and talks with that deep-throated swallowing enunciation, same as Eden does. But I understand him reasonably well. Bevin is a tough guy. He doesn't know, of course, that your dad has been dealing with that sort all his life, from building trades to coal miners. So he won't be new.

Marshal Stalin and Molotov are coming to see me this morning. I am hoping we can get things in shape so we can quit about Tuesday. If we do, I may be home a week from today—and how I'll like it. The next thing I'll want are a couple of truants back in the White House.

[4]Reference is to the colorful, controversial, and hulking president of the United Coal Miners union.
[5]Anthony Eden, Bevin's predecessor as British Foreign Minister.
[6]Republican Senator William Langer of North Dakota.

Kiss your mamma for me and lots & lots of 'em for you.

Dad

OOOOOOOOOOOOOOOOOOOOO

X X X X X X X X X X

After the Cold War had intensified between East and West, Truman evaluated his relationship with Joe Stalin.

Note to Eben Ayers
[October 1951]

[James] Forrestal[7] says in his diary that Byrnes told him that Stalin did not like me. That I can't believe. Stalin and I were able to get along all right. We had no disagreements whatever except over the treatment of our people in Bulgaria and in Rumania. That was the first of all the broken agreements.

The broken agreements concerned Stalin's reneging on pledges he made to Roosevelt at Yalta and again to Truman that defeated German satellites like Bulgaria and Rumania would be left free to shape their own postwar destiny. Ultimately, Russian occupation forces shaped it for them instead, and in the Soviet communist image.

"And I liked the little son of a bitch," Truman wrote of Stalin in a letter he didn't mail during his

[7]Secretary of the Navy.

retirement years. "He was a good six inches shorter than I am, and even Churchill was only three inches taller than Joe! Yet I was the little man in stature and intellect! Well, we'll see."

On a different note, on his way home from Potsdam, Truman felt obliged to have lunch with England's King George VI. Later, upon the King's death, he recorded the event in his official White House diary:

February 6, 1952

He was a grand man, worth a pair of his brother Ed.

The King entertained me at Plymouth on the return from Potsdam. Lunch was served on board the *Renown,* a British cruiser. I had an hour talk with the King before lunch. When the luncheon and the conference was over, I went back to the *Augusta.*

The King and his staff came to the *Augusta* about 3 P.M. He inspected the honor guard, stood for the salute, and then came to my quarters. He told me that the Queen and his daughters were collectors of autographs—they would like to have mine! I gave him three White House autograph cards, properly signed.

Elizabeth, the King's daughter, will be a good and great Queen. She is a grand person—and so is her consort.

XXII

"The Hill Gets Higher and the Climb Steeper . . ."

Too busy to write by hand to Cousin Nellie when he got back from Potsdam, Harry dictated her a letter. On the bottom, he jotted "The hill gets higher and the climb steeper every day, but we've got to make it someway."

Japan, sent reeling by two atomic bombs, had just surrendered. The French general, Charles DeGaulle, was visiting Washington. A myriad of postwar economic problems had to be tackled. And if that were not enough, the President also confronted an economic crisis within his own family.

THE WHITE HOUSE

Aug. 23, '45

Dear Baby:

Mamma says you're busted—not physically but financially—so here's a little of the circulating medium to tide you over. She said to send you twenty bucks, so I'm sending twenty for her & twenty for me. As my mamma says, "Now you behave yourself." You'd better come home some of these days or send me a picture or something—I've forgotten how you look. I expect to see your hair gray if it's much longer before I see you.

Mr. DeGaulle was here last night. He's a real "high pockets." 6 ft. 6 in. tall, and a pinhead really. Looks to me like he wears a 6⅝ hat, but I may be mistaken.

I pinned 28 medals of honor on 28 soldiers this morning. Your ma has gone to Shangri La to see what it's like.[1] We may go up there Friday.

Tell your grandmas hello for me, and also your sundry uncles, aunts, and cousins. Lots of love.

Dad
X X X X X
O O O O O

By mid-September, things settled down enough in Washington to permit a flight home. Bess swallowed hard, and bravely left the ground with Harry aboard the Sacred Cow. *But when they got to Independence, she stayed put. Harry returned to the White House to grapple with domestic affairs. He also had a physical examination scheduled with his new physician Wallace Graham, a young Army surgeon, son of the Trumans' old family doctor.*

[1]Shangri La, the presidential retreat in the Maryland mountains, was named by FDR. President Eisenhower later renamed it Camp David.

Sept. 17, 1945

Dear Bess:

The flight yesterday was ideal—not a jolt or a bump anywhere, and the landings and takeoffs were perfect as usual. The trip would have been perfect had you been along as you were going out. . . .

When we landed at Paducah there were several thousand people awaiting to see Mr. Barkley off. He said they always met and saw him off that way! But he said my being along may have had something to do with the warmth of his welcome. He was late in arriving at the field, and I had shaken hands with about a hundred by the time he arrived. He had a car accident—not serious—just drove over a high curb and couldn't get back in the road again. He brought his mother down to the plane— a lovely old lady eighty-seven years old and spry as a kitten. She had gotten dinner herself Sunday for Barkley and baked him his favorite custard pie.

It's a lonesome place here today. Had Schwellenbach over for lunch and heard all the pain in the labor setup.[2] Hope to fix it tomorrow. Should have done it 60 days ago. Snyder is also having his troubles too.[3] But I guess the country will run anyway in spite of all of us. Saw Rayburn, McCormick, Barkley, and McKellar on the state of the Congress

[2]Lewis Schwellenbach had become Secretary of Labor.
[3]John Snyder had become Director of War Mobilization and Reconversion.

this morning—it's in a hell of a state according to all four. But I'm not so very much worried. Clarence Cannon is coming to see me at 9:15 in the morning about appropriations. Don't think his visit is of much help. [Also] had a session with my Secretary of Agriculture, also with [the] Atty. Gen.

The new doc gave me a physical at 5:30. Blood pressure 120—74, heart action good, lungs clear, gall bladder working a little overtime as usual, glands etc. normal. Said he might as well go to the poor house if he depended on my sickness for a living. Said a lot of people thought themselves into sickness and that Unity[4] or Christian Science were good for that sort. He's a nice boy and knows his onions. Said there is more in prevention than in cure.

Hope you and Margie are having a grand time— I'm not.

Kiss my baby—love to you,

Harry

Problems with Roosevelt-appointed staff members plagued Truman and kept him busy. "I'm sick of having a dozen bureaus stumbling over each other and upsetting the apple cart," he told Bess. "I'm either going to be President, or I'm going to quit, one [or the other]." And he cancelled a November visit to his mother because "the Congress are balking, labor has gone crazy, and

[4] A religious movement founded in Kansas City in the late 19th century.

management isn't far from insane in selfishness."
Various short excursions had to do.

THE WHITE HOUSE

Oct. 21, 1945

Dear Mamma and Mary:

. . . They gave me the [Masonic] 33° honorary [in Alexandria, Va.] on Friday evening. There was quite a large class of high officials and economic royalists there—most of them were anti-me and anti-Roosevelt. Aside from the Secretary of Agriculture and Generals Arnold and Doolittle, I don't think there was a friend of the administration present. But I am endeavoring to restore real harmony in the whole organization, and from what I heard after a little talk from me, I hope we are on the road.

Had a very pleasant time at the White House photographer's dinner last night. It is an annual affair. I was there with Mr. Roosevelt last year. The President hands out the prizes for the best snapshots of the year in some four or five classifications. The grand prize of the whole thing went to a timid little boy (forty maybe, but he doesn't look it) who took a picture of Mamma and me in front of the plane when she and you came here. It is a nice picture.

I am going to the 1st Baptist Church today, quietly if I can. I've been to both the Army and Navy chapels, and to the big Methodist Church, so I have to give my own crowd a chance to gawk and stare—so I'll do that today.

Write when you can, and both of you keep well. How does the coupe operate?

Love to you both,
Harry

The coupe was the 1941 Chrysler that Mary's now-famous brother had bought after his '40 senatorial race. No longer able to use it, he gave the car to Mary.

For the rest of that year, Truman continued to be so busy that he felt like a prisoner in the Oval Office. Thanksgiving was spent at the White House, and he almost didn't go home for Christmas. It was Margaret rather than her father who got to ride the trains these days.

THE WHITE HOUSE

Dec. 23, 1945

Dear Margie:

You'll never know how much your dad appreciated that nice letter, written on the train. It must have been rough over the mountains. I have been in that rear car when the booster engine went to work. It really does shake you up. Sometimes they put it ahead of the diesel, but I imagine the train was too long and they were afraid of pulling the diesel too. So you had a good shaking up. Mr. Clark told me that he saw you on the train. He is one of my cabinet [members] who is for the President and what he's trying to do. . . .[5]

I just now went out and took a walk. It is cold as mischief. I looked over the Christmas tree, and walked around the back yard—four Secret Service men and two policemen came along—to keep me from slipping on the ice I guess. A crowd did collect at the back fence. So I guess they were right.

The stage is set up south of the fountain, and one of the pine trees down by the fence is all decorated, and I have to light it and make a speech to the nation tomorrow at 5:16 P.M.

Hope to see you the next day. Kiss Mamma and tell all your aunts & uncles hello, and call up your country grandma and say hello to your city one.

Lots of love,
Dad
X X X X X X X
OOOO

He flew home Christmas morning, and that day ate three turkey dinners: one with his Truman kin in Grandview, one with Bess and the Wallace Clan, and one across Delaware Street with the Nolands. After staying in Independence overnight, he flew back to Washington, and his whirlwind tour put him in the dog house with Bess, so much so that he wrote her an apology and then didn't mail it. He felt, he said, "like a last year's bird's nest which is on its second year." She would never understand,

---

[5]Attorney General Tom C. Clark.

he conjectured, how he felt after working so hard, to come home "and have the only person in the world whose approval and good opinion I value look at me like I'm something the cat dragged in and tell me I've come in at last because I couldn't find any reason to stay away."

By early summer the next year, Harry could write home, "Things have eased up somewhat, but not enough to justify a vacation for me. Since I'm not accustomed to vacations, it won't matter much." Then he thought better of it, and considered a trip aboard the presidential yacht U.S.S. Williamsburg to Puerto Rico. But that changed. "Puerto Rico is out," he reported. "I have decided to leave here next Friday, Aug. 16, and cruise up the east coast, through Long Island Sound, Nantucket Sound, to Portsmouth along the Maine coast and back here Sept. 2." But that changed too when too many New England politicos asked for an audience with him.

He finally settled on a cruise to Bermuda.

[To Bess, Bermuda]
[August 22, 1946]

So here I am in a beautiful blue harbor with no U.S. politicians in reach. The Gov. Gen. has called & I'm returning it at 5 P.M. I shall tour the Islands on Saturday, and that ends my troubles. All I'm to do for a week is to eat, sleep, swim, walk, and enjoy the sunshine (I hope, I hope, I hope).

305

I've never seen a lovelier place—but I'm sure it would eventually become very tiresome. Went fishing Friday and caught some beautiful sea fish and took a ride over the Islands yesterday. They are nearly all connected by causeways. Stopped at the town of St. George in the extreme northern end of the group, and visited St. Peter's Anglican Church, founded in 1620. They have a silver communion service dating from that era. Two pieces given them by King William III in 1625 and one earlier than that and one later. The service [was] appraised some 20 years ago as worth £40,000. About two hundred thousand dollars and they don't even keep it locked up, and it is also kept in what would be a tinder box if fire started. The chandeliers were very beautiful, brass candle holders, and dated from the sixteen hundreds. In the historical museum adjoining the church was a Breeches Bible. There are only a very few [of] them in existence—and it was not in the fireproof place either. Visited the old Masonic Hall too. The lodge is over two hundred years old and their Bible had been autographed by George Washington. Some American tourist tore the signature out for a souvenir. They had to replace it with mine!

[August 26, 1946]

I am having a real rest. Go ashore every morning

and walk, have breakfast, usually at eight, do my usual working bit on the mail, reports and papers to be signed, then if the sun shines take a sunning on my deck, swim, have lunch, a nap, and then a social gathering in the lower lounge about 5 P.M.

[August 28, 1946, 1st letter]

Well, our fishing trip yesterday was a complete failure, only one fish caught, and that inside the bay only a couple of hundred yards from the anchored *Williamsburg*. The weather was stormy, the sea rough, and our boat rocked around like a cockle shell. We went out fifteen miles from land over the reef which surrounds this place, but had to turn right around and come back. I got wet as a rat and had to change clothes from the skin out.

[August 28, 1946, 2nd letter]

Vaughan, Graham, Clifford, Allen, and Marks all went to town to buy presents for their families. The ship looks like a pirate's must have after a successful raid. Tomorrow will be our last day here, and I am rather sorry to leave and face the grind again. It will be a grind too.

Back in the White House, a tanned Chief Executive arranged a dinner party for his Bermuda traveling companions.

THE WHITE HOUSE

Dear Mamma and Mary:

. . . I've been covered to the ears in work. Will be caught up by Monday I hope. I always say every time I go anywhere that I'll never go again because I simply pay through the nose for it by piled up work.

Had a nice party Friday night for the reporters and guests who went on the trip. They all seemed to enjoy it and I think they did. I gave them a regular "State Dinner" except for tails and white ties and an orchestra. They showed all the newsreels of the trip. Gen. Vaughan had taken some two or three hundred feet of colored film which was excellent, and the Navy had taken a lot of footage, most of it rotten, and the newsreel men had taken a lot too.

The party was over by ten, and everybody left sober so I guess it was a success. . . .

Love to you both,
Harry

XXIII

"Dear Mamma"

It would be difficult to find a man more influenced by or more devoted to his mother than Harry Truman. Martha Ellen Truman taught her son to choose right from wrong and to act accordingly. "Since a child at my mother's knee," Truman wrote in his diary, "I have believed in honor, ethics, and right living as its own reward."

"What is the right thing to do?" Averell Harriman remembers the President asking when he pondered diplomatic matters. That, former Ambassador Harriman maintains, is far different from "What are our options?," the catch phrase used by more recent foreign policy architects.

The last six years of her life, "Aunt Matt," as the Truman cousins affectionately called Harry's mother, lived with Mary in Grandview. Each month her eldest son religiously sent a check to help cover expenses, and just as religiously her daughter Mary Jane nursed her. When Mary attended an occasional Eastern Star meeting away from home, she had Mamma stay with friends.

"I have lost Mrs. Lester's address and so can't write to Mamma," a distressed President wrote

Mary during one such trip. But then he found it.

THE WHITE HOUSE

Oct. 1, 1946

Dear Mamma:

I had intended to send you a letter before you left home, but so many things were piled up on me I could not get it done.

Had a nice trip to West Point and saw a football game between the cadets and Oklahoma. . . .

They showed me through the library and museum. They have an original letter from Edgar Allan Poe addressed to the superintendent asking for an introduction to Lafayette, and they also have some original sketches by Whistler. Both failed to graduate, but both are better known than any of their classmates.

They showed me Goering's guest book which Gen. Patch had captured. It has the signature of Herbert Hoover and Lindbergh in it. I would wager that they wished it didn't.

I know you are having a nice time. Remember me to Mrs. Lester and to Marian. As you tell me, "Behave yourself."

Lots of love,
Harry

Several weeks before, Harry himself had not behaved very well. In what he privately called "one of the worst messes I've ever been tangled up in," he had fired former Vice President Henry Wallace from his cabinet post as Secretary of Commerce. Wallace had made a foreign policy speech that questioned the administration's increasingly hard line against the Soviet Union, and while Wallace had given the speech to HST to read beforehand and to approve, Truman uncharacteristically hadn't done his homework. After reading one paragraph and glancing at the rest, he had given Wallace the okay. But Secretary of State Jimmie Byrnes hit the roof over the speech, and Harry was caught in the middle.

THE WHITE HOUSE

Sept. 16, 1946

Dear Bess:
Well, this is income tax day, and what a jolt. I went to church yesterday. Just walked up there and the preacher and everybody seemed glad to see me. He talked on a timely subject too, Romans 8—28. Said our troubles and mistakes today may be looked upon later as blessings. Do you reckon Henry & Jim will look back with pleasure on my last fiasco? I don't think I will.

Your letter came about 4 P.M. while I was reading Gray's Elegy. Really nodding over it. I'm glad you've set the day of return. I'll meet you at Silver Springs as we did before. Be sure and wear a red carnation in your hat so I can recognize you—and I'll wear a blue suit with a blue handkerchief and black shoes.

It was nice to talk with you even if you did give

me hell for making mistakes. Looks like I'm a natural for making them. Hope Margie had a nice time at the party with Joe Crowe. It's a good thing his name isn't Jim.

If things calm down, I may go up to Shangri La for the weekend and try to get some outdoor exercise. My physical condition was never better. Weigh 171 and spent an hour on the roof yesterday. So if I can just get the brains in shape things will work out.

I guess the cabinet always did quarrel and bicker. Cleveland had almost as much trouble. So did Wilson. And old Andy [Jackson] really set 'em back—over a lady.

Lots of love. Tell everybody hello.

Harry

His mother celebrated her ninety-fourth birthday on November 25th that year. But then her health began to fail. She caught a bad cold in February, and her son, no stranger to that malady, commiserated with her and Mary. "I have been fighting one for two weeks," he wrote, and he blamed it on "all this handshaking with the sneezing public."

The following Thursday, Mamma slipped, fell, and broke her right hip. By noon next day, Harry, along with his personal physician Wallace Graham, stood by her bedside. When he returned to Washington to prepare for a state visit to Mexico, he saw that a stopover in Grandview was included in his trip's itinerary.

THE WHITE HOUSE

Feb. 27, 1947

Dear Mary:

I've been trying for two days to write to you but the things are piling up here sky-high. It is always that way when I get ready to go somewhere.

I was glad to talk to you last night and to hear that Mamma is getting along all right. . . .

Things have been happening here in a hurry. The Republicans get in deeper and deeper, and that is what we want, but they are causing me and the departments a lot of bother for which they'll have to pay later.

Foreign affairs are in the usual turmoil just before a big conference. I am spending every day with Marshall[1] going over our policy and hoping we can get a lasting peace. It looks not so good though right now. . . .

See you Sunday. Lots of love to you both,

Harry

The medical reports promised that Mrs. Truman would be up and about in two months' time. The broken hip showed signs of mending. "I was glad to get your letter and hear about the X rays for Mamma," Harry thanked Vivian.

But a few weeks later, when the doctor tried to

---

[1]General George C. Marshall had just replaced Jimmie Byrnes as Secretary of State.

sit Mamma up in a wheelchair, the pain was too great. She grew weaker, and Harry prepared to fly home. On his return to Washington, he planned to bring Bess's brothers George and Frank back with him because their mother, Madge Wallace (who lived with Bess and Harry in the White House), longed for a family reunion. And to firm things up, the President wrote a letter.

THE WHITE HOUSE

May 8, 1947

Dear George:

They've moved the clock up on us here, so I'll want to leave a half hour earlier than I thought. If you and May and Frank and Natalie could be out at Mamma's at 11:45, then we can get off the ground at 12 or 12:15, and that will put us here at 5:30 Eastern Daylight Time.

I'm looking forward to a nice visit with you. We'll have lunch on the plane. I wrote Frank a good stiff letter. So I hope he'll come. We've arranged to have a nice time while you are here, and all of us are looking forward to it.

Your mother is particularly anxious for all of you to come.

Sincerely,
Harry

Her son's quick visit acted like a tonic; Mamma Truman sat up and her hip showed renewed signs of healing. So, while Bess departed Washington in time to spend the Fourth of July at home, excerpts from Harry's letters home show that for him it was business as usual.

[To Bess]
[July 1, 1947]

You know what I had to do? I had to check up on myself to be sure I wasn't dreaming when I talked to you last night. I'd read King Henry IV of France and the study of prehistoric civilization which Margie gave me for Father's Day until I'd had to put drops in my eyes to keep them open, and finally at 11:30 put the second call in for you. I'd already called Frank and George at 9:30 and received no answer, so I judged that they were at the station to meet you. The RR company had informed me you would get through, but I never spent such a bad four hours except when Margie was to sing. Then to top it all off, at 11:45 I went sound asleep, and . . . I mean sound asleep, and when you answered I wasn't sure I hadn't dreamed I talked to you. So I had Rose[2] . . . check with the Secret Service, and they reported you had talked to me—then I knew I hadn't dreamed it.

[July 2, 1947]

Well, I'm through another big day. Interviews

[2]Rose Conway, his personal secretary.

315

with congressmen, senators, national committeemen on every subject under the sun. But most of them went away in a good frame of mind.

They are painting your room and have finished painting Margie's . . . Talked to Mr. Crim[3] about the metal awnings for the south porch. Suggested he build a portico with entrance from the Monroe room and have the metal awnings extend from it. He liked the suggestion, but I doubt it will be done.

[July 8, 1947]

Give me Fred's address and ask Margie if she has ever written the Naval Academy about their invitation to sing. They are holding up the programs until she decides because they want her to have the choice place if she sings there.

Glad Mamma is looking so well. Hope your paper hanger came. Ask Margie if she has a pen or pencil. I am trying out one that Sol Bloom sent me today. He said Roosevelt pocketed a $50 [one] he brought to him to sign a bill. I told him to try me out! He did, and I have the pen.

[July 11, 1947]

Mary called this morning and said Mamma has

[3]White House architect.

316

had a setback, but that she is recovering from it. . . . My blood presure has been up to 130—Congress, I suppose, and my weight is off four pounds.

[July 14, 1947]

Well, summer has at last arrived—and how. I went walking this morning for 20 minutes instead of my customary 30, and when I arrived back upstairs, I looked as if I'd been dipped in the pool, clothes and all.

Went to the French Embassy at 4:45 (to arrive promptly at 5:00) to be present at the presentation of the highest French medal to Mrs. R. for FDR. I wore my white silk suit and sat in state as Marcus Aurelius or Constantine would have done while the French Ambassador made the presentation and read the citation. All of 'em had to stand but me! . . . I came away as soon as I could so they could drink champagne & have a good time. I don't like it—even if it is French best.

[July 15, 1947]

It looks as if each day is just a bit more hectic than the one before, and I suppose that will be the case until this awful Congress quits. I really do not think I can possibly come home this weekend because of all these things piling up on

317

me. So, if you want to stay a few days longer, do it. And I'll try to make it the next one.

[July 16, 1947]

Had the usual number of customers including a Royal Prince from Yemen, a little country in S. West Arabia, and an interesting one. They raise citrus fruits, and other agricultural products, are mostly at an elevation of 7,500 feet and have a good climate. Have more loot as a result of his visit—another scimitar & dagger, four beautiful silver lace bonbon dishes hand-made, an immense brass tray about 30 inches across, and a most interesting ring dating back to B.C. It is some peculiar stone with the tree of life carved upon [it], but too small for me to wear, so I guess Margie will get it for a dinner ring.[4]

[July 21, 1947]

Talked to Dr. Graham, Vivian, and Mary after I talked to you. . . . I have feared all along that the end is approaching, but I feel we've done everything possible to postpone it. I had hoped she would get up after that first bed sore healed, but it doesn't look so good now. All seemed to think I'd better finish up this terrible Congress before

[4]When Truman left the presidency, all gifts bestowed upon him were given to the American people, and they are displayed today at the Truman Library.

coming home. So unless there is an immediate emergency, [I'll] do that.

[July 22, 1947]

The reason I can't come home Saturday is the likelihood of Congress adjourning. There are fifty bills. . . . All these must be signed or re-jected—the rejected ones must go down before adjournment, hence I must be here Saturday in case I veto some bill in a hurry that day. Of course, the easy way would be just to let 'em die, which they do ten days after adjournment if I don't sign 'em. But I don't want to do that, only when I have to. I have faced the music, and have never failed to take a positive stand when nec-essary. So I'd better stay and finish the job.

The President arose early as usual on Saturday morning July 26th and wrote a light-hearted letter to Bess. "This is Turnip Day and Nellie Noland's birthday," he began, and he told her how on this day in 1901 his "old bald-headed uncle, Harrison Young" had planted turnips all over his farm on the theory they'd break a drought. 1901 was also the year he and Bess graduated from high school, he remembered. "You see, age is creeping up on me. Mamma is 94½ because she never lived in the past. I'll never be 94½, but I'm not going to live in yes-terday either."

A postal clerk hammered the Washington, D.C.,

postmark across the airmail special delivery enve-
lope at 11:00 A.M. But Harry beat the letter home.
A phone call told him Mamma's condition had
turned critical. He was airborne by midday. Some-
where over Ohio he dozed off, and dreamed of his
mother. The pilot received a message, and Wallace
Graham handed it to an awakened President.
Head bowed, Martha Truman's son spoke quietly.
"Well—now she won't have to suffer any more."

Ironically, nine years later to the day, Harry
would attend the funeral of another mother. "No
one in the world can take the place of your
mother," he consoled his friend Rufus Burrus after-
ward. "I am sure that yours felt the same way mine
did towards me—nothing that I could do was
wrong."

Well, maybe. Because during her son's junior
year in high school, Martha Truman, in her only
surviving letter, wrote her sister-in-law:

Now, Matt, don't sew too hard or with your feet
cold. I think it is nice you can get the work. Do
it nice like you do, and [I] feel proud of you for
it. But my dear child, I'll say just as a sister, I
only mean for you to take care of your health. I
am in no hurry for my skirt, could do all sewing
on it myself, only want you to bring your pleater,
and just cut it for me. Anytime you can come,
but [I] don't want you to think I don't want you
to come. And when you *do* come [you] must sew
some for yourself. We won't let Harry fix the
machine next time. He enjoys that yet and

laughs. He has just taken up three new studies. Last night he made him a gallon of ice cream. He eats it like a pig . . .

The hot midsummer day Mamma died, as his airplane droned on toward Kansas City, her son Harry took up pen and paper and drafted a two-page obituary. "Martha Ellen Truman," it began, "born Martha Ellen Young, November 25, 1852, on Parrish farm now 36th and Prospect, Kansas City, Mo." It ended: "Survived by two sons and a daughter, six grandchildren, and three great-grandchildren—four sons and daughter of J. V. Truman and [one] daughter of Harry."

"I am enclosing you a picture of the flowers on Mamma's grave," he wrote Mary after the funeral. "I thought you would like to have one of them."

XXIV

"Bess: I'd Like to Go . . ."

The Cold War intensified over Russia's strong-arm tactics in eastern Europe in 1947 and Harry Truman decided he'd best mend fences with America's western hemispheric partners. So "Good Neighbor" trips were set up for Mexico, Canada, and Brazil. In early 1948, the President also visited Puerto Rico, the Virgin Islands, and Cuba.

Mexico came first. Never before had an American President paid a state visit there. "I have wanted to return to Mexico ever since November 1939," he said, recalling his senatorial trip. He brought with him a mathematics textbook that an American soldier had filched a century before during the Mexican-American War in order to return it to the Mexican military academy. His hosts were even more surprised when Truman laid a wreath at a monument to the cadets of Chapultepec. They had died rather than surrender to invading Americans in that war, and Truman explained that "Brave men do not belong to any one race or country. I respect bravery wherever I see it."

Of course, he also wrote home.

[Mexico City]
March 4, 1947

Dear Bess:

We arrived on the dot at 10 A.M. Left K. C. at 3:04 and had to slow down so we would not arrive too soon. . . .

The airport was lined with people and the Mexicans put on a real show for me. The Mayor of the city and Gov. of the Federal District (the same man) made me guest of honor and presented me with a solid gold medal weighing a half pound with the arms of the city on one side, and a replica of an Aztec calendar stone on the other. I wore it all day to the delight of the Mexican President.

He has a most beautiful home where I called on him, and three lovely children, two boys and a girl. I met the First Lady of Mexico and she is a charming person. . . .

Last night's affair was a colorful one. The streets were packed from the embassy to the palace and at least 10,000 were in the square in front of it. The President & I had to greet them from the balcony in Franz Josef style. Never had such a welcome.

Hope everything is going well. Tell Margie to behave. Lots of love.

Harry

Canada came next. "Bess: I'd like to go and I'd like you to go too. What do you say?" Harry jotted a note when the idea first arose. It took some coaxing, of course, because Bess didn't like pomp and circumstance. But she finally agreed. Margaret made it a trio, and their reception there was over-whelming. "I've read about royalty walking on red carpets, but I never had that experience before I came here," the President told the Canadian Par-liament.

The big event was to be Brazil in September. And again Bess and Margaret agreed to go along. They traveled there in a new presidential airplane, its fu-selage painted to resemble the head of an eagle. Dubbed the Independence *in recognition of both the country's revolutionary heritage and Truman's hometown, the new DC-6 flew at an astounding 400 miles an hour. "We landed safely," the Presi-dent assured his sister Mary. "We have had one go around here," he added later.*

[To Mary, Rio de Janeiro]
[Sept. 7, 1947]

We went to the Presidential Palace (and palace it is) to a state dinner that night after which some beautiful dances were put on. We sat at one end of a beautiful pool of water lighted all the way around by candles and on which four swans swam, and at the other end was a stage. The pool was flanked by royal palms at least a hundred and fifty feet high.

In between the pomp and circumstance, Harry, along with Wallace Graham, climbed part way up

*Rio's Corcovado. They made the hike after eluding
the Secret Service, and, as Margaret remembers it
in her biography of her father, they picked flowers
from the mountain's slopes. In France, three decades before, Harry had braved German bullets to
pluck two poppies from below Fort Donoumont.
This day he bore a half dozen orchids.*

*The Truman entourage returned home on the
battleship* Missouri, *and when they crossed the
equator, King Neptune held his traditional court.
And the ship's No. 1 polliwog, Harry Truman,
loved the ceremonial jostling.*

*When it was all over, however, Bess and Harry
decided they'd had enough ceremony. He wrote
Mary:*

[November 1, 1947]

I had to call a halt on parties, dinners, etc. There
is nothing more wearing. I shook hands with
some 5,000 people in Mexico City, at least a
thousand in Canada and Brazil, and some 10,000
during the year here in the White House. Bess
was about five thousand ahead of me in White
House shakes. So we called off a lot of functions.
I used to like to meet people. Now I almost hate
the sight of 'em. It is a bad way to get . . .

*A persistent cough also plagued the President
when they returned from Brazil. Bess left for home
and Harry coped with a touchy larynx.*

[To Bess]
[September 26, 1947]

Yesterday was a hectic day. My conference lasted from 9 to 10:30 and then we weren't sure we were ready for the terrible press conference. But it turned out to be one of the best ever.[1] Things clicked 100% and the questions helped instead of hurt. The headlines in both evening and morning papers seem to be all that could be desired—except, of course, the sabotage sheet.[2] That dirty traitorous outfit gives Taft first place in an attack on the foreign policy.[3] Taft, you know, is trying for the support of Bertie [McCormick] and Cissy [Patterson].[4] He is welcome to it. Both should have been shot for traitors in the war.

Had some bank examiners from 48 states in the backyard yesterday. They had looked over the White House and seemed to like it. I told 'em that it is the finest, most expensive jail in the

[1]The news conference focused on the President's requests for an emergency program to help alleviate world food shortages, and economic assistance to war-torn western Europe, known later as the Marshall Plan.
[2]Truman's catch-all phrase to describe his press opponents, including the Scripps-Howard, Hearst, and McCormick-Patterson newspapers.
[3]Republican Senator Robert A. Taft of Ohio, a leader of Truman's congressional opposition.
[4]Publishers of the anti-Truman Chicago *Tribune*.

world, and that contests were held for men who were pining to get into it.

I'll do some broadcasting tonight at 11 P.M. for the Community Chests. I hope I can get by without giving them a graveyard cough! It is better this morning, and I imagine with some of Doc's spray, cough drops, etc., I'll get by.

[September 28, 1947]

Believe it or not, I went to church this morning! Had a hundred thousand words to read for tomorrow's conference with the congressional leaders and the reorganization commission—so decided to let the words go to hell and I'd go to church. Didn't get up until 8:30 daylight time, but fortunately they'd set the clocks back at 2 A.M. and I still had time to read a lot of words, morning papers, have breakfast in state in the family dining room with a grate fire, and then walk to the Baptist Church at 16th & O. They were having a Sunday School graduation and I was asked to say a few words to the kids, which I did.

[October 6, 1947]

I have had a hectic two days. I suppose I might say customarily hectic. Seems to me that the last seven or eight hundred days have been hectic or something. My throat has been giving me hell all week and the doc used heroic measures to get me by last night. Think we made it O.K. I think maybe a couple of days in bed would do the trick. But it can only be done at the weekend, and you see what happened to this one.

[October 8, 1947]

I have to speak to the women today at 1:30, and I hope I can do it without a cough. I have a terrific one on occasion, but it only comes by fits and starts. Had a good night last night after a visit to the Baptist Church to hear about six speeches on the location of the headquarters of the Baptist World Alliance here from London. Charlie Ross[5] & I went, and aside from too much hot air it was a good meeting. . . . A Dane, a Norwegian, a Canadian, and an Australian made excellent short talks and then old Lewis Newton, the old hypocrite who is president of the Southern Baptists, made a silly talk. He's the one who is always after Vaughan. But take it as a whole the meeting was all right. If I'd felt better, I could have enjoyed it more.

[October 11, 1947]

Well, I'm feeling much better today. Took my usual swim and beating up by the sergeant yesterday afternoon for the first time in a week or

[5]The President's press secretary.

more and went walking this morning too.[6] So I'm just about back to normal, cough and all.

We are getting an aluminum canopy over the back door. It looks fine. White on top and green inside. If we get the new porch, everything will be lovely. Looks as if we may get it.[7]

Hope everyone is well. Will call you tomorrow as usual. Almost did it last night. I dreamed about you and it was most pleasant. Woke up and you weren't there—a great disappointment.

A few years later, after he'd left the presidency and begun writing his memoirs, Truman reread his letters to Mary Jane. On the envelope of one he scratched "Bess and Margie name a tugboat. Winchell tells a lie, and I propose to start for Virgin Islands and Key West." The letter read in part:

[February 11, 1948]

Bess and Margaret arrived from New Orleans Monday. They had a grand and strenuous time. Stopped in Biloxi and saw the Luxiches with

[6]The "beating up" was the President's way of describing a massage.
[7]They did, and the White House's new south porch became so controversial that supporters of Thomas E. Dewey's 1948 presidential bid chanted, "Truman was screwy to build a porch for Dewey."

whom they lived some fifteen years ago. Margaret christened a tugboat named for me at New Orleans. It is said to be the most powerful river tugboat. The paper said it required two bottles of champagne to name it. Headline said, "Margaret Christens a Two-Bottle Boat."

Margie went on to New York for a visit with the Watsons and a trip to the opera. She's got the fever. One of these lying columnists, Winchell by name, announced her engagement to a boy out in Michigan whom she's only seen a couple of times. If I could have gotten my hands on him, I'd have tried to break his neck (Winchell's).

On Friday 20th, I'm leaving for Key West, Puerto Rico, St. Thomas, St. Croix, and the naval base in Cuba. . . . I'm so tired and bedeviled I can't be decent to people.

Valentine's Day arrived, and so too did a nice heart in the mail.

THE WHITE HOUSE

2-14-48

Dear Margie:
It was a perfect valentine. I've heard the Enesco Rhapsody over the radio a couple of times. He's not a noise composer—thank goodness.
In days past your dad could get what he wanted when he wanted it. Now it has to be done by a

"messenger." So—you & your mamma got no sentimental cards from me. Read some of the old ones—they are still good.

OOXXXXXXXOODad

The Independence *flew the President to San Juan, Puerto Rico. From there he toured other U.S. Caribbean possessions aboard the* Williamsburg, *ending up at Guantanamo Bay, Cuba. Then he returned to the States by air.*

Key West, Fla.
Feb 26, 1948

Dear Bess:

I started a letter to you on the ship at St. Thomas and you should have had it today from Cuba (I can't spell that naval base), but I became indisposed due to the rocking and pitching in the straits between Puerto Rico & the Virgins, and never managed to finish it. In the rush from then on this is the first time I've been able to sit down long enough to write.

The receptions in all the Islands were all that could have been asked. Their beauty is a revelation, and the people the kindliest yet. Someday the idle rich will discover the climate and the beaches and then the prosperity of those parts will be assured. Charlotte Amalie and Christiansted on St. Thomas & St. Croix are just simply dream towns. It never becomes warmer than 90° nor colder than 68° winter and summer—the same is true of San Juan, Puerto Rico. . . .

Spent last night signing bills, protocols, etc., and reading Washington and N.Y. papers. Will be going to the beach this morning and [will] read high-class *literature* the rest of the day. . . .

Remember me to your mother, kiss or spank Margie—whichever she needs, and loads of love to you.

Harry

XXV

"We Are Going to Lick 'em and Lick 'em Good!"

"Senator Barkley and I will win this election and make these Republicans like it—don't you forget it!"

It was 2 A.M. on a mid-July morning in the packed Philadelphia convention hall. It felt like noontime, it was so hot and muggy. But these words jolted the wilted Democrats to consciousness. They had just nominated Harry Truman as their 1948 presidential candidate, and, as he addressed them, he knew he faced the fight of his lifetime.

For nearly two years, a Republican-controlled Congress (Truman called it the "do-nothing" 80th Congress) had opposed his domestic reform ideas, and he had vetoed dozens of its anti-administration bills. Learning about a Republican Capitol Hill strategy caucus in mid-1947, the President predicted to Bess, "They intend to smear me as their fundamental campaign program! Pretty dirty—but they are dealing with a completely smeared & unsmeared expert."

Then, too, most of the nation's press pitted itself

against him in 1948. Truman was Franklin Roosevelt's lackluster errand boy whom fate had made a transitory occupant of the White House, editorialized the big newspapers. And the political pollsters confirmed their assessment. Harry Truman, they said, didn't have a chance against Republican presidential hopeful, New York's governor, Thomas E. Dewey.

Even a good many Democrats conceded defeat. Sniffing the political winds, some of the party's bigwigs had organized a "dump-Truman" movement. "Some of my so-called friends have been getting the jitters and [are] running out on the Democratic Party," HST wrote Mary in March. "But that is to be expected under the circumstances."

More Democrats bolted by mid-year. Some followed the banner of Progressive Party candidate Henry Wallace, whom Truman had fired from his cabinet. Still others, members of the Democratic Party's conservative southern bloc, marched out of the Philadelphia convention after adoption of a strong civil rights plank. Quickly dubbed "the Dixiecrats," they held a convention in Alabama, organized the States Rights Party, and nominated a presidential ticket of their own.

Early on, Truman himself doubted he could win. "I'd be much better off if I were out or licked, and I suspect you and Margie would be much more pleased," he wrote home philosophically. "I'm ready to go to Tucson, Phoenix, Springerville, or even Yuma in 1949," he joked on another occasion. To his sister, he counseled, "Don't worry about the political outcome. I shall stick to my guns and won't shed a tear if I lose. That would be the best thing that could happen to me."

A few weeks later, however, a more confident candidate outlined some of his campaign plans. "I am considering a cross-country trip taking in Chicago, Des Moines, Omaha, Butte, Mont., Seattle, San Francisco, Salt Lake City, Denver, and Kansas City," he informed Mary in April. The White House billed the trip as "nonpolitical," a presidential inspection tour prompted by an invitation from the University of California. The President would receive an honorary degree at its June commencement exercises.

In reality (and everyone knew it) Harry Truman wanted to test the political waters. He also needed the train trip, with its many scheduled "whistle stops," to practice speaking informally. "I've been experimenting with 'off the cuff' or extemporaneous speeches," he confided to his sister shortly before the tour began. "There has been much talk that my prepared speeches don't go over, but that when I talk without notes they go over."

The presidential entourage, aboard a special sixteen-car train, rolled out of Washington's Union Station the morning of June 4th. For the next two weeks, the Ferdinand Magellan, a walnut-paneled, armor-plated car built originally for President Roosevelt, served Truman as haven and rostrum. Two steps out its back door brought him before a microphone connected to three speakers mounted to the roof. Before trip's end, Harry spoke in eighteen

states to an estimated two and a half million peo-
ple. It didn't matter whether it was 7 A.M. or 11
P.M.—impressive crowds greeted the President.

The only place where the turnout was poor, in
fact downright embarrassing, was Omaha. Be-
cause people had gotten the false impression that
his appearance there was a private affair, only the
front seats of Omaha's cavernous Ak-sar-ben Col-
iseum were filled.

Afterwards Truman summed up his impressions
of the trip's first leg.

SUN VALLEY LODGE
Sun Valley, Idaho

June 8, 1948

Dear Mary,

. . . The Omaha celebration was a real one and I
appreciated it. But one mistake was made, and that
was going out of town to that big hall without special advertising. Of course, the mean columnists
will try to make something out of it. But the welcome on the streets offset it. The chief of police
told me that it was the biggest turnout Omaha ever
had.

Along the way at Grand Island, Kearney, North
Platte, Sidney in Neb., and Cheyenne, Laramie,
and Rawlins, Wyo. the whole town turned out. It
was 11:00 P.M. at Rawlins, yet all were out. They
told me that at a little town in Idaho at 5:15 A.M.
the whole town was out. I wasn't up. At Pocatello,
Id., at 7:15 there were 2,000 people and at Ket-

chum, the P.O. for this place, everybody in the country was there.

We are going to lick 'em and lick 'em good!

Take care of yourself. . . .

Lots of love.

Harry

Bess and Margie want to be remembered.

Bess and Margie were also aboard the Ferdinand Magellan, *and Dad introduced them to the crowd, that is, unless it was before nine* A.M., *their accustomed waking hour. "I have been up since a quarter to six looking over this trail that the Union Pacific follows up here," he told an early morning Idaho crowd. He had come amongst them, he said, "so you can look at me and hear what I have to say, and then make up your own mind as to whether you believe some of the things that have been said about your President." "I wish I could stay longer," he told an Illinois crowd near the end of his tour, "but . . . I have to get back to Washington to veto some more bills."*

The trip was a great success. The big turnouts, the public's warm reception to his folksy informality buoyed Truman's spirits. "It has certainly been a relief to me, and an education to me," he sighed.

So too were the final deliberations of the Democratic National Convention in Philadelphia. The party gave him its nomination, and despite the southern bolt, he felt that, with Alben Barkley of Kentucky as his running mate, he could win in November.

Following his acceptance speech in Philadelphia, he returned to the White House at 5:30 A.M., got three hours of sleep, ate a quick breakfast, and then, as he had promised at the conventon a few hours before, officially requested that the Republican 80th Congress reassemble into special session. It would reconvene, Truman directed, on July 26th, "Turnip Day" back in Missouri.

Calling the special session was blatantly political. The President schemed to focus the country's attention on the record of the Republican legislators. "They sure are in a stew and mad as wet hens," Harry gleefully told Bess. "If I can make them madder, maybe they'll do the job the old gods used to put on the Greeks & Romans."

While the 80th Congress fussed and fumed in special session, Harry flew back to Missouri with a quick stop in New York City to dedicate Idlewild Airport. "O'Dwyer, Mayor of N.Y., met me for the first time! He's either been sick, out of town, or too busy before. It's a good sign because he's a bandwagon boy."

Then it was back to Washington for a startling discovery—the White House was collapsing! Earlier that year, the President had asked that the second-floor living quarters be examined for structural soundness, and he now explained to Mary:

[August 10, 1948]

The White House is still about to fall in. Margaret's sitting room floor broke in two but didn't fall

338

through the family dining room ceiling. They propped it up and fixed it. Now my bathroom is about to fall into the Red Parlor. They won't let me sleep in my bedroom or use the bath. I am using Old Abe's bed and it is very comfortable. Mr. Searles, one of the ushers, told me that when the Lincoln bed was in Margaret's sitting room [Franklin] Roosevelt's mother always slept in it. He'd always ask her how she and Old Abe got along and she'd always say, "fine, Franklin, fine—if you do as well I'll be proud."

Next day, the White House developed more problems, and Harry wrote Margaret about how, among other things, he had to pitch in and help the staff mop up a mess:

THE WHITE HOUSE

Aug. 11, 1948

My dear Margie:

I am in the so-called Lincoln Room—the southeast room. Your uncle Vivian called it the southeast 40 acres of the White House! I have been staying in this room at night because my bedroom is about to fall into the Red Parlor. Ain't that something? It is—I'd say.

I've had one "great" day. Signed the bill giving the U.N. 65 million dollars to build their building in N.Y. Had Tom Connally, Dr. Eaton, Trgyve Lie, Byron Price, Mayor O'Dwyer of N.Y., Warren Austin all present. The Senator from Michigan was not here, but Sol Bloom was. I gave all of 'em pens with which I had signed the bill. There were nine pens. I make an *H* with one, *arry* with one, *S* with one, *T* with one, *ru* with one, and *man* with one, write *Approved,* and the date, and I have some to spare!

Then I had to review the budget for an hour, talk to the usual aide, the military aide, the Secretary of the Intelligence Service on the Atomic Bomb, and some others. I shook hands with some 250 people at 12:45, made them a speech, and finally arrived at my 1 P.M. luncheon for Barkley et al. at 1:15.

Worked all evening after 5:30—no swim, had a club sandwich and a terrible rain. Water blew in the balcony door in gallons, into your bathroom, your mamma's bedroom & mine in torrents. I finally managed to put the windows down and shut the balcony door. Beals finally came up with my sandwich & buttermilk, and told me that the state dining room had two inches of water in it, and the pantry was flooded. Nothing hurt—so they say. Furguson finally came up with a mop and soaked up some of the water in the study and the Lincoln room where I am sleeping. I'd already soaked up most of it with bath towels!

This end (southeast 40) is certainly "haunted." More noises than a subway.

I shall count on you to help me out on Labor Day.

Lots of love.

X X X X X X X X X X Dad
O O O O O O O O O O

With the Labor Day speech behind him, and a two-week western campaign swing ahead, Truman boarded the U.S.S. Williamsburg *for one final diversion.*

U.S.S. Williamsburg
Sept. 11, 1948

Dear Mary,
I was glad to get your letter of day before yesterday just as I left the White House to come aboard. . . .

I loaded my secretaries on the yacht and we've been working on my western speeches. . . .

We are anchored off an island at the mouth of the Potomac where Lord Baltimore landed in 1634. . . .

A Baptist preacher from New Bern, No'th Ca'lina came to see me yesterday and gave me a gavel made from a cypress tree that was standing [here] in 1710 and still is alive. He was on his way to Bern, Switzerland to give the Mayor of that town one. The N. C. town was founded by emigrants from the old Bern in 1710. . . .

Lots of love.

Harry

His first full day of whistle-stopping began at 5:45 A.M. at Rock Island, Illinois ("I don't think I have ever seen so many farmers in town in all my life!"), and it ended fifteen hours later after a dozen speeches had been given before thousands of Iowa farmers. Next day, Harry, Bess, and Margaret enjoyed a refreshing Sunday morning at home in

Independence, then boarded the Ferdinand Magellan *for their western swing.*

The turnout was more impressive than in June.

Ogden, Utah, 11:15 P.M.—"You know, those eastern newspapers just won't believe it when they are told that past 11 o'clock there are 10,000 or 12,000 people out to listen to me in Ogden!"

Merced, California, 6:55 A.M.—"I didn't get up quite as early this morning as I usually do. I missed a great crowd back at Tracy, but I have to have a little sleep, I can't go all night and day too."

Sanderson, Texas, 10:06 P.M.—"I started in at El Paso this morning and it looked like half of Texas were present in El Paso. But that was not the case, for at every other stop the other half has been at each one of these other cities—and it looks now as if everybody in the neighborhood is here!"

Shawnee, Oklahoma, 7:35 A.M.—"I can't tell you how very much I appreciate this wonderful turnout at this time of day—and the train [is] 15 minutes ahead of time!"

Montgomery, West Virginia, 10:43 P.M.—"I never expected to see a crowd like this at this time of night. . . . I want one of you expert photographers to come up here and take a picture of this crowd, because this picture ought to go in all the newspapers in the country."

In June, Truman had stressed Republican misdeeds on Capitol Hill. Now, because G.O.P. legislators had predictably refused to do his bidding during their special "Turnip Day" session, Harry hammered away at what he called the "do-nothing, good-for-nothing 80th Congress."

In a lighter vein, he also appealed to the voters' generosity. Vote for me in November, he said tongue in cheek, and "I won't be troubled by the housing shortage—I can stay in the White House."

When his train stopped at Shelbyville, Kentucky, the President recalled a little family history. "My grandfather Truman ran off with Mary Jane Holmes and was married here in Shelbyville, and lived on an adjoining farm out here west of town," he explained. "Then he went to Missouri—was afraid to go back home. And about 3 or 4 years after that, why, his father-in-law sent for him to come home, he wanted to see the first grandchild. That settled things and they got together."

What the President probably didn't know was that his grandfather, after becoming widowed, had taken another, this time melancholy, journey back to Shelbyville. A rare, recently discovered letter written by Anderson Shipp Truman three years before H.S.T. was born shows a few misspelled words and lots of Truman grit:

Bagdad, Shelby Co., Ky.
July 2, '81

My dear Emma & Roch,

I am now at my old home and it makes me very sad to think of the past. But Will and all the family are kind to me yet. I look round and see some old rellicks and I no how they got them [and] it makes me feel bad. But there is no remedy and I have to stand it.

I have seen the Great Beauty.[1] She is nothing in comparison to my girls.[2] She is gross and her face is one sided. She is common. [She] pouts on write smart. But when I showed [pictures of] you and Matt and my boys they never said a word. Only that you was good looking. . . .

Tell John and Matt[3] that I want to see them very much. Tell Matt they wanted me to send for her just as soon as they saw her picture.

The crops in this state [are] not half a crop. Wheat is poor. A great deal won't make five bushel per acre. . . .

Nothing more from your old pa.

A.S. Truman

P.S. Roch. Give me all of the news and how the crops are and how the wheat is and the general news. Yours as ever, AST

---

[1]Reference is apparently to his brother William's daughter.
[2]Anderson Shipp had three girls, one being Emma.
[3]The President's father and mother, John and Martha.

The country's general news two generations later was that a spunky, plain-speaking fellow named Harry Truman didn't have a chance to win the presidential election. But following his western tour, Harry was more confident than ever.

The Nolands didn't hear much from their cousin these days. When they did, it was usually a hastily dictated letter. But his fascination with travel and good humor still came through occasionally. Signing a typed letter to Ethel as he sped across the country aboard the Independence, *HST added a postscript:*

I am signing this at 17,000 ft.—over 3 miles up— at Cincinnati! Moving at 270 mi per hour—using 385 gallons of gas to do it! I'm economy minded.

The Independence *didn't log too many presidential flying hours during the campaign, because in 1948 candidates still chose the train. But before making his final whistle-stop tour across the upper Midwest and into New England, Truman flew to Miami. There he addressed the American Legion, and, on his return flight to Washington, he stopped in Raleigh, North Carolina, for two more speeches.*

THE WHITE HOUSE

Oct. 20, 1948

Dear Mary,

. . . I've had quite a time since I last wrote. We left

here in the rain Sunday morning at 6:10, but in fifteen minutes we were up about eighteen thousand feet and it was beautifully clear with the sun rising on one side and the full moon setting on the other.

We arrived in Miami at 10 o'clock and I had one of the most enthusiastic receptions in the campaign on the streets. There must have been 200,000 people out and it was eighty in the shade and no shade for me. The Legion gave me an ovation. There were at least 30,000 in the audience and that many outside. The meeting was in an old airplane hangar fitted up as a hall. It must have covered two acres at least.

We took off at 4:15 and arrived in Raleigh two hours and thirteen minutes later. Went to the hotel and stayed all night. There were people all along the way from the airport, which is fifteen miles out of town. It was cold too. Yesterday I spoke to 50,000 people from the Capitol steps and as many more at the fair grounds in the afternoon.

We've got 'em on the run and I think we'll win.

Take care of yourself. I'll see you Sunday Oct. 31.

Lots of love.

Harry

One week before Election Day, writing from Chicago's Blackstone Hotel (where he and Bess had spent part of their honeymoon), Harry looked ahead to the campaign's finish.

Chicago, Illinois
Oct. 25, 1948

Dear Mary,

. . . We arrived here at 2 P.M. today. Had the usual ride on the back of the open car waving at the populace. The welcome was most enthusiastic. Former Mayor Kelly and the present Mayor Kennelly rode with me. They both said that the demonstration was better than any ever held here including FDR and all the rest. . . .

We go from here to Cleveland tomorrow. From Cleveland to Boston, Boston to Providence, R.I., to New Haven to New York. Then to Brooklyn and on Friday night we leave for St. Louis. Saturday night while your party goes on I'll be winding up the campaign with all I have in the old conservative Mo. metropolis. We leave St. Louis at 11:30 and arrive in Independence at 7:30 A.M. Sunday. I'll call you when I get to the house.

I expect to sleep all day Sunday, but I'll see you Monday A.M. On Monday night at Independence I'll broadcast from the house. I want you and Vivian and all his family there. You tell him. Tell Ralph too so he can come.

Take care of yourself. Lots of love.

Harry

The American people were about to witness (and themselves make possible) the greatest political upset in modern times. Pollsters predicted Harry's

defeat right up to Election Day. But he, and thou-
sands of others, weren't listening.

[Longhand note, 1948]

. . . Jim Rowley and Henry Nicholson, first and second in command of the White House detail of the Secret Service, drove me over to the Elms Hotel at Excelsior Springs. I took a turkish bath and went upstairs at 6:30, had a ham sandwich and glass of milk, and listened to some eastern returns and went to bed. I was some thousands ahead.

I awoke at midnight and again listened to the radio broadcast of Mr. Kaltenborn[4] and I was about 1,200,000 ahead on the count, but according to the broadcaster still undoubtedly beaten.

About four o'clock Mr. Rowley came into my room and advised me to listen again to Mr. Kaltenborn's broadcast. At that time I was over 2,000,000 ahead, but the broadcaster couldn't see how I could be elected.

I told Jim and Nick we had better go back to the Muehlebach Hotel in Kansas City because it looked very much as if we were in trouble for another four years.

We arrived at the hotel in K. C. about six o'clock A.M. Wednesday morning and at 10:30 we received a telegram from Gov. Dewey congratulating me on the election. I was very glad

[4]Commentator H. V. Kaltenborn.

I'd had a good night's sleep.

We had not been accompanied to Excelsior Springs by any reporters or newsmen. They were all preparing to celebrate with Dewey!

XXVI

"X Marks the Spot Where I Sleep"

By 1948, Key West, Florida, had become Harry Truman's favorite cold weather retreat. There, he got up later than usual, donned wildly colored tropical shirts, took walks under rustling palms, read a bit, swam a bit, and enjoyed an afternoon nap. In the evening, with a glass of bourbon by his side, he played poker.

His quarters were located on the Navy's submarine base. Built in West Indian style, with its top floor boxed in by a louvered screened porch, the white ten-room frame house looked more like a barn than a presidential residence. But it suited Harry Truman's tastes just fine.

"This place is what I hoped it would be, and what I was certain it wouldn't be," he wrote home approvingly on his first stay there in November 1946. "I'm seeing no outsiders," he vowed. "I don't give a damn how put out they get. I'm doing as I damn please for the next two years, and to hell with all [of] them."

His bravado subsided, but Key West afforded a welcome escape from the Washington scene.

We have breakfast on a sub in a few minutes and will in all probability go down under. That has not been published yet, but I thought I'd better tell you. I've been up 17,000 feet around the top of Popocatépetl and I should go the other way to be even.

[November 22, 1946]

Yesterday morning we went down in a new German sub. There was no sensation to it and nothing could be seen except the inside of the ship and the teamwork of the crew, which was excellent. We went down 450 feet.

[November 29, 1946]

The sun shines with terrific force down here. My face and head are as red as a beet, but the rest of me is brown except for a strip around the middle which is white. I told Santiago[1] that as soon as I watched him in color, I'd take no more sunbaths.

Glad at least one maid stayed on the job [in the White House] while the "haunts" were walking. There's no more lonesome hole in the United

[1]J. Santiago, chief steward of the *U.S.S. Williamsburg*.

351

States than is that old barn commonly called the President's House. I sure hated to go away and leave you alone there because I know how it feels.

I had a "tea" myself yesterday afternoon for the thirty newsmen. . . . For once we have no S.O.B.s with us. Shoop[2] couldn't come. Ed Lockett[3] is sick. I hope it's smallpox—and the Chicago *Sun* could send anyone. Therefore the men here are the best of the lot. Some of the locals may be haywire, but they can't hurt us.

It was during his next Key West visit that the President heard Margie make her national singing debut over the ABC radio network. At first, he thought he might miss it; Key West didn't have an ABC affiliate. But John Spottswood, owner of the local Mutual network station, arranged to pipe the ABC program from Miami to his station and thence to Truman's quarters.

This, plus a momentous foreign policy speech he'd just made asking Congress to abandon postwar traditional American isolationism, became the subject of a letter home.

Key West, Fla.
March 14, 1947

Dear Bess:
. . . I had no idea I was so tired. I have been asleep

[2]Duke Shoop of the Kansas City *Star.*
[3]Edward B. Lockett of *Time* magazine.

most of the time. Didn't get up until 8 o'clock yesterday and 7:30 today so you know I'm rather all in. Even drove to the beach instead of walking as I did before. Had a forty-minute sunbath at eleven o'clock, and will have another one this morning of one hour.

I am very much in favor of Margie's coming back to Washington next Monday. Then we can take stock and decide what's best to do. I hope she shows you my letter to you.[4]

They are running a special wire in here from New York so I can listen to her without interruption, so I guess I'll stay over a day or two beyond Sunday if it is all right with you. . . .

Hope the [Truman Doctrine] message will be for world peace.[5] It was a terrific step to take and one I've been worrying about since Marshall took over the State Dept. Our very first conversation was what to do about Russia in China, Korea, and the Near East.

As far as I've seen [in] the papers, there has been a favorable reception except by the crackpots headed by Henry [Wallace] and his crowd. I don't believe they can get a following. It was pleasing the way the Congress reacted—didn't you think it was

[4]The letter, dated March 13, 1947, appears in Margaret's book, *Letters From Father,* and wishes her well in her debut.
[5]On March 12, 1947, the President spoke before Congress advocating U. S. aid to Greece and Turkey to forestall a communist takeover there.

nearly unanimous?[6] How I wish you and Margie and your mother were here. The ship is tied up right in front of the house—just half a block away. Maybe I'll come home aboard it if it doesn't take too long.

I'm looking for a letter! *Lots & Lots of Love*

Harry

But, alas, not everyone agreed that Margaret's talent warranted a singing career; not even her voice instructor. "Margie should have no future handicap by having her music teacher say she had to go on charity to get a career," her irate father agreed with Mamma, recommending that the teacher be paid off and sent scooting.

Margaret opened a concert tour in Pittsburgh, and Dad gave her some advice.

THE WHITE HOUSE

Oct. 21, 1947

Dear Margie:

I have just been reading the clippings from all the Pittsburgh papers. The write-ups were excellent except for some of the critics. If I ever meet one of them, I'll bust 'em [in] the nose.

One of them was kindly and constructive. His name is Ralph Lewando and he is with the *Pitts-*

[6]Although controlled by Republicans, the Congress endorsed the Truman Doctrine.

burgh Press. If I were you, I'd read what he says and weigh it carefully. I'm telling you this because I'm more anxious for your *complete* success than you are, if that is possible.

You should finish this tour and then carefully take stock and do whatever you do, but I want you to do what will be most likely to take you to the top of the ladder. It is a long hard pull and takes work and more work. Your dad ought to know. . . .

We sure miss you around here. If I was not at the White House, I think I'd adopt a couple of little girls!

Tell grandmother, Aunt Mary, and all your uncles and aunts hello.

Lots of love,
Dad

O O O O O O O O O O O O O O O O O O O O O O
X X X X X X X X X X X

Later, when Washington Post *music critic Paul Hume wrote that Miss Truman's voice was "flat," and that he was mystified that people kept paying to hear her, Dad had a fit. He wrote Hume a letter that made people gasp, calling the music critic lower than a "guttersnipe," saying he hoped Hume would "accept that statement as a worse insult than a reflection on your ancestry."*

But the diversions of Key West allowed the President to cope more easily with such attacks, whether directed at him or at his family.

Had a press conference and it turned out well—believe it or not. The setting for it was beautiful and the press boys showed their appreciation. Only one smart aleck present, John O'Donnell, and he got no answer to his question.

Went to the beach and had a good swim, had lunch at 12:30, and went fishing. We drew sides, Adm. Leahy[7] in charge of one side, and [me in] charge of the other. . . . We made up a pot, putting [in] $5 apiece. $10 to go for the longest fish, $10 for the heaviest fish, and the balance to be distributed among the people on the side that caught the most fish by weight. On our side, Dr. Graham caught two, a barracuda & a grouper, [Clark] Clifford[8] a nice grouper, & Bill Hassett[9] a 25-pound amberjack. Total weight, 42½ pounds. Capt. Dennison[10] caught [a] beautiful mackerel, weight 29½ pounds and about 3 ft. long. So he won both prizes of $10, but our side divided up the pot. I made a dollar, getting six back for my five.

[7]Fleet Admiral William D. Leahy, Chief of Staff.
[8]Special Counsel to the President.
[9]Correspondence Secretary.
[10]Captain Robert L. Dennison, naval aide.

[March 4, 1948]

The weather here is ideal. It is hell to have to go back to slavery and the bickerings that I'll have to face from now on. But it must be done.

[March 6, 1948]

I sure felt badly when I left you at the airport in D.C. Those d——d reporters and photographers wanted something embarrassing to happen. It did not. So I told Col. Williams[11] to beat them here for the landing. He did. I stood at the steps of their plane and asked them about Molotov, Vishinski, and *Novakane*.[12]

[March 13, 1949]

We are debating whether to go to church at 11 o'clock and then go to the beach, or to go to the beach at ten and *hope* to get to church later or some other day. The latter will probably win.

Wish you and Margie were here. They have fixed you up a palatial bedroom next to mine. You've

[11]Pilot of the *Independence*.
[12]The President's pique, turned to humor, stemmed apparently from the press's attempt to capture him and Bess in a farewell embrace.

357

never seen a nicer one. The place is all redecorated, the porches have been leveled up, so there are no steps from the dining room, new furniture, and everything. I've a notion to move the capitol to Key West and just stay.

In time, however, the "Winter White House" took on a more formal air. This happened after two Puerto Rican nationalists tried to assassinate the President in November 1950. Taking no chances, additional security guards were assigned to protect Truman wherever he went, including his stays at the already tightly guarded Key West sub base.

After returning from a visit there, the President shared his recollections with the Noland sisters, and, as in days gone by, "Horatio" included a picture postcard that showed what his vacation abode looked like.

THE WHITE HOUSE

April 9, 1951

Dear Ethel,
Your letter of April 1st has been in my unanswered letter file since the 3rd. For some reason I am finding it more difficult to be prompt with my personal correspondence. For the last year or more things have piled up on my desk—maybe it's sixty-seven that's haunting me!

My purported vacation was a farce—except for

a change of scenery. I'm enclosing you a postcard showing the house I occupy at Key West. X marks the spot where I sleep. It is a beautiful bedroom with the screened and latticed porch on the sides marked. There are half a dozen bedrooms with twin beds where my immediate secretaries stay. Press, appointment, correspondence, legal, special, etc. etc. ad lib. I keep them all busy. I have to in order to get in my 600 signatures a day. Then I have executive assistants by the half dozen. Military aide, Naval aide, Air aide and *their* assistants, a Medical aide–Air Force, a Medical aide–Naval with assistants, who dose me, beat me and keep me generally healthy—which I'd be anyway.

What I'm saying is that the business of the government never stops no matter where the President goes—it follows him. In addition to all the secretaries, exec. assts., medical aides, and their helpers, I have sixteen Secret Service guards who see that I don't get shot or shot at, and at the house in Key West there are forty-odd Marine Guards who stand stiffly at attention at all the entrances and salute me punctually when I go out the front door, the back door, or anywhere else. At the Blair House and the White House there are forty blue-coated policemen who do the same thing. This, you must remember, is a *"free"* country. Of course, getting shot at and having a man killed and two wounded hasn't helped the situation any, and I'm very docile since that event. It's terrible to have men killed and wounded in your behalf. . . .

Was Margie any good? Of course you can't say no!

My best to Nellie.

Sincerely,
Harry

Cousin Harry exaggerated his Key West routine, of course. His stays there were not quite so harried. There was more time for contemplation. Once, sunning himself on the sea wall, gazing at the incoming surf, he turned to White House economic advisor Dr. John Steelman and mused, "John. Just think what a great country we live in. Here you and I are—a farmer boy from Arkansas and a farmer boy from Missouri—and look where we are. Do you realize if you and I went swimming out there right now and both of us would drown, this great country would move right along without a ripple. Might be a little ripple, but not much of a ripple. This great country is too big for both of us. It's too big for anybody."

XXVII

"I Am in the Midst of the Most Terrible Struggle . . ."

He figured he'd traveled 31,700 miles during his presidential campaign against Dewey. So in 1949 Harry Truman let people come see him *for a while. Except for a return to Key West, he didn't venture any distance from Washington until mid-year. Then he attended the annual reunion of his old 35th Division. He wouldn't miss it. The Battery D boys were there, and so too was Cousin Ralph. "I don't think that red-headed cousin of mine will believe this," he said, "but I don't think I have missed a meeting of the 35th Division Reunion since the First World War, with possibly one exception."*

The Flying White House
June 11, 1949

Dear Bess:

We are moving along at 19,700 feet in the air at about 300 miles an hour. The visit to Little Rock was a complete success. Five thousand people were at the airport when we came in yesterday, 100,000 (conservatively) were on the route of march this morning, and between ten and twelve

361

thousand were at the Memorial Stadium in 100-degree sunlight to listen to the speech at 2:30 P.M.

I gave them all I had because my heart was in it. Charlie Ross, Dennison, Harry Vaughan, Snyder, and Bill Bray all said the delivery and the speech were in Class A-1. Bill Bray said only St. Louis in the campaign could come anywhere near to topping it.[1] I've never worked on a speech as hard as I did on this one. The whole Arkansas delegation in Congress were there except one. Both Senators listened intently. I hope it had the desired effect.

I couldn't call you, but I told Nick and Jim to wire you of my arrival. I was completely surrounded every minute I was in Little Rock. I'm sorry I didn't run 'em out and call you. But you'll have to overlook it this time.

Mary Jane, Ralph, Canfil, my aides and all had a good time. Will call when I get in tonight. Love as always,

Harry

His Arkansas speech dealt with America's problems with Russia. A few months later, when the Soviets exploded their first atomic bomb and mainland China fell under communist control, those problems intensified. To add to the President's woes, labor chieftain John L. Lewis threatened a crippling coal strike for early 1950, the press began accusing Harry Vaughan of peddling his influence

[1]Bray did advance work for presidential trips.

*in return for gifts, and a demagogue in the Senate
named Joe McCarthy stepped forward to accuse
Truman of shielding communists in the State Department.*

*The United States entered the season of Mc-
Carthyism, an era of suspicion and fear. And Harry
had to do something about it.*

Key West, Fla.
March 26, 1950

Dear Ralph:
This is a letter I wish I didn't have to write. First
of all I want you to understand that I appreciate
from the heart the sentiments which caused you to
want to give me a dinner in Washington for our two
birthdays.

But a President never can do what he wants to
do or what he'd like to do. I am in the midst of the
most terrible struggle any President ever had. A
pathological liar from Wisconsin and a block-
headed undertaker from Nebraska[2] are trying to
ruin the bipartisan foreign policy. Stalin never had
two better allies in this country. I must make an
effort to stop that procedure.

After long consultations with the Cabinet and my
secretaries it has been decided that I must make a
cross-country tour and nail the lies and bring back
some confidence. The date set to start is May
7th. So that knocks out two of the most pleasurable

[2]In addition to McCarthy, the reference is to Republican
Senator Kenneth S. Wherry of Nebraska.

363

dinners I was anticipating. Tom Clark's[3] and yours.

Let's try and get together this summer at home and have our family celebration as you visualized it on a postponed basis.

I'm terribly sorry, but as I said before I can never do what I want to.

My best to Olive.

> Sincerely,
> Harry

It was indeed necessary for Harry Truman to "bring back some confidence." He packed his bags for another whistle-stop tour that took him to the Pacific Northwest to dedicate Washington State's Grand Coulee Dam. The first full day out (his 66th birthday), the President made ten stops as he crossed Illinois, Iowa, and Nebraska. In all, during the trip, he delivered 75 speeches.

"I am talking to you now as your hired man," he said. He hadn't gone "high-hat" since 1948, and he wanted to present "the facts as they really are." Even though following the '48 elections Democrats had taken control of Congress, he still had problems there. Those legislators who blocked his reform ideas like expanded social security to include health insurance were "pullbacks" and "reactionaries." "The cry of socialism is as old as the hills," Truman told them, counter-attacking those who, like McCarthy, equated his "Fair Deal" domestic

[3]Supreme Court Justice who had traditionally given the President a birthday dinner.

reform proposals with godless communism. Without mentioning McCarthy by name, the President also warned against returning to isolationism as after World War 1.

A Republican spokesman charged "This trip of the President's is a medicine show attempting to sell fake nostrums by guile and deception." It was, he claimed, a political trip, "replete with name-calling, presenting the Truman version of the New Deal." The trip was nothing of the sort, the President retorted, and, adding insult to injury, he invited the gentleman whom the Republicans had hired to tail him to join his entourage. ". . . If he will buy a ticket and get on the train," he chuckled, "I will take him along."

In the weeks following his return to Washington, it was business as usual. Bess went home to Independence, and Harry stayed in his oval office. "Another day—but I have not received my dollar!," he wrote his lady, and that day he also got hopping mad over something he'd read. The Kansas City Star, *founded seventy years before by William Rockhill Nelson, had just published a commemorative tabloid edition, and after examining it, Harry wrote home, "It must have been written by [Westbrook] Pegler because it is full of lies and makes your old man a very small potato. . . . A good book you should read if you want to get good and mad."*

Of course, to him the Saint Louis Post-Dispatch *wasn't much better. Referring once to its publisher, Harry told Cousin Ethel, "If [Pulitzer] and his ilk are in heaven, I want to go to hell!"*

Consequently, when Bess learned that Harry had agreed to receive an honorary degree from the University of Missouri at Columbia, she reminded him of a little history. "You are right about the Un. of Mo. being late in every particular," Harry replied. "They have always taken their cue from old Joe Pulitzer and Bill Nelson's successors." Still, he had "other fish to fry." Besides, it was convenient. The 35th Division's annual meeting opened in Saint Louis the next day, and both occasions gave him a chance to talk about containment of world communism.

Afterwards, he wrote Bess in part:

[June 11, 1950]

The St. Louis meeting was a most successful one. The Battery breakfast was short, dignified, and to the point. There were seventy-five of them there. We marched from 17th and Olive to the old court house—about a mile and a half. It was hot but no one fell out. The Governor, the Mayor, Louis Johnson,[4] and all my fat and thin aides had to march also.

The speech at Columbia and the one in St. Louis make a complete resumé of the foreign policy of the United States. No one can misunderstand it

---

[4]Secretary of Defense.

or garble it. Acheson[5] will make six speeches in the next month, and I am sure there will be no misunderstanding of our position. It has taken five years to get to this point. I am hoping two more will wind it up. Think—Byrnes, Baruch, Marshall, Molotov, Vishinski, Attlee, Bevin, Mackenzie-King, Churchill—and now Dean Acheson, Schuman, St. Laurent, and Stalin. Byrnes, Molotov, Vishinski, and Bevin have been anything but constructive. The others have brought us to this point. I hope all of us who are left may take us to the right conclusion. It's an awful responsibility. That's what I was thinking when I looked down on those 2,000 young people in the rain on Friday.

[June 12, 1950]

Have had the usual busy day. Big Four at ten. Looks as if we are going to have an 81st Congressional record. . . . Had a cabinet luncheon with Bob Patterson[6] and Averell Harriman as special guests. We had a grand time and finished at 1:10 P.M. Had a forty-minute nap and went back to try and persuade Lovett[7] to go to Europe for me. He could not go—still has trouble with his gall bladder, which has been extracted! The St.

[5]Dean Acheson, who had replaced Marshall as Secretary of State.
[6]Robert P. Patterson, Secretary of War.
[7]Robert Lovett, Under Secretary of Defense.

Louis trip seems to have been very successful politically. Hope that's true. . . . I am going to Quantico on Wednesday night to review the Marines on the morning of the 15th. These military men are the greatest prima donnas. What's the masculine for prima donna?

He reviewed combat field maneuvers at Quantico, Virginia, little knowing that those Marines would soon fight in a real war. Nine days later, the President flew to Kansas City for a weekend rest at home. "I'm so tired, I can hardly wait to get into the house," he said at the curb when he arrived. That evening, the phone rang. The North Koreans had attacked South Korea. Harry Truman had been home just eleven hours, and next day he had to return to Washington.

June 26, 1950

Dear Bess:

We had a grand trip back after we were in the air. [My pilot] Col. Williams was fooling around waiting for Landry[8] to show up. Landry had gone to some golf course, after asking me if it would be all right for him to play Sunday afternoon. But he should have left the name of the club where he intended to play at the hotel. Evidently he arrived at the airport shortly after we were in the air and reported to us about the time we were over St. Louis that he was fifteen minutes behind us. I told the

[8]Presidential air aide, General Robert B. Landry.

communications officer to tell him to go back to K. C., get in touch with Gen. Vaughan and Ted Marks,[9] and bring them in tomorrow. . . .

The crowd at the Washington Airport was made up of the Secs. of State and Defense and Army, Navy and Air.

Had them all to dinner at 8 and the dinner was good and well served. . . . My conference was a most successful one, and there is a chance that things may work out without the necessity of mobilization. Haven't been so badly upset since Greece & Turkey fell into our lap. Let's hope for the best. . . .

I've canceled my sailing trip [on the Potomac]. Don't want to be too far away. . . .

Lots & lots of love and many happy returns for the 31st year of your ordeal with me. It's been *all* pleasure for me.

Harry

[9]An old friend from Battery D days.

XXVIII

"Let's Shoot Him. God Knows He Should Be!"

Back in 1918, Captain Harry Truman, Field Artillery, had looked into the future and thought maybe he'd become "a congressman or something where I can cuss colonels and generals to my heart's content." As it turned out, he did more than cuss a general. In one of the most controversial acts of his presidency, Harry Truman fired a general.

He never liked Douglas MacArthur. Two months after Franklin Roosevelt's death, Truman pondered over "what to do with Mr. Prima Donna, Brass Hat, Five-Star MacArthur." It was, he said "a very great pity we have to have stuffed shirts like that in key positions."

When in 1948 some Republicans advanced the general as their presidential candidate, Truman disliked him all the more. After the MacArthur-for-President boom fizzled that year, Harry gleefully shared with Mary a joke "about the Almighty going back on his boy Mac." It concerned a meeting between Admiral Chester Nimitz and MacArthur. "Nimitz said he couldn't swim but he didn't want it known. Mac said he couldn't walk on water but the Admiral should keep it a secret."

But MacArthur, ensconced in his downtown Tokyo headquarters as U.S. occupation commander in Japan, was a logical choice to oversee American military involvement in Korea. So Truman, taking his cue from a United Nations resolution that the U.S. direct armed resistance to the North Koreans, named MacArthur Supreme Commander of U.N. forces.

In October, after a U.N. counter-attack seized the initiative in Korea, Truman flew to Wake Island in mid-Pacific to confer with the general. The North Koreans were in retreat, and he had to decide whether U.N. forces should penetrate into North Korea. If they did, Communist China, and possibly even the Soviet Union, which also bordered Korea, might intervene, and the President had to weigh the risk.

His recounting of the Wake Island trip afterwards for Cousin Nellie belies the gravity of the situation. Weighing more heavily upon Harry's mind was the recent attempt on his life by two Puerto Rican extremists.

THE WHITE HOUSE

Nov. 17, 1950

Dear Nellie:

I appreciated your letter of Nov. 1 very much. You see my name was not up on that day. I was most happy to see you and Ethel at the luncheon, and I'm sorry I did not get a chance to talk to you both at that time. But as I told Ethel this morning, I'm under a very heavy guard, and while I can send 'em away, if anything should happen they'd be to blame. So I have to "grin and bear it."

You'll be interested maybe in my Wake Island trip. I left here at 2:30 P.M., arrived in St. Louis at about five o'clock. Went to Mary's [Eastern Star] installation, where Vivian & I escorted her to her station. Had lunch with her and her Grand Officers at noon the next day.

Left St. Louis airport at 2:30 C.S.T. and went to an airport between San Francisco and Sacramento where we landed at about 5 P.M. P.S.T. When we went over Kansas City, I could see Atchison, St. Joseph, Topeka, Grandview, and Independence. We were 21,000 feet up. We went from K. C. to Salt Lake in two and one half hours! Grandpa Young took 3 months to make that trip. We landed at an airport called Fairfield between the two California towns named above. I inspected the hospital and shook hands with a lot of Korean wounded.

Boarded the *Independence* about 10:30 P.M. Pacific Time and went to bed. When I awoke the sun was coming up over the Pacific. I went up and sat with the pilot and watched the Hawaiian Islands come into view. We could see all of them from 200 miles away. We landed at 8 A.M. Hawaiian time, went to the Naval Commandant's Hdqs. and then inspected Pearl Harbor. Saw the *Utah* and the *Arizona* in their sunken condition. There are 1,190-

odd men still in the *Arizona* and several hundred in the *Utah* and they can't get to them. Isn't that awful to contemplate?

I called Bess and Margie at 12:30 P.M. H.W. time and it was 5:30 Washington time. We left the H. I. at midnight Saturday and arrived in Wake at 6:30 Sunday next week. MacArthur met me at the landing field and we went to a quonset hut and talked for an hour, then had a session of two hours with Gen. Bradley, Ambassador Jessup, Dean Rusk, Adm. Radford, and my own staff. It was a most satisfactory session and everybody left the conference feeling it was well worth while.

I left Wake about 11:00 A.M. and landed in Honolulu about 5 P.M. I tried to call the folks from Wake but couldn't because of static. Instead of being 5 hours behind as in Honolulu, I'd have been a day ahead. I had two Saturdays and two Sundays in the same week! It just can't happen but it did. On the second Sunday in Honolulu I went swimming, toured the Island, and went to bed at 9:30. Left there at 6:30 the next morning—Monday, landed in San Francisco at 5 P.M. Spent Tuesday going over my speech. Left S. F. about 10 P.M. Tuesday and land[ed] in Washington at 10 A.M. Wednesday. Actual flying time about fifty hours for 14,404 miles. Grandpa wouldn't believe me!

Hope you are well and everything going well. Margie comes down tomorrow. I go on the ship and won't see her until Sunday.

My best to you both,

Harry

Ominous reports began coming in from Korea. At Wake, the President had given MacArthur the green light to attack into North Korea. But as advance units probed northward, they met resistance from a new quarter, Red China. "We face an entirely new war," General MacArthur cabled Washington in late November as thousands of Chinese "volunteers" swarmed into North Korea in massive counter-attack. "General MacArthur is in serious trouble," Truman noted in his diary. "We must get him out of it if we can. . . . It looks very bad."

Next morning, a Sunday, the President picked up some scratch paper and jotted:

Dec. 3, 1950

I slept an hour later this A.M. Arose at 6:30 instead of 5:30. Read all the papers, news, editorials, and even some of the liars (columnists). Looked over the financial reports as they affect government bonds because there is financing to do.

Read the book reviews and tried to weigh the news reports from [the] front with my own inside information. When newspapers stick to news and advertising they are excellent public servants. When [they] editorialize and let liars write editorials for them they are prostitutes of the public mind.

I finally became impatient and called Dean Acheson. He said that he, Gen. Marshall, Gen. Bradley, and Mr. Harriman would be right over.

They had been in conference all morning with the Chiefs of Staff, Secretaries of Army, Navy, and Air and others. Gen. Collins had been delayed on his way to Tokyo and could not report from there until later.

We discussed the situation and Prime Minister Attlee's visit for two hours. No decisions as yet. . . .

His decision, made several days later, put Harry Truman on a collision course with Douglas MacArthur. MacArthur, trained in the tradition of no-holds-barred war and politicians deferring to military leadership, pressed for the bombing of selected Chinese targets and a naval blockade of China's coast. Truman refused. He chose instead to contain the war, to retreat to the 38th parallel that separated South from North Korea, to make a stand there and seek a status quo antebellum—*two Koreas separated at the same place as before. Europe, not Asia, was our first line of defense against world communism, the President maintained; Russia, not China, our chief concern.*

MacArthur would not yield. The general, despite a presidential directive against such public statements, urged a "conventional" military response in Korea. "There is no substitute for victory," he wrote Republican congressional leader Joseph Martin.

Harry Truman fired the general five days after he learned about the letter. He explained why in an unmailed defense intended for a journalist.

The attached editorial—it contains a double-barreled bare-faced lie which I've marked with a red line. I fired the great MacArthur for insubordination and for his effort to tie us up in an all-out war in Asia. I took a 14,000-[mile] air trip in order to have an understanding with him. He told me that the Korean situation was under control, that the Chinese would not come in, that he would release one of our regular divisions for occupation duty in Germany on Jan. 1, and that he would not further make a "chump"—his word not mine—out of himself by dabbling in Republican politics. I believed him. I'd no more than arrived home when Joe Martin published Mac's letter to him.

I fired MacArthur for insubordination and a misstatement of the facts to me at Wake. Of course, truth means not one thing to Roy Howard[1] or your snotty little *News*—but these are the facts.

Working on his memoirs later, Truman sent the section dealing with the MacArthur controversy to Dean Acheson, his former Secretary of State. In his evaluation, Acheson questioned whether the President had presented a strong enough case against the general. He reminded Truman of a statement attributed to Emerson, "If you strike at

[1]Publisher of the Scripps-Howard newspapers.

a king, you must kill him." "MacArthur can be shot right through the heart," Acheson advised. "I do not believe that this text does it." "Something to that," Truman penned in the margin of Acheson's critique. "Let's shoot him. God knows he should be!"²

For the public's part, its initial reaction to MacArthur's firing had been violently anti-Truman. He and Secretary of State Acheson were burned in effigy in cities across America. But within a month, Truman detected a change of mood.

THE WHITE HOUSE

May 19, 1951

Dear Ethel:

Your letter, mailed May 8, has been here some days, but I have had so many chores to do besides my regular 18-hour-a-day commitments that I've just now had the chance to answer. The birthday remembrance came yesterday. It was beautiful and useful. My *good* handkerchiefs somehow disappear and these two are very welcome. Thank you and Nellie very much. . . .

I've had rather a strenuous time even for me in the last three or four weeks. It was necessary to

²The final published account of the MacArthur affair does not, however, differ appreciably from the draft Acheson critiqued. It remains a bland recitation of presidential responsibility and prerogative. See *Memoirs II,* pp. 432-50.

recall the Big General from the Far East if I expected to be President to the end of my term. I knew that the opposition and the crackpots would have a field day and of course they have. But thinking people now seem to understand what was toward.

When stories like this one begin to circulate the country's safe. It seems that a mental expert knocked on St. Peter's Gate and asked for admission. When the expert had stated his case and his background, Peter invited him to come right in. The old saint said that the services of such an expert were needed. He said God had been acting queerly lately and it was the consensus of the saints that the situation should be examined. God had been talking as if he thought he were MacArthur.

Sacrilegious, but American. . . .

Sincerely,
Harry

XXIX

"It Won't Be Long Until You'll Have Neighbors"

The assassination attempt in November 1950, plus the crisis in Korea, put a damper on presidential travel. Feeling more than ever a prisoner in the "Great White Jail," Harry turned his thoughts increasingly to home and family. He wrote more often to cousins Ethel and Nellie, and he sounded a lot like that high school boy Horatio who had penned "Courage is not always in facing the foe but in taking care of those at home." He asked Ethel: "Did you ever stop to think that the troubles of your own family are the troubles of every family? And that if you help alleviate your own, you can and should help as many as you are able to help?"

Looking anxiously toward a quick trip home at Christmastime, he wrote:

THE WHITE HOUSE

Dec. 20, 1950

Dear Nellie:
Was most happy to have your letter of the 16th. I'm glad the folks arrived home safely and in good

shape. I've been afraid for four years that every trip Mrs. Wallace would take would be her last. But we have a very able young doctor, an assistant to Dr. Graham who does hardly anything but look after her. She likes him and he's been able to persuade her to do what she should. You know that she and Bess are allergic to M.D.s since old Krimminger[1] died. I can make Bess do what she should, but it's harder with Mrs. Wallace. But she's alive because Dr. Graham and his helper have seen to it.

Glad you like[d] my Emergency speech. It had to be told.[2]

Hope you have a fine Christmas dinner—with plenty of sugar in the cranberry sauce!

Expect to be home Friday for a real go around. Looks as if everybody wants to control my movements out there, and only the Secret Service can do that.

I'll see you soon.

Sincerely,
Harry

While home, he dedicated a new Baptist church in Grandview.

Jan. 20, 1951

Dear Nellie:

I appreciated your good letter very much. It has

---

[1]Dr. C. E. Krimminger, the Wallace family physician.
[2]Because of Chinese intervention in Korea, on December 16 the President declared a state of national emergency.

been like spring here for the last few days too. I always enjoyed looking at those famous seed books in spring. But I could never get things to come from the seeds as the colored pictures in the books showed them.

Thanks for the piece about the dedication of the Grandview church. I had a letter from a man over at Barny in Platte County giving me the early Masonic record of Grandpa Truman. He joined the lodge over there nearly a hundred years ago. Then in 1872 moved his membership to Raytown. The Raytown records were burned up when the Lodge Hall burned down about 30 years ago. . . . .

Say hello to Ethel.

Sincerely,
Harry

Then he had some information for Ethel, the family historian.

THE WHITE HOUSE

May 4, 1951

Dear Ethel:

Enclosed is a piece from the Herkimer *Evening Tribune* of Herkimer, N.Y. It was sent to Joe Short[3] by Lee Allen, the managing editor. It is interesting to say the least. You know, there once was a Harry L. Truman who lived at Independence, Kansas. I sometimes received his mail.

[3]Presidential Press Secretary.

These N.Y. Trumans were bankers and tall-hat citizens. There is a town in the neighborhood of Utica called Trumansburg. Can't you see the top banker there squirm when someone asks him if he's kin of that low occupant of the White House?

My best to Nellie and all the family & you too.

Harry

"I sent Ethel a book from Ky. which showed that our great grandfather paid his taxes," he later wrote Nellie. *"That's really something. I wonder if my great-grandson goes to jail if I'll get the credit. I probably will."* He added:

Now this seventy business seems to be a delicate subject. You, Ralph, and Myra are there. I'll be there soon, and so will Ethel, Vivian, Mary, and all the rest. We'll have to take it.

He never missed a 35th Division reunion, except in the summer of '51. "I can't be present in To-peka," he wrote Ralph. "The Secret Service have received more than the usual number of threats to rub me out," he explained. While he didn't fear so much for his own safety, "what worries me is that some good fellow who has three or four kids may get killed—to keep me from that fate. You've no idea how it feels to have a grand man killed and two more badly wounded protecting you. So I'm not coming."

Margaret meanwhile toured Europe, and her

Washington-bound father enjoyed her trip vicariously.

THE WHITE HOUSE

June 12, 1951

Dear Margie:

It was nice to talk to you Sunday and I'm looking forward to the same experience next Sunday. Here are a couple of pictures of your mamma which appeared in the *Mayflower Magazine* for June. I'm always sending her pictures of you in London and other places, so I thought turn-about would be fair play.

The reaction here to your English visit has been perfect—fantastic, in fact. I've had numerous pieces from papers in England, all favorable, and letters and reports from people who have seen you at various places; General Bradley, Bob Sherwood,[4] to name a couple. You must have had a grand time at Old Lady Astor's party. I am glad you went to Stratford and the Tower. I imagine the Tower [of London] was better than the Astor party.

I am hoping that you may have as interesting [a] time in Holland, Belgium, France, Luxembourg, and Italy as you have had in Britain. If the damned French will let you alone, you should have a grand time in Paris. There's lots to see in that town. . . .

When your dad went to France in 1918, he was under wraps, but he saw many interesting and

[4]Robert Sherwood, former Roosevelt speech writer.

beautiful things. . . . Hope you will be able to look at my command post across from Ft. Taranne at Verdun; you probably won't.

When you go to Rome, be very careful. Your dad's a Baptist, the most democratic of religious organizations and sometimes the most bigoted. You'll see the head of the most autocratic of religions. He's a great man, but he stands for autocracy in the minds of men where the worship of God is concerned. Remember your English Church statement "that where two or three are gathered together for worship of God, there He will be," whether Pope, Bishop, Priest, or Rector is present.

So, don't be taken in by the glamor of the Archbishop of Canterbury, the Bishop of Rome, or any other self-appointed Vicar of the Prince of Peace. Just be the great daughter that you are of a Missouri farmer, Grand Master of Masons, and Roger Williams Baptist.

Have all the fun you can now, because in 40 years you'll be sixty-seven! Your dad was twenty-seven once!

Lots of love,
Dad

He did get away to make a dedication speech at a new air research center in Tennessee. He wrote Bess beforehand, "I'm going to tear the Russians and the Republicans apart—call a spade just what it is, and tell Malik[5] if Russia wants peace,

[5]Jacob A. Malik, Soviet U.N. representative.

peace is available and has been since 1945." As for his enemies at home, the McCarthyites, Truman demanded they stop their "political smear campaign." "Lies, slander, mud-slinging are the weapons of the totalitarians. No man of morals or ethics will use them."

But he also had trouble with Democrats. While Congress remained in their hands after the 1950 elections, conservatives had gained strength. Aided by the exigencies of war, they blocked the President's Fair Deal proposals.They also held up requests for stiff price controls.

This, plus the protracted fighting in Korea, concerned Truman one weekend as the U.S.S. Williamsburg glided toward Chesapeake Bay.

U.S.S. Williamsburg
[June 30, 1951]

I go on a weekend "rest" Friday, June 29, 1951. Have quite a schedule for the day. Several extras not on the official list. At 5:15 P.M. I depart for the *Williamsburg*. Have Chief Taylor give me a rubdown after a hot and cold shower. Sit on the fantail from six-fifteen after calling Bess at six. It is as hot as ninety probably, with a slight breeze.

Because of the Russian-Chinese-Korean situation, the Secretary of State, Mr. Acheson, the Secretary of Defense, General Marshall, the Deputy Secretary of Defense, Mr. Lovett, the chairman of the Chiefs of Staff, General Bradley, and Asst. Sec. of State, Dean Rusk, come aboard at 6:45 and have dinner. After dinner we discuss a directive to General Ridgeway. After much discussion, a directive is approved and my guests leave at about 9:30 P.M. I call Short[6] and inform him that no important policy matters were discussed. Talk to Senator Ernest Mc-Farland[7] and tell him in no uncertain terms what I think of last night's performance in the Senate.

Go to bed about 11 P.M. and sleep like a log until five in the morning, when we have a thunder storm and a very heavy downpour of rain. Go back to bed and sleep until seven. Get up, shave, dress and have breakfast at 8:15. At nine I call Mr. Murphy, Mr. Stowe and Mr. Hopkins.[8] After talking to them, the barber of the ship gives me a haircut. Then I talk to Mr. Averell Harriman about Yalta, Iran and China.

Commander Bill Rigdon brings me various documents to sign. Captain MacDonald had brought me letters to sign to Senators McKellar and McFarland and Congressman Cannon as a result of my conversation with Sen. McFarland last night.[9] I try to sit on the upper deck and relax—no soap. So I come back to my desk, clean out the file, read the quarterly report of the De-

[6]Joseph H. Short, Secretary to the President.
[7]Democratic majority leader from Arizona.
[8]White House staff members.
[9]Reference is to requests Truman sent these legislators asking for committee action on bottled up legislation.

fense Production Administration and get ready for lunch.

Some rest! No President ever had any real rest! Why should I try.

Except for a quick jaunt to Detroit to commemorate the city's 250th anniversary in July, Truman stayed close to his desk until autumn. "Wish I could come home like anybody else and do as I please," he lamented to Bess as he prepared to fly to San Francisco to open the Japanese Peace Treaty Conference in early September. "Hope you and Margie are having a nice evening—not as lonely and homesick as mine. I have your groceries all assembled. If we stop for gas in K. C. on the way out, I'll unload them and send them to you."

Returning from San Francisco, he stopped off at Independence for a few days. Then for the family it was back to Blair House, because the White House was still under construction. He wrote Nellie:

Oct. 14, 1951

I've just finished off a dinner of roast beef and browned potatoes, and a good nap—so I suppose I've gained a pound and a half, and Doc is mean as he can be about that. I'm half starved all the time!

Bess, Margaret, and I went over to "the House" just before dinner and surveyed it from cellar to garret. Hadn't been in it for two weeks

and believe it or not, they are making *some* prog-
ress. We may move back into it a *few* days before
my term expires. If the damned Congress had
been willing to trust me to do the job, I'd have
had it done a year and a half ago for two million
less money!

His next visit home was at Christmastime.

[Diary, New Year's Day, 1952]

What a year this 1952 may be. . . .
    The evening of the 24th I acted as installing
officer for Grandview Lodge 618, A. F. & A.
M. of Missouri. I started that organization in
1911, was its first elected Master in the fall. My
appearance on the 24th 1951 was the fortieth installation under its charter.
    We had a grand Christmas as usual. Presents
from the family opened around ten o'clock.
Then a big turkey dinner with all the trimmings.
I visited my cousins across the street, my
brother and sister at Grandview, and went to
bed early. Had [also] spent some time at work
on the message on the State of the Union.

*His last year as President, his travel schedule
was lighter. A speech in New York and a Key West
vacation in March ("I've had some rest and a
change of scene, but I still sign my name 600 times
a day!"), a flight to Omaha to inspect flood damage in April, another New York speech and trips to
West Point and the U.S. Naval Academy in May,*

388

and, in June, Harry revived his acquaintance with the 35th Division in Springfield, Missouri.

The Chamber of Commerce gave him an "Ozark Hillbilly Medallion." He made the usual march up the avenue with his comrades. And they in turn heard a speech, this time about America's defense posture vis à vis the Soviets.

Of course, Cousin Ralph was there. In fact, Ralph and Olive lived in Springfield, and Harry stopped by the house.

THE WHITE HOUSE

June 21, 1952

Dear Ralph & Olive:
I have been covered up since the Springfield Reunion—hence the delay in writing you.

I think we had the greatest meeting we've ever had—thanks to you. . . .

It was a pleasure to sign all the books and programs. Tell Henrietta[10] to send me copies of the pictures she made. . . .

Things have been in a turmoil since I returned. I suppose we'll work things out—we always do. When I go away for a day, my 600 signatures become 1200 and it takes me two more days to catch up. . . .

Take care of yourselves.

Sincerely,
Harry

---

[10]Ralph's daughter by a previous marriage.

389

1952 was a presidential election year, and Harry Truman wasn't running. Nearly two full terms in the White House was enough for him. He had written Nellie the year before:

Bess and I will spend our time across the street from you and Ethel, I hope after 1952. Maybe we can come over and finish up that Cicero and Caesar lesson. I'm sure you can still give us the necessary information. I'm looking forward to retirement with the rest of you, and to ten years of a happy existence with all of you.

While he wasn't pleased with Adlai Stevenson, the Democratic Presidential nominee in 1952 (he wrote Stevenson two unmailed letters threatening to withdraw his support), Truman's distaste for GOP candidate Dwight Eisenhower and his loyalty to the Democratic party dictated his actions. Before joining battle in the campaign, and still smarting over failure to legislate a national health insurance program, he wrote Nellie, who had just returned home from the hospital.

September 14, 1952

Dear Nellie:

I am more than happy that you will be walking again soon. You have found out by awful experience what I have been working for in hospital and health care. Doctors are made up of a cross section of humanity as it is. There are good ones, honest ones, conscientious ones, false front ones, and

390

plain incompetents. I am sure happy that you have found a good, competent, and conscientious one. That is what my health program means, to try to educate more honest, conscientious, and able doctors and arrange things so that they can be adequately paid for their work and their knowledge. If that is wrong, then so am I.[11]

I'll make you a bet that Dan Deets will make the Plymouth run like a new one. He is an honest car doctor. . . .

Margie is somewhere between New Mexico and Los Angeles. She'll be on a show with Jimmy Durante, Sept. 20 at 8 o'clock our time. I think that is 6 o'clock your time. After the show she is coming back here to go with me on my northwest campaign. I leave here on Sept. 27 by train for Montana by way of Chicago, St. Paul, Fargo, Glasgow, Mont., and intermediate points. Then to Spokane & Seattle, Washington, San Francisco, Utah, Colorado Springs, Iowa, St. Joseph, Sedalia, Jefferson City, Buffalo, N.Y., Harlem and back to the capital.

I'm in doubt about the good it will do. People are funny, sometimes phoney. Members of labor

---

[11]Medicare, signed into law by President Lyndon B. Johnson in a ceremony honoring Truman at the Truman Library in 1965, contained part of HST's original design. For the story of Truman's fight with the American Medical Association over this issue, see the editor's *Harry S. Truman Versus the Medical Lobby: The Genesis of Medicare* (Columbia, University of Missouri Press, 1979).

unions vote against their bosses in politics—Ohio for Taft, Wisconsin for McCarthy. Look what Mo. did to the no-good candidate I endorsed.[12] I hope they won't put Stevenson in the same class!

Tell Ethel to be a good *girl*.

Sincerely, Harry

In San Francisco, on Fairmont Hotel stationery, the President described the first week of the campaign.

Sunday, Oct. 5, 1952

We arrived here Friday evening, Oct. 3rd, after a trip across the continent from Washington beginning Saturday night, September 27th. Went to church in the oldest one in town—140-year-old Baptist church—Bethany Church of Wooster. The preacher had an impediment in his speech—but when he started his sermon it was forgotten. He gave us a lesson I won't forget.

We started the political campaign at Fargo, North Dakota early in the morning, 8:30 A.M. Not so early by farmer standards, but by eastern getting-up time, very early.

It was necessary to set the pattern of the "Whistle-Stop Campaign" at the first official

[12]Truman had unsuccessfully backed Missouri Attorney General J. E. "Buck" Taylor in the state's Democratic primary for the United States Senate race. Taylor's opponent, Stuart Symington, ultimately won the Senate seat.

392

stop. We did it by changing the Republican slogan "Look ahead Neighbor" to "Look out Neighbor." That slogan was stressed all the way across North Dakota and Montana.

At Spokane, Washington, we really started the Whistle-Stop technique. From there it was tops.

When he got to Buffalo, New York, again he made use of hotel stationery.

Had a grand reception and an enthusiastic meeting here yesterday. The kept press tried by every hook and crook to make it appear that the visit was not a success.

The morning and afternoon sheets which pose as newspapers are owned by the same outfit and controlled by anti-administration interests. But they have no political influence.

In my state, the St. Louis *Post-Dispatch* wobbles always. In 1932 that paper supported Roosevelt, in 1936 it was against him. In 1940 the *P.D.* was for Willkie. In 1944 it was for Dewey, and in 1948 it was for Dewey for the same reason. Now that character assassin sheet is on our side. It is no asset.

Eisenhower clobbered Stevenson in November. For the first time in twenty years a Republican prepared to move into the White House.

Fifty-six days before he and Bess turned over the "Great White Jail" to Ike, Harry wrote his final letter as President to Nellie. He didn't mention it, but it was also the centennial of his mother's birth.

THE WHITE HOUSE

November 25, 1952

Dear Nellie:

I was most happy to have your good letter. This business of leaving the presidential office is quite a job. Ike came to see me and he was not at all happy when he left. He found that being President is a sort of a working job and Ike doesn't like to work—either mentally or physically. What a fool he is to have left "social security" in the form of lifetime pay and emoluments of a 5-star general and move into the most controversial and nerve-wracking job in the world!

I have had a lot of fine letters from people I've never heard of and none of the mean sort. The public isn't right sure what it has gained. The fear is that something has been lost. I wonder. We'll have to wait and see.

I'll be home about Jan. 23, '53 and go on from there. . . .

It won't be long until you'll have neighbors.

Sincerely,
Harry

XXX

"I Took the Grips Up to the Attic"

[Interview, Phoenix, Ariz.]
[Nov. 15, 1978]

EDITOR MONTE POEN: Now, you were the mayor of Independence. I've heard the story that when the President got home he took the luggage up to the attic. Is that the kind of man he was?

BOB WEATHERFORD: That's right. I asked him the next morning. I said, "What was the first thing you did, Mr. President, when you got home?" And he said, "I took the grips up to the attic."

The newspapers said Harry Truman went home to retire. They were wrong. Over the next decade his grips were usually out of the attic and on the road. He kept on the move campaigning for Democrats, speaking at fund-raisers to build a presidential library, accepting various honors, lecturing at colleges, and making three trips abroad.

First, Harry and Bess took a vacation cruise to Hawaii. Margaret went along, and in Hawaii the three enjoyed the hospitality of oil millionaire Edwin Pauley, who turned his private preserve,

Coconut Island, over to them.

Pauley's children were on the island too, and a former President got a big kick out of their playful antics, so much so that he joined in and created a mythical "Coconut Cabinet." Every kid became a member and Harry later sent each an engraved, signed certificate. One read:

Stephen Pauley, Secretary of Mischief, whose authority runs to short sheeting, frogs and snakes in beds, and whatever else causes laughter and ridiculous situations.

His job is to persuade the Secretary of Defense that all things in his department are necessary for the happiness of the inhabitants of Coconut Island.

Back in Independence, Harry and Bess planned another trip, this time by car to visit old friends in Washington. "Isn't it good to be on our own again, doing as we please as we did in the old Senate days?" Bess said, as Harry propelled them along Missouri's Highway 24. Yes, indeed, it was grand, he replied. But their experience as ordinary tourists was short-lived.

HOTEL McLURE

[Wheeling, West Virginia]
Friday, June 19, 1953

Left home at 7:15 A.M. in the new Chrysler New

Yorker. It was a very hot day from the start. Drove on Highway 24 to Monroe City where we went into [Highway] 36.

Had lunch at Hannibal at the junction of Highways 36 and 61. It was a good fruit plate with iced tea for the drink. We thought we were getting by big as an unknown traveling couple until we went to the counter to pay the bill. Just as we arose from the table, some county judges came in and the incog[nito] was off.

His second year out of office proved hectic and frustrating. There were memoirs to write and a library to build, but both projects had to wait. One summer evening, as Harry and Bess enjoyed music in Kansas City's Swope Park, a gall bladder attack folded the President in pain, requiring immediate surgery.

Recovered by December, he flew to Philadelphia to speak at a postponed library fund-raising dinner. Because his airplane had mechanical trouble, Bess and Margaret saw him off twice on this trip. Harry's problems getting off the ground that day no doubt stiffened Bess's resolve made years before to stay firmly on it.

THE BELLEVUE-STRATFORD

Philadelphia, Pa.
Dec. 12, 1954

. . . Arrived at the K. C. airport at 4:05. The head

of TWA was ready to receive us. The plane on which I was to go was not coming in until 4:10 P.M.—due at 3:20 P.M.

When it came in at 4:20 the man in charge of TWA at the K. C. airport took me aboard. Started off and then came back—an engine, No. 4, was out. The nice stewardess said 10 minutes would be the delay. I dismounted and Bess, Margie, and I sat around until 6:30 when I left on another TWA flight.

Arrived in Chicago after a flight of an hour and forty-five minutes. When we were ready to leave the Chicago airport after a thirty-minute transfer, the new plane had to return to pick up the baggage which they'd left without! Arrived in the City of Brotherly Love at 12:15 A.M., Dec 13, 1954.

The mayor, Mr. Clark, and a whole delegation had stayed up to meet me. I still can't understand why people want to treat me as if I were the No. 1 citizen of the country. Of course, I'm not. Ike is. . . .

At 11:30 we went down to Independence Hall and I presented a portrait of Benjamin Franklin to Mr. McKay, Sec. of the Interior, who has charge of public parks. The picture was made back in the 1770s by a sixth-great-grand nephew of Cardinal Richelieu. It was presented to me by Gen. De Gaulle when he was president of France. . . . Since old man Franklin made his fortune and his reputation in Philadelphia, I thought Independence Hall was the proper place for the picture.

Wanting to visit Europe again, yet with memoirs to finish and speaking dates to meet, the best Margaret Truman's father could do was to enjoy hearing about her trip there.

Kansas City, Mo.
August 19, 1955

Dear Margie:

Your mamma & I were most happy to have your two letters—one from the ship and one from the Woodwards.[1] You must have had a fine crossing and you seem to be having a grand time. I am glad for both.

It must be a lovely country from your description. Hope to see it some day along with Venice, Milan, Florence, and Rome. I am anxious to see Vienna and Istanbul too. If things work out as planned, maybe we can see them together along with your mother. . . .

I'm still reading proof, both for you and me. Yours is excellent. I'm not so sure about mine. It's going to stir up the animals, but I don't care. Have some speaking to do in Indiana, Michigan, & Calif. in a week or two, and that'll do some stirring too.

My best to the Woodwards. Let us hear from you & often.

Sincerely & lovingly,
Dad

[1]Margaret was house guest at the Austrian estate of Mr. and Mrs. Stanley Woodward.

Kansas City, Mo.
August 20, 1955

Dear Margie:

I sent you a letter yesterday but it was written in a big hurry. There was a Mennonite preacher waiting to give me a book he'd written and to ask me about Guam where he was going to teach history. The book is good but I couldn't reciprocate because I've never been to Guam. I did try to give it civil government, and did—over the violent protest of the Navy.

I also gave Puerto Rico home rule and insisted on setting up the Republic of the Philippines over protests of special interests. I appointed a native to be governor of the Virgin Islands too. Ike sent an Iowa Negro to the Virgins and he failed dismally, and now he's sent a California one. He just doesn't know the history of home rule and self-government.

Look magazine has come out with a pack of lies about the relations between Ike and me. It is funny as can be. Ike's gone fishing, Congress has adjourned, and your dad is about the best news source to pick on, I suppose.

I'm getting letter after letter asking me to go back to 1600 Penn. Avenue—but I'm not going, and that's not saying I couldn't. Wish I could be 50 instead of 70. I'd take 'em around the bend you bet. Your mamma's in better shape than she's been since we left the Great White Jail, and I'm not going to put her to bed by going back there.

Wish we could be with you. I want to see Venice

& Vienna (Wien) so badly. Hope you'll make it clear to the Woodwards that your mother & dad highly appreciate their hospitality to you. Keep us informed as much as you can. We miss your phone talks. Almost called you Sunday.

I'm going to a synagogue tomorrow. Mamma says I should join and be a rabbi!

Lots of love,
Dad

Oxford University offered him an honorary degree, and in 1956 the former President tied the invitation in with a tour of western Europe. Before he and Bess could go, however, two things, one painful and the other a delight, had to be accomplished—finishing the memoirs and attending Margaret's wedding.

Margaret, who had abandoned her singing career to become an NBC television personality (including a stint as Edward R. Murrow's replacement on a "Person to Person" program wherein she interviewed her parents), "had found a grand man," her father decreed, referring to New York Times *journalist Clifton Daniel, Jr. Following Margaret's wedding (in the same Episcopal church where Harry and Bess had exchanged their vows), the long-awaited European trip began.*

They sailed to Le Havre, France, and from there traveled to Paris, Rome, Naples, Florence, Venice, Salzburg, Munich, Bonn, Brussels, and The Hague. They concluded the trip in England, where Harry received the Oxford degree and visited with former Prime Minister Sir Winston Churchill.

Philadelphia mayor Joseph Clark, Jr., in England to write a series of newspaper articles, observed the English people shower accolades upon their wartime ally. It made him proud to be an American, Clark wrote in his piece about the Oxford ceremony, and he later sent Mr. Truman a copy.

Touched deeply by what Clark had written, the former President penned a reply and kept a copy for his files:

> Kansas City, Mo.
> July 28, '56

Dear Mayor Clark:

I came downtown this morning to sign some books and a lot of mail the office force had prepared for me. My correspondence is terrific, the largest for an individual in this part of the country.

I opened it, read it, read the column you enclosed, and did exactly what I did at Oxford. I wiped my eyes and my glasses.

You know, I'm a damned sentimentalist who is as contrary as hell in fundamental things, but who can be deeply touched on a personal basis.

That column of yours hit me where I live and I'll never forget it. . . .

> My best to your family,
> Harry

While in Europe, Truman himself wrote newspaper articles. If he hadn't, he and Bess wouldn't have gone. Congress was still debating whether former presidents deserved a pension, and until it legislated one, Harry had to depend upon money generated by his writing and speechmaking. He could have parlayed his position into a six-figure income (advertisers beseeched him to endorse their products), but he refused—the presidency was not for sale. He did share in the proceeds when his mother's farm in Grandview was sold (Harry had helped reclaim it years before, after the 1940 mortgage foreclosure), but with an office to rent, a secretarial staff to pay, and stamps to buy, the money dwindled rapidly.

Writing to a rich Illinois friend, the former President lamented: "One of my difficulties is that I have had no opportunity for a stay in Florida or to cross the ocean on a ship or to do anything for rest and relaxation." He was constantly bombarded, he said, by people wanting him to make appearances. "You millionaire lawyers can go away when you feel like it and come back when you feel like, and perhaps one of these days Congress will fix up former Presidents so that they can act like other retired people, even if they can't save any money."

Congress came across in the summer of 1958. It granted former Presidents an annual pension of $25,000 and additional money for office and staff. Harry and Bess celebrated by returning to Europe, this time for just "rest and relaxation."

Sam and Dorothy Rosenman accompanied them. Sam, a New York lawyer, had served Franklin Roosevelt as a speech writer, had stayed on to *help Truman when Roosevelt died, and now during HST's post-presidency handled legal matters for him.*

The Rosenman's were inveterate travelers, but as Dorothy remembers, vacationing with Harry and Bess was something special.

[Interview, New York City]
[December 15, 1980]

When we went to France, we went in the expectation we were going to lead a very private life. We really did, with a few exceptions, but it was an endeavor because every place [the President] went, he was recognized. As soon as we went to the Matisse Chapel at Vence the nuns recognized him. We had to see every single solitary thing. They took out all the robes and everything.

[Unknown to the Trumans, Sam had also made arrangements for them to visit Picasso, who lived near Cannes.]

One morning we were sitting out on the terrace having breakfast, and I said, "If we're going to see Picasso, we'd better call and make an appointment." And at that (the President had gone inside for a moment) Bess said, "I don't think we ought to go see Picasso." I said, "Why not?" Bess said, "You know what Harry thinks about modern paintings." [Sam and I] both said, "You've got something there." When [the President] came back, I said, "Bess raises a point," and I repeated it. He said, "Of course I want to

404

go. He's the foremost painter of the time; of course I won't say anything to hurt his feelings."

[After viewing Picasso's latest work, the party left his house and entered the garden.]

I was walking with Picasso; Sam was walking with the President, and [Mr. Truman] mumbled, "How can Dorothy rave about those things? They're God-awful!"

Picasso asked, "Have you been to the pottery works?" We said, "No, but we're going." He hopped in the car and rode along. [Arriving there] Picasso said to Mrs. Truman and me, "Will you each select a plate?" That plate over there [nodding in its direction] is what I selected. It's quite a conventional plate. Mrs. Truman selected one with a design that was truly Picasso. I mumbled to her, "Why do you select that? You know you don't like that type." She said, "If I'm going to have a Picasso, I'm going to have a Picasso!"

Then Picasso asked, "Have you been down to my museum?" We said, "No, but we're going there." So we went along. I didn't notice, but you enter it through a chapel. When we came out, Bess said, "It won't do her any good! It won't do her any good!" After we got in the car and had left, I said, "What did you mean?" Well, they had noticed that Jacqueline [his secretary] had crossed herself as we went into the chapel. She was not married to Picasso at the time but was living with him, and Bess said, "It won't help her; it won't help her a bit!"

They spent a month at a château in the South of France, making excursions like the one to see Picasso, visiting historical spots, and savoring the food at various restaurants.

Each day, the President took his brisk walk before breakfast, and finally, after making a number of concessions, he persuaded Sam to go along. At Sam's insistence, they started at "a decent time," eight o'clock instead of six. Huffing and puffing alongside Truman, Sam said, "My children will never believe this!" and he kiddingly demanded some kind of proof.

Next morning, Sam arose to find that the President, waiting for him, had written up a "diploma" of accomplishment for his hiking companion. Upon Sam's further insistence, Harry even got the "diploma" notarized.

SS)
France)

Now comes Harry S. Truman, who being duly sworn, doth depose and state as follows, to wit:

That on certain days between the 7th day of June 1958 and the 30th day of June 1958, twelve days in all, Samuel I. Rosenman, a person well known and highly regarded as to truth and veracity by said Harry S. Truman, did arise at an early hour on each of said days and walk over certain parts of the Alpes Maritimes in the southern part of France from eight o'clock until ten o'clock for a distance each day of 2.7 kilometers or nearly two miles at a hundred and twenty steps per minute, duly timed and counted, without stopping until the whole distance was covered: that said Samuel I. Rosenman did this of his own free will and accord without coercion; and further deposent saith not.

(signed) Harry S. Truman

(seal)

When they returned to the States the former President again plunged into the whirligig of politics. 1958 was a congressional election year, and because Adlai Stevenson had lost a second time to Eisenhower two years before, Democrats still considered Truman titular head of their party.

Charlie Murphy, who helped schedule HST's campaign appearances and who went along, recalls:

[Interview, Washington, D.C.]
[December 11, 1980]

We had a lot of fun really, on his campaign trips. That was before there was any such thing as Secret Service protection for former Presidents, or staff assistants and things of that kind. So, our travel arrangements were . . . not very elaborate, I would say. Most of the time we traveled by commercial airlines, and from time to time by borrowed private airplane. We would borrow almost anyone's plane who would lend us one and some of them were quite nice and some were not so nice, but President Truman never complained. . . .

He, of course, was well along in years [in 1958], and this was rather strenuous activity. When I got to Kansas City and Independence, I found out that his staff there and also Mrs. Truman were rather worried about his beginning this strenuous period of activity. I was right much troubled by that and I began to worry also, but all things considered, I did not try to get him to call it off. So, we started out on our travels. It seemed to me as time went on during those six weeks that he got younger and more vigorous, and I got older and all worn out.

Truman's campaign pace can be sensed from two notes he drafted in New York City.

Sept. 16, 1958

Arrived in N.Y. City at 5:15 P.M., an hour late. Clifton Daniel met Mrs. T and me, along with Bill Hillman,[2] Mr. Mooney of the Mo. Pac., a representative of the Penna. R.R., and reporters and photographers. Went to the Carlyle Hotel and then to Clif & Margie's apartment across the street to see the grandson. He was up and waiting. Walking now and saying words. He is very

[2]Hillman served as a speech writer.

408

intelligent, at least his grandfather thinks so.

Had dinner at the Carlyle with Mrs. T & Clif and went to bed early because tomorrow will be a go-around.

Sept. 17, 1958

Had breakfast with Gov. Harriman, Frank Hogan, candidate for Senate in N.Y. State, and Murphy, Hillman, Dave Lloyd, Sam Rosenman, and Don Donahue. It was a most interesting breakfast. Harriman & Hogan had an argument over Hogan's successor as Dis. Atty. of N.Y. County. The governor appoints the successor. It was a hot one and Sam Rosenman was in the middle. [I] finally stopped it, and went over to Margie's apt. for breakfast with Clif and the baby.

Came back to the Carlyle and answered phone calls, fixed up a speech for Baltimore, and at 11:30 went to the N.Y. Adv[ertisers] for luncheon celebrating 50th anniversary of Mo. University School of Journalism. Had a chance to tell all the stuffed-shirt editors and publishers what I thought of them. The Cowles outfit, *Detroit Free Press,* K. C. *Star,* Chicago *Tribune, St. Louis P-D,* and every other magazine and newspaper that had circulated lies and character assassination articles about me. For me it was a most satisfactory meeting. I had them where they couldn't run out and had a chance to talk very frankly to them.

Had to hurry to the airport and fly in a private plane to Atlantic City for the meeting with the Steel Workers Union. Never had a happier or a more cordial meeting. Dave McDonald, the president, gave me a marvelous introduction. Never at any meeting have I had a more cordial & enthusiastic welcome.

Flew back to N.Y. and had dinner at the Carlyle with Clif & Mrs. T.

The elections over, his pace hardly slackened. "I really don't know how he stands up under the constant harrassment (photos, interviews, autographs) of an admiring public. He is a wonder!*," an exhausted friend wrote Truman's secretary after making a trip with him. The secretary replied, "The President took off again this morning—this time by Army plane with Gen. Wally Graham—for Houston, Missouri down in the Ozarks where he will dedicate a new hospital. He has to be back again to finish up this month's article for North American Newspaper Alliance which must be telegraphed in before 5:00 P.M. today."*

Fittingly, Grandpa Truman's first letter to Margaret's firstborn, Clifton Truman Daniel, Jr., included photos of vintage airplanes.

Independence, Mo.
September 24, 1959

Dear Kiffie:

Here are some plane pictures that your grandfather found in a magazine. I am very sure you will like them, so I am sending them to you for your pleasure and entertainment.

When you grow up you may have a chance to ride in one of them. I hope you will enjoy that ride.

Give your father and mother a big hug and kiss for

Grandpa

He liked to stay at the Carlyle Hotel on his visits to Kiffie and the family, and from time to time there were things forgotten ("Please mail my laundry." "That cane I left in the hotel is my favorite walking cane."), and things that went awry. Stuck once in the hotel's elevator, Truman later assured the Carlyle's manager that no apology was necessary, that he "spent a very pleasant few minutes talking to the people on the second floor through that part of the elevator door which could be opened."

From Washington D.C.'s Mayflower Hotel, on Jan. 7, 1959, he wrote the last letter home to Bess that has surfaced to date. He had come for a political strategy meeting. "As you know," he told her, "we are up against it for a winning [presidential] candidate in 1960. After much discussion we come to the conclusion that, at the present time, Stuart Symington is the best bet."

Symington, a United States senator from Missouri, remained Harry's choice through the 1960 Democratic convention (which, Truman claimed, was rigged by John F. Kennedy's rich old man). When Kennedy won the nomination, Truman belatedly joined ranks with the young senator from

Massachusetts and effectively campaigned where Kennedy needed help most, in the South.

Two years later, Truman participated in his last campaign. This time it was Idaho Democrats who needed help. They were fighting amongst themselves, and the former President went to Idaho Falls to urge party unity. "From what I've found out, the ticket is in one terrible fix," he penned on hotel stationery. He intended to tell them, "Now you get your nominees together, get behind your whole ticket before you ask me to come back to Idaho." If they didn't, he warned, the Republicans will "just make chumps out of you and beat the whole ticket. If that is what you want, go ahead and stick your tongues out at each other."

But when he got to Pocatello, tough words yielded to good fun. During a banquet there, he donned an Indian chieftain's headdress, and when he got back to Independence he learned that the Pocatello Chamber of Commerce had designated him "Chief 'Give 'em Hell' Harry." Affixed to their proclamation was a picture of the chief, one Harry S. Truman, grinning beneath his Indian regalia. "And I've laughed at a former President!" Truman chided himself, thinking back to a similar picture of Calvin Coolidge. "Got hooked on this one," he confessed to his secretary.

He would also remember 1962 as a time of deep personal loss. Cousin Ralph died in April. "Can a person die over a broken heart?" Ralph's widow Olive asked their doctor after the general suffered a massive coronary. "Yes, it's possible," the doctor *said, and Olive added:*

[Interview, Kansas City, Mo.]
[November 12, 1980]

I told him, "I think that's what killed him because they're tearing up the 35th Division, and it was just killing him seeing that division torn all to pieces." There was just a brigade left in Missouri, and a brigade left in Kansas, and they had taken Nebraska out of it entirely.

[She called to tell Harry of Ralph's death.]

He was shocked. I know, I could tell that he started to cry. He came down to Springfield . . . , and I asked the President, "Will you go up to the funeral home and to the cemetery with me?" And he said, "Yes." He rode with me in the car, and sitting up there at the gravesite he held my hand so tight that I thought he was going to break it part of the time. About the time the service was over, he leaned over to me and he said, "Olive, I'm not going back to the hotel with you. I'm going to leave right now because if anybody says anything to me I'll cry, and I can't stand to see a man cry. I just can't stand it."

And so he got up and left.

The following year, replying to friends who wrote him from Teheran, Iran, Harry said, "That is one place and one country I want to see before the 'long call' comes!" But he never did. His last overseas trip was to Athens in 1964 to attend, at the

413

request of President Lyndon Johnson, the funeral of King Paul of Greece. As Margaret remembers:

[Interview, New York City]
[December 16, 1980]

My husband went with him. I was having some child or other—I was always having children in those days. [My father] stayed up half the night, not thinking of the difference in time. He stayed up half the night playing poker—General Vaughan was along.

He got there the next day, and he went sightseeing—he wanted to see the Acropolis. Then, all of a sudden, the king, the then King of Greece, King Constantine, decided he would have a dinner party for the visiting dignitaries which hadn't been specified—black tie. My father had to borrow a black tie from Henry Lubolise, who was our Ambassador.

He went to that dinner party, he went to the funeral obviously, he toured around Greece as much as he could in and around Athens, came home and immediately went into his eightieth birthday celebration. And then wondered why he was tired. He felt a little bit tired. He couldn't figure out why. He was serious, he couldn't figure out why. Maniac—for work, that is!

It was dark when he landed in Washington aboard Air Force One *on his return from Greece, and at the bottom of the plane's ramp a lanky fig-*

ure waited to greet him. "Who are you?" Truman snapped, as the shadowy hulk thrust a hand at him. Much to the old statesman's embarrassment, the hand belonged to Lyndon Johnson, President of the United States. "I was blinded by a light beamed to my face," he apologized to LBJ afterward.

Now the funerals came oftener, and they were not for foreign potentates. Brother Vivian died, and Jim Pendergast went too. "The tree is falling apart, Doctor," he told Wallace Graham. "You have no idea how it affects me."

In October 1964, entering his bathroom, Harry tripped, fell against the bathtub, gashed his head, and broke some ribs. From that time on his own health declined.

For the last six years of his life, the man who loved to travel remained confined largely within the walls of the old house that Bess's grandfather had built, reading about other people's adventures. If he did venture out, it was usually to see Mary in Grandview. His driver, John Martino, who worked most times as a Truman Library grounds keeper, picked him up at the house, and invariably the old President said, "Take the back roads." He didn't want to ride the freeways. He preferred the roads that a former Jackson County judge had built three and a half decades before.

"Truman was a great man," Martino believes. "He treated people just like you and I. You know, he didn't have no friction with them. He knew what was right and what was wrong. If they didn't speak *the right way, he'd walk away from them, and that was all she wrote!"*

His last motor trip was to Kansas City's Research Hospital on December 5, 1972. Sensing the end was near, he told Wallace Graham, "Doctor, we're going to have one hell of a time!" His mind was coming and going, and for months Graham had been fighting to save "the kidneys, then the heart, after the heart function was fine, then the lungs. It was just one thing after another. He had a general multiple tissue breakdown."

Harry Truman's odyssey ended the day after Christmas, 1972, in Kansas City, Missouri.

About the Editing

With few editorial trappings, what you have read are the words penned by Harry Truman, and in the manner he put them on paper. Misspelled words have been corrected, style regularized, and in some instances, especially in his early letters, occasional long sentences and paragraphs have been shortened. The one document that I did alter significantly is "The Military Career of a Missourian," an unpublished 34-page "diary" HST wrote during his senatorial years describing his national guard experience. Because he composed this remembrance in the third person, I changed his references to "our young soldier" to the first person.

Where repetition or other distractions cropped up, such as mundane family matters and overly detailed descriptions, I deleted them, but of course used ellipses to indicate where the omissions occur.

M.M.P.

The publishers hope that this
Large Print Book has brought
you pleasurable reading.
Each title is designed to make
the text as easy to see as possible.
G. K. Hall Large Print Books are
available from your library and
your local bookstore. Or you can
receive information on upcoming
and current Large Print Books by
mail and order directly from the
publisher. Just send your name
and address to:

G. K. Hall & Co.
70 Lincoln Street
Boston, Mass. 02111

or call, toll-free:

1-800-343-2806

A note on the text
Large print edition designed by
Bernadette Strickland
Composed in 16 pt. Times Roman
on a Mergenthaler 202
by Compset Inc., Beverly MA